The Natures of
John and William Bartram

The Natures of
John and William Bartram

THOMAS P. SLAUGHTER

PENN

University of Pennsylvania Press
Philadelphia

SCI
QK
31
.B3
S58
2006

PENNSYLVANIA PAPERBACKS

First published 1996 by Alfred Knopf, Inc.

Copyright © 1996 Thomas P. Slaughter
Maps copyright © 1996 David Lindroth Inc.

Pennsylvania Paperbacks edition published 2005 by arrangement
with Alfred A. Knopf, a division of Random House, Inc.

Printed in the United States of America on acid-free paper.

10 9 8 7 6 5 4 3 2 1

Published by
University of Pennsylvania Press
Philadelphia, Pennsylvania 19104-4112

ISBN-10: 0-8122-1934-1
ISBN-13: 978-0-8122-1934-0

A Cataloging-in-Publication record is available
from the Libary of Congress

To my family,
Denise, Jasmine, and Moses,
with love,
and to the memory of Willie,
who was family, too

In a word, I cannot foresee a single extraordinary event that is likely to occur in the whole term of my sojourn. . . . I tell this honestly to the reader, lest when he find me dallying long, through every-day . . . scenes, he may hurry ahead, in hopes of meeting with some marvelous adventure farther on. I invite him, on the contrary, to ramble gently on with me, as he would saunter out into the fields, stopping occasionally to gather a flower, or listen to a bird, or admire a prospect, without any anxiety to arrive at the end of his career.

Washington Irving,
Bracebridge Hall

Contents

Acknowledgments

I am grateful for the financial support of the American Council of Learned Societies, the American Philosophical Society, the John Simon Guggenheim Memorial Foundation, the Library Company of Philadelphia, and Rutgers University. For their ongoing support of my work, I thank Paul Clemens, Richard Dunn, Douglas Greenberg, Philip Greven, Stanley Katz, Louis Masur, John Murrin, and Michael Zuckerman.

The Library Company of Philadelphia provided me the opportunity to work there as a resident research fellow at an early stage in the project. This is the second time I enjoyed that privilege and, just as the last time, immersion in that institution's unmatched collections shaped the book in fundamental ways. James Green proved an inestimably valuable source of information on eighteenth-century books and publishing. His generous sharing of information and time saved me from errors and made me aware of both manuscripts and books that became essential to my analysis of William Bartram's *Travels* and the larger world of eighteenth-century natural history. I am deeply grateful to Green, John Van Horne, and Philip Lapsansky for their help and the Library Company's support of this project.

I am equally fortunate to have enjoyed the hospitality and support of Martha Wolf and Joel Fry at Bartram's Garden. Their knowledge of the house and grounds, their generosity with time, access to the house and their collection of Bartram materials, and encouragement of my research provided an introduction to the Bartrams' ghosts and the enchantment from which the book greatly benefited. Fry's unsurpassed archeological knowledge of the site provided insights to the architecture that I would never have discovered.

At the American Philosophical Society, I thank Beth Carroll-Horrocks, who took time on numerous occasions to answer my questions about the Society's collection of William Bartram drawings, and Roy Goodman, who helped me locate books and journals, and who introduced me to research on CD-ROM. At the Academy of Natural Sciences, Karen Stevens was especially gracious in providing me access to William Bartram's garden diaries. At the University of Pennsylvania, Nancy Shawcross helped me pursue unattributed books from the Bartram family library, as did Holly Lucas in the Biomedical Library. Thomas Horrocks and Charles Greifenstein were similarly gracious during my time at the College of Physicians of Philadelphia Library. Ian MacPhail at the Morton Arboretum, Jane Alling at the Pennsylvania Horticultural Society, archivists at the Natural History Museum of the British Museum, and Brenda Burgess, librarian for the Earl of Derby, all helped make the research for this project the joy that it was.

Those who attended public lectures at the Library Company of Philadelphia and participants in the Washington Area Seminar in Early American History and the Philadelphia Center for Early American Studies Seminar thoughtfully engaged some of the ideas shared here and in the book on which I am now working. I am grateful to John Van Horne, Alison Olson, and Richard Dunn for the opportunity to speak before their respective groups and for their generous hospitality.

For their readings of the manuscript, I am deeply indebted to Paul Clemens, Jane Garrett, Philip Greven, Sara Gronim, Louis Masur, Jean Soderlund, Denise Thompson-Slaughter, and Cami Townsend. All were helpful in making this a better book than it was when they read it; several made suggestions that led to significant restructuring. Lou Masur's reading and re-readings also gave me greater insight into myself, which has enhanced the meaning of this project immeasurably in ways that I can't, but know I don't have to, repay.

If Denise didn't read this book quite as closely as she did the last two, it's because without her this one couldn't have been written at all. With the death of my mother; the delightful, if always demanding, presence of our three-year-old and our baby; and me writing a book this past year, it has certainly been the busiest twelve months of our relationship and the most stressful. Her great gift was the three hours somehow carved out of our mornings for me to work. In return, I fear that she has gotten an emotionally drained husband ungratefully grumpy about the shortness of his workday. Sorry. Love. Next year will be better.

Introduction

John (1699–1777) and William (1739–1823) Bartram, father and son, were the leading American horticulturalists of their time. John was a traveler, gardener, herbalist, botanist, author, and purveyor of plants. He was a founding member of the American Philosophical Society, and in 1765 George III appointed him botanist for Britain's North American colonies. John was a "philosopher" of nature in both eighteenth-century senses of the word; he was a scientist and an enquirer into the meanings of life as revealed by the natural world. He was an eminence in Philadelphia's intellectual community and in the international solidarity of "curious" men who wanted to know more. John Bartram's garden, the plants he collected, the journals he wrote, his correspondence, and, most importantly, his personal style and patient instruction of others in the ways of nature made him the most beloved American naturalist of his day.

William Bartram was the first native-born American to devote his entire life to the study of nature. He was heir to his father's knowledge and philosophy, accompanied him on collecting expeditions, and as an adult embarked on his own to unexplored terrains. He was a nature artist of international repute and wrote the most remarkable American nature and travel book of the eighteenth century, *Travels Through North and South Carolina, Georgia, East and West Florida, The Cherokee Country, The Extensive Territories of the Muscogulges, or Creek Confederacy, and the Country of the Chactaws.* Bartram's *Travels* inspired the poetry of Coleridge, Wordsworth, and other Romantics, who drew images directly from the book, provided settings for the novels of

Charles Brockden Brown and James Fenimore Cooper, and influenced the nature writing of Emerson and Thoreau.

This book is about the "natures" of John and William Bartram in that word's various meanings, and the plural form isn't chosen idly. Raymond Williams calls nature "the most complex word in the language," and I agree that contemplating the "nature" of anything or anyone, let alone the nature of Nature itself, is a prodigious undertaking.[1] What complicates the task even more is a desire to plumb the relationships between the natures of John and William—the influences of father and son on each other—and the sway of Nature on the natures of the two men.

This is an essential complication because a sense of the Bartrams' humanity enhances appreciation of their naturalism. Knowledge of their naturalism deepens comprehension of their private struggles to live in the world. This book views the Bartrams' natures as men through their naturalism, and it explores their natural philosophy through the prism of their lives. It is, then, less about nature as a biological entity than it is about the imaginative construction of nature by these two eighteenth-century men. It is more about interior than exterior exploration, but ultimately it is about the relationship between imagination and experience.

Largely about the Bartrams' interior lives, the book explores the ways that they thought—their frailties and strengths, their hopes and fears, and the aesthetic and ethical qualities remarked on by so many of those who knew them. They were no more consistent and no less flawed than the rest of us. The major triumphs of their lives were against their own natures; their heroism came in small victories of their best selves over what they saw as their worst.

How they dressed, spoke, wrote, lived, and laid out their gardens challenged contemporary style in a number of ways. George Washington, for example, was horrified that the Bartrams didn't pull weeds from their garden, and saw such behavior as a profound challenge to contemporary notions of order and beauty. William spoke often and powerfully against hunting for sport, anthropomorphizing the beasts of forest and field. The Bartrams were appalled by attempts to eradicate rattlesnakes from settled areas and wilderness alike, and justified their stance on religious, philosophical, and what we call environmental grounds. In all these ways, the Bartrams were eccentrics who were ahead of their time, and behind it in some ways, too.

The differences between them are as striking as their shared beliefs. John had unsatiated ambitions for public accomplishment. William was a private man in an age of great public figures. He declined both a professorship of botany at the University of Pennsylvania and an appointment as a naturalist for President Jefferson's Red River expedition, choosing instead to draw, work in his garden, commune with nature, and talk to his friends. John's principal influence on others was during his lifetime; William's came largely after he died. William was an emotional man in an age of rationalism; John, in this sense, was more a man of his time. William was afraid of the wilderness he romanticized; John was even more frightened than his son. John despised Indians; William admired them more than did any other white American of his day. John was practical to a fault; William was a visionary. Both adored nature, but each in his own way. John's published nature writings were chronicles of fact; size, distance, number, and practical uses for plants were the themes of his wilderness journals, while his correspondence contains passages that admire nature more in the language of poets than of the new science that influenced him. William drew and wrote about nature in an emotional manner that evokes both Gothic and Romantic imagery. John's writings were blueprints for exploiting the wilderness; William's were celebrations of wild nature just as he found it—uncleared, unplowed, unfenced, and scary—but he favored development, too. John saw plants; William's wilderness teemed with human and animal life. Both men believed that plants have volition, and each crafted a unique personal philosophy based upon his relationship with flora and fauna. The Bartrams are unique and exemplary, and the quality of surviving prose written by, to, and about them is such as to enable the telling of an intimate story about the lives of two eighteenth-century men.

No pondering of nature and natures is without its dark side; crises are the most emotionally revealing moments in anyone's life, when whatever intellectual accommodations we make with the universe are dealt ferocious, sometimes even fatal, blows. William and John had conflicts between them and with others, and they confronted ambition, failure, self-doubt, danger, and fear. Neither of them was always up to the challenge, and their personal crises sometimes brought them to their knees. John, who was orphaned as a child, was hopelessly insecure as an adult; his ambitious, acquisitive, and sensitive nature grew from an insatiable need for reassurance that his life had meaning as measured by the father figures whom he collected. William suffered from an unresolved crisis in his teen years, when he felt betrayed by adults who had encouraged his artistic talents and then wanted him to abandon his art for a more "practical" career. He may also have endured attacks of melancholia, what we call depression, which made it impossible for him to fulfill the expectations of his father and of himself.

This book is about nature and natures. It's about a father and son who loved each other and sometimes hated each other. It's about how people faced the joy and the anguish of life in another time and philosophical place. It's about connections among two men and a natural world that no longer exists.

The book begins with the "Ends" that brought John and William's lives to a close. By inverting chronology in this way, the first chapter introduces themes pursued in the rest of the book and establishes a reflective perspective that unites author and reader in a shared sense of where the story will go. From "Ends" the telling moves to "Foundations" upon which other chapters build. This, the second chapter, and the two that follow it address John's life independently of William's in a fashion that takes seriously the chronological relationship between the life of a father and that of a son, while maintaining the topical focus that provides richer analytical possibilities than a linear alternative would. "Foundations," "Visions," and "Business" relate John's character, his views of the world, the influences on the ways he thought and lived, and how he made his way in the world. These three chapters lay the groundwork for reconnecting the two lives in chapters five and six, which are about "Beginnings" and the significance of "Snakes" that come between father and son. These lead to an independent consideration of William, who was never free from the influence of his father, but was his own man nonetheless. "Journeys," "Perspectives," "Travels," and "Gardens" tell about William from different vantages that were important to him and represent aspects of the complex man that he was.

The last, as yet unmentioned, connection is that between this project and me. The use of first-person paraphrasing throughout the book suggests how closely my life, consciousness, and nature are entwined with my interpretation of the Bartrams. This method is intended to enliven the narrative, but it also exposes a belief that my experience provides an authority supplementing that of the sources mentioned in the Notes. Writing history is, of course, a creative process of focus, selection, interpretation, and expression, one that should be understood in personal terms. The sources listed in the Notes are filtered through my life; they have no independent standing as evidence apart from my understanding of them.

I have chosen to minimize contexts that other authors might have shared more fully with readers; I decided to focus on the emotions upon which human rationalities are built. The Bartrams' story seems to me to warrant such an emotional recounting. John's heartfelt, if unlettered, prose and William's impassioned drawings of animals and plants gave me access to the deeper feelings that define who we are and determine what we do no matter how we comprehend our actions or explain ourselves to others. Those are connections between their stories and mine.

That said, a little more self-revelation is called for here. The kind of book this is—as much emotional and reflective as it is intellectual and analytical—warrants a greater explicit sharing of self than I give elsewhere in the book. I offer this information with some trepidation, recognizing that both the act and the content risk providing ammunition for overdetermined readings of my epistemology and of who I am. I'm a Quaker. I'm a mix of Native-American, French-Canadian, and English heritages. I'm a father and, in common with all of my gender, I've been a son.

This project crystallized in my consciousness during a year in which my father died and my son was born. Before I started writing, my maternal grandfather and my mother died, too. Halfway through a first draft, my daughter was born. Days after I completed the last chapter, before I wrote the conclusion, my good friend and dog, Willie, died, ending a companionship of thirteen years. If death and life stalk these pages together, if the book combines melancholy with a seemingly inexplicable good cheer, that's because such emotions contribute to who I am and thus, unavoidably should I have wanted to avoid it, to what the book is as well. These aren't necessarily contradictions, tensions, or inconsistencies in my epistemology unless you read them that way. All the things that I am and that have happened to me contribute to what this book became, what it is. In ways that I can only glimpse, this project is a chapter in my life, a connection to those long since and only recently dead, and to all of those who, for me, continue to live. This includes John and William Bartram, both of whom live for me.

The Natures of
John and William Bartram

CHAPTER ONE

Ends

THE END CAME SUDDENLY, as he walked from the house to his garden, or he died slowly, breathing his last while reposing under a weeping ash tree. He died alone or in the arms of his niece's husband. It's not even certain where relatives and friends buried him—in his beloved garden or in the cemetery of the Quaker Meeting, where Friends registered his birth and that of his twin sister more than eighty-four years earlier. "William and Elizabeth the son and daughter of John Bartram and Ann his wife was born the 9 day of the 2d month."[1]

The ninth day of the second month was April 9 as Darby Meeting reckoned dates in 1739.[2] "Was" born—a simple grammatical slip, perhaps, the consequence of a singular habit not coming to terms with the somewhat unusual plural birth; or "was" one twin already more visible than the other, about whom I know only that her father called her Betty, that she married William Wright in 1771, moved to Lancaster County, and died there in 1824. I wonder about Elizabeth's life, about the connections between these two children, about the sister who leaves no written record and the brother who, in voluminous surviving writings, never even wrote down her name. I wonder many things about William, too, but I can write about him in ways that I cannot write about her.[3]

William Bartram died on Tuesday, July 22, 1823; that I do know. I can imagine, from the records he left, the nature of the hours preceding his death. From his garden diary I know that William's habit was to retire shortly after 10 p.m. and rise before dawn. There's no reason to suspect that he deviated from the habits of a lifetime on his last day.

A light sleeper, like his father, William apparently missed little that passed during the night. He heard thunderstorms that began before dawn, at 2 a.m., and at 10 and 11 p.m.; felt the sultry heat of a summer's night and knew it broke at 5 a.m.; and heard and felt the wind change direction at midnight. He saw a halo around the moon at 10 p.m. and smelled a "light shower of rain" that came in the night, even when a sprinkle fell between 3 a.m. and sunrise. He witnessed a snowfall's end at 10 p.m. and at midnight, saw the Northern Lights appear at all times of the evening, gazed at a comet on three consecutive nights, saw a total eclipse of the moon, and watched the stars in all seasons. He heard the spring frogs and summer insects from his bed, the migrating geese of autumn fly over his head, and the calls of night birds in winter outside his window. All this during ten of his last eighty-four years, and all of it in the same place just outside Philadelphia. Had he lived but one more day, William would have witnessed—for the third time in his life—a total eclipse of the moon.

After awakening each day, he meditated and prayed, perhaps before dressing, but surely before leaving his room. William's meditations, or "reflections," as he called them, were sometimes "serious" and sometimes "idle," as is true for us all. Where did his mind travel on his last morning, backward through memories across time and space or forward to the hours before him into a future that he knew to be short in a place that he would never again leave while alive? Undoubtedly his mind wandered both forward and back, but the mix we can't know and the feelings we can only imagine. I hope that William's mind allowed him to live for the day, without fear or regret; but that's only a dream I wish for myself.[4]

As the sun rose on each day of his life, William prayed to Nature's God, "the soul of the creation of the Universe." Here, in the title he gave his God and in his prayerful writings, we get a final glimpse of William's belief in the unity of all nature. His prayers, on this day as others, were to the animating and visible soul of all life, the connecting spirit uniting us with other animals and plants.[5]

On this, his last day, the struggles of William's youth were past, but scars remained. His youthful and middle-aged failures, his self-doubts, the knowledge that he had not fulfilled the expectations of others and, worse yet, of himself, remained a painful part of who this man was. He still brooded over all this—failed business ventures, a disastrous and

near-fatal attempt to establish a Southern plantation, flight from creditors that led to his five years of exile in the wilderness, his father's
harsh judgment of him, lack of recognition by the European scientific
community of his botanic discoveries, the poor sales and hostile reviews
of his book, and the disbelief and resulting ridicule of those who found
his tales of roaring, steam-belching Florida alligators in that book preposterous at best or charlatanry at its worst. He brooded less than he
might have and less than he once had, but he would take his regrets and
his sensitivity with him to his grave, wherever his grave is.

As the narrator tells us in Cormac McCarthy's *The Crossing,*
"doomed enterprises divide lives forever into the then and the now."
William accepted this division in his own life with grace over time. By
his lights, doomed enterprises plagued his more public young adulthood; private triumphs against his weaker self characterized his garden
years, the last forty-six spent in the comparative solitude of that one
peaceful place. William's final days weren't just reflections on a lifetime
of failure; he wasn't a brooding old man. He had accomplished much,
even by his own measure, but his achievements as he understood them
were largely private ones, not the sort appreciated by the rest of the
world. His attempts to conquer ambition, forgive his enemies, and
lead a simple, virtuous life—goals that filled the pages of his commonplace books—were, to all appearances, achieved. This was a lot, if not
enough, for any man, and William was proud of what he had accomplished in the last four decades of his life—in his garden, in his heart,
in his mind, in his soul—without ever leaving his home.[6]

For what did this eighty-four-year-old man pray on what he
couldn't know was his last day? His wants were few, his character fixed,
and his days numbered. He prayed for others, as his correspondence
shows—for his niece and nephews, his siblings and friends. Perhaps he
prayed as well for his garden, for the plants and animals that shared his
part of the natural world. They were certainly much on William's
mind, as his garden book attests, through every season, every day of
the year. He thanked God for the blessings bestowed on the garden's
inhabitants, for the warming sun, the refreshing rain, and the time and
health that enabled him to continue his work and to chronicle the natural rhythms of the garden into his old age.

Then there was death; always there is death. William contemplated it much during his young adulthood and middle age; wrote

about it much less frequently during his last twenty years. Virtue and death are principal themes of his commonplace books, and it's the juxtaposition of the two that gives these more private writings their meaning: "Is it not strongly persuasive that Virtue makes us happy daily and removes the fear of death from our eyes antecedently." Maybe; or perhaps these were the hopeful jottings of a middle-aged man whistling in the dark to keep the monster at bay. Later, in his early fifties, William reminded himself "that is the best thing for a man which God sends him and that is the best time that he sends it. . . . Manage all your thoughts and action in such a manner as though you were just going out of the world." Lastly, as William approached his sixties: "Says Montaigne, if I study it is for no other science than what treats of the knowledge of myself, and instructs me how to live and die well." Then no more, not a word about death for twenty-five years.[7]

Was he convinced? Is that why he stopped quoting others and writing down his own thoughts about death? Had he reached the sort of accommodation to which he, and all thoughtful people, aspire? Possibly the fear of life growing shorter each day was simply too much and he chose, consciously or not, to dwell less on the greatest fear a person can have. Perhaps William was simply determined, as the poet Donald Hall tells us he was upon receiving a death sentence from his physician, to write about something besides death and dying. Like Hall, William found solace, redemption, and meaning in work—gardening, writing, drawing, teaching others to see and to render nature in pencil and ink, observing and chronicling nature's cycles in the garden. Was it enough? Did William's faith give him hope? Did his virtue grant him peace? In his youth he had quoted himself a biblical reminder: "The wicked is driven away in his evil, but the righteous has reliance at his death." If William had reliance, he hadn't known that he would.[8]

William also had moments, and longer periods, of despair—when he glanced into the abyss, shivered, and blinked. "What a poor impotent contemptible creature I am," he wrote one day. What did he do or what could he not do? There were other times, too, that he felt just as badly about himself for no reason discernible in the surviving record, which is not to say that there wasn't just cause. Memories of past mistakes no doubt haunted him. Patient man that he was, he suffered his own faults impatiently. He had his reasons, born of temperament and humanity, for having doubts about his self-worth.[9]

William seldom committed to writing the pain he suffered from loss. If the death of loved ones led him to despair, he kept it to himself or shared his anguish in face-to-face encounters. His father, mother, siblings, and friends died without mention in William's correspondence, garden diary, or commonplace books. Perhaps the pain, however great, was relieved in private reflection and interpersonal exchange. In a letter, now lost, William mourned to a friend, who tried in response to help recapture his acceptance of the workings of nature. "The storms of affliction do not last for ever," wrote the ornithologist Alexander Wilson, "and sweet is the serene air, and warm sunshine, after a day of darkness and tempest. . . . How many millions of beautiful flowers have flourished and faded under your eye; and how often has the whole profusion of blossoms, the hopes of a whole year, been blasted by an untimely frost."[10]

In this letter Wilson hit the right notes, for William tried to accept death with a resignation born of his lifelong immersion in nature. The seasonal cycles were his cycles, just as they are for the farmer and fisherman who live by their rule. William not only lived the earth's rhythms; he studied them, meditated on them, drew them, and wrote them as well. His life's work was as surely an orchestration of nature as a composer's is an orchestration of sound. For him, nature's cycles were more than a metaphor for life; more truly, his life is a metaphor for them.

The death of William's beloved nephew provides a rare glimpse of his struggle to accept that everything dies that ever has lived. Perhaps this, the death of a young person, seemed unnatural and hence more jarring, so contrary to William's expectation that he should die first. Knowing that some birds expire in the egg having never quite lived, or fall to their deaths without ever taking wing, didn't help him this time. Read William's notice of that death: "*18th* [of April, 1818]. Cool wind high, blustering from NW. NB. died this morning Dr. James Bartram of Kingsess, grandson of the celebrated John Bartram the Botanist & naturalist."[11]

This entry is in William's garden diary, and comes as a note to the diary's central function, the recording of the nature of days. The obituary interrupts only briefly the larger pattern of natural events as he reports them, the seasonal cycles, the daily changes of weather, bird migrations, freezings and thawings of the Schuylkill River, animal habits, and the annual appearance of insects, flowers, and plants. It's an interruption only in the limited sense that William noted no other human deaths in this diary—of siblings, dear friends, or the great men with whom he was acquainted. In other ways the entry expresses quite eloquently the place of one human life within its natural setting—the direction of the wind, the temperature of the air, the coming of spring. The brevity of the notice belies the grief revealed by its very existence. This time, William needed to remind himself of the workings of nature and our powerlessness to resist.

It is also revealing that William triangulated the loss in relationship to another over forty years past. If the publicly meaningful identity of his nephew, and of himself, came from lineal association with a man of renown, the personal meaning of his father's existence was, for William, also of another kind. Curiously, as we see his father's public identity commemorated in a private writing, William's most affectionate testament to his father comes in a published biographical sketch that he wrote at the request of a magazine editor. Only once in nine pages does William abandon the factual tone of the chronological narrative, and he does so to give a very private accounting of the great man.

> Mr. Bartram was a man of modest and gentle manners, frank, cheerful, and of great good-nature; a lover of justice, truth, and charity. He was himself an example of filial, conjugal, and parental affection. His humanity, gentleness, and compassion were manifested upon all occasions, and were even extended to the animal creation. He was never known to have been at enmity with any man.[12]

This is the model, one of private accomplishments rather than public ones, by which William measured and led the second half of his own life. This is the ideal, however in conflict with the image of John Bartram that emerges from his writings and voluminous correspondence, to which William aspired. The quoted passage gives more insight to the nature of William than to his father. The eulogy helps explain William's introspective focus by cataloguing his father's public accomplishments—John's appointment as Royal Botanist in the colonies, his recognition by scientific societies in Europe and America, and his standing as one of the greatest collecting botanists of his day. It illuminates why William rejected all public roles cast before him once his travels had ended. In his own mind, he simply couldn't be as great as his father; he had to focus if he were to become almost as good a man. Late in life, if not still on his last day, William struggled with what it meant to be John Bartram's son.

It is with such thoughts about himself in relation to his father, to nature, and to nature's God—some of them conscious, some of them imbedded in his adult self, some of them articulated in prayerful reveries, and some of them worn on his sleeve—that William dressed in the plain clothes described by visitors and descended the stairs at or before dawn's early light. The descent was painful and difficult. The right leg, broken in a near-fatal fall when he was forty-seven, ached. He limped, always, leaning heavily on a walking stick. His eyes, always weak, grew weaker over the years. They had given him near-constant problems ever since a temporarily blinding affliction incapacitated him during his travels; and the house, in any season and at every time of the day, is dark. He carried eyeglasses, useful only for reading and other close work, in his pocket or wore them on the top of his head.

How he looked, where he looked, and what he did when he reached the bottom of the stairs were of a piece with his sense of connection to God and our place in the natural world. On this particular morning, after he prayed and dressed, William may have measured the temperature and discerned the direction of the wind, as was his habit for years; or maybe he stopped doing this six months earlier when he made the last entry in his garden diary. It's unclear why he ceased this ritual part of his day, so central to his life for decades on end. It doesn't seem that he'd grown too enfeebled, for he continued to write and to survey his garden, but maybe he felt not up to the task. Possibly, with his eyes growing weaker and the pain strong in his leg, he no longer had the discipline of body and mind. Perhaps the keeping of such a record was no longer meaningful to him, clinging as he was to the edge of life's great abyss, knowing that soon he would fall into a chasm where weather, seasons, and the passage of time no longer have the same meaning that they once had for him. Whatever the other reasons he had for ceasing to write in his diary, the end of the garden chronicle was William's prediction that his own end was near, a prescient estimation that he would not live to see a new year. This old man knew the rhythms of nature, the cycles of time, the signs that the life of a tree, a plant, a flower, a bird, or his own body was coming close to the end.

On his last morning, William hobbled to his desk, eased himself into the chair, set his cane close by, adjusted the glasses on his nose and over his ears, and turned his gaze to the manuscript on which he was working—the natural history of a member of what he called "the vegetable kingdom." As the story goes, he finished the article in that sitting, but I smell more romance than truth, an odor of poetic rather than literal end, in that tale. Not even the name of the plant has survived. Why, if there was a completed essay, wasn't it cherished, preserved, and published by those who valued William's life and his work?[13]

At some point he rose, slowly, painfully, reversing the order in which he dealt with paper, pen, glasses, cane, desk, chair, and the frail body that stiffened while his mind and hand worked. The next steps on William's morning routine took him toward the garden that he loved. His habit surely varied with the seasons, whim, and the day of the week. He was a man both of routine and of whimsy. He stuck to his course unless something "curious" led him another way. If his eyes locked on the struggle of an ant with a large load, if he sniffed the perfume of a bud blossoming for the first time that season, heard the call of a bird that he wished to sketch, or felt drawn to the banks of the river, there went whatever plans he had for the day.

William spent a great deal of time outside. The garden book reveals that even less passed him unnoticed during the day than at night. Often, he recorded the temperature at daybreak. When the fog cleared at 8 a.m. or the mist at 10:00, he was there. He felt a misty rain at 7:00 and the heat of summer at 9:00. He watched spiders "darting their webs" in January and bees searching for flowers in February, measured the depth of March snow, charted the arrival of April flowers and migrating birds, and observed a bull frog devouring a mole during May. He celebrated summerlike winter days and lamented cold snaps that brought the end to frail blossoms in spring. He recorded the arrival of "sultry" weather in June and the death of a bird found five miles away, the ripening of apples, the flowering of lilies, and the chirping of crickets in July. He noticed that the partridges' song changed during an August drought. He witnessed the course of yellow fever during the summer and fall, each species of bird as it passed south, the first frost, the first ice, and the first and last solid freezing of the Schuylkill each year. He remembered how the patterns compared to the past; he knew when it was time to hope for a change. He clearly liked moderate weather best, but was capable of describing "beautiful white frost," a July day cold enough for him to sit comfortably by the fire, and weather so warm that it was fit only for sitting under a tree. His highest compliment to the elements was the label "serene," and, not surprisingly, he found serenity in all seasons.[14]

William made it outside and died in the garden. Whether drawn there by habit, pain, sound, sight, or smell, I don't know. An artery burst in his lungs. He was alone, but not undiscovered for long. He lay under a tree in this man-, God-, and nature-made forest of plant and animal life. This is the story I tell. He's buried in the cemetery, I think, although I would have buried him here, in the shade, with a good view of the plants, river, and house. Wednesday's newspaper invited friends to the funeral, "from Bartram's Botanic Garden, Kingsessing, this afternoon, at 3 o'clock." "From" the garden, not in it—too bad.[15]

The earth eclipsed the moon while William's body lay in the house. "We have witnessed many similar events," the same newspaper reported, "but never one which occasioned more admiration and delight." William would have delighted in this natural event as much as anyone, had he just one more day. "All nature seemed to have sunk to rest—scarcely a leaf waved upon the trees, and 'the clear blue vault of Heaven' was unobscured by a single cloud." William's romantic style of writing about nature, so ridiculed by reviewers forty years earlier, was now journalistic fashion. "The Moon rose in full majesty, from the horizon, and shed her silver radiance around us, with almost the brightness of day. Her rich mellow light was alone sufficient to attract observation, and to draw off the mind into the range of 'spheres and planetary worlds.'" William could have written these words, this sort of appreciation of nature, himself. No longer did such "rhapsodical effusions" seem "disgustingly pompous"; no longer was such writing "too luxuriant and florid" or "too luxuriant and poetical" for popular tastes. "But what imagination can do justice to a scene like this, without the aid of observation?" One recently living; one with the sensitivity of an artist, the talents of a gifted writer, and a poet's soul.

> How grand and imposing is the view of
> the march of worlds casting their dark
> shadows over the lights of Heaven as
> they range round in their mighty orbits;
> teaching to man the vast plan of
> creation, how 'stars on stars their
> brightness shed,' and worlds on worlds
> are multiplied, put in motion and
> sustained, and the vast Omnipotence of
> Him who made and controls them all. Oh
> Man! Man! how insignificant a being art
> thou, in the great scale of creation, to
> wear a Maker's image, and meet the care
> of kindness of ALL NATURE'S GOD.

Yes, just as William Bartram himself would have said, just as he had said in words and in drawings over the course of his life.[16]

BY ALL INDICATIONS William's father was ready for his own end, which came in his house on September 22, 1777, the same house outside which William would die. Family tradition has it that anxiety hastened John's death, that he feared invading British soldiers would destroy the garden that he had labored half a lifetime to grow. Doubtless he worried about his family as well—his wife; the recently returned prodigal, Billy; and the rest of his offspring, all grown to adults and now, with the exception of Billy—always Billy—with families of their own. He need not have worried; the only lingering evidence of war in the garden was a solitary cannonball that remained on the grounds for half a century, at least.

The enemy eventually repelled, General Washington would sit under the weeping ash tree, so the story goes, chatting with the French ambassador. What kind of nut is that? enquires the diplomat jovially, gesturing toward the ball. It is a nut too hard for John Bull to crack, the general retorts. As always, it seems, there's a second version of the story. In this one Washington is eating one of John Bartram's prized pears. What description of fruit is this? the French ambassador asks Washington, pointing at the cannonball. Ah Count, the great man replies, that is a fruit hard of digestion. John would have liked the story in either version and retold it himself, possibly adding yet another variation, many a time. He would have been proud that Washington, first among other great men, sat in his garden; and John always liked a good joke, particularly one where nature was featured as part of the fun.[17]

The pain of loss shaped John's concern for his children as his life was ending. Two had died during childhood—Richard (1724–1727 or 1728) at age three, and the first Elizabeth (1734), as an infant barely out of the womb. One more sad ending came in the same year as John's; his youngest daughter, Ann, named for her mother, died at age thirty-six. Ann had married in 1764, so we might guess that either childbirth took her or one of the maladies to which a weakened body is prone. Whether Ann's death came before or after her father's, whether they were ill at the same time or worried about each other, one can only guess.[18]

The rest of the now-adult children made out just fine. They all survived the Revolution without injuries related to war. John Jr., to whom John had turned over the house and garden in 1771, continued and enhanced the family's business in plants and seeds. The two other daughters, Mary and Elizabeth, were married, apparently well, at least by their father's lights; Isaac and Moses, the latter of whom also had his problems settling down, prospered in the apothecary business. And William—yes William, not Billy, now that his father was dead—became the best man he could be right there in the garden, without a wife or any profession at all. John's wife, William's mother, also lived out her last years in that house, surviving her husband by about seven years in the same anonymity that marked the rest of her life.

It's not until John's mid-fifties that I can see in his writings engagement with his own death. That's not to say that he, who lost his parents at such a young age, didn't contemplate mortality in general and personal terms before he reached fifty-six, but there are visible moments of change as he considered anew his own end. "Time is now far spent with us both," he wrote to Peter Collinson, the English merchant who helped John market his plants. "We are all mortal," he reminded his friend.[19]

Two years later came the flood. As he began his fifty-ninth year, John dwelled on the meaning of his life and its end. Long-held beliefs, which always had the potential to run him afoul of the Quaker discipline of Darby Meeting, brought problems now. A combination of his circumspection and the tolerance of Friends for their beloved member John had previously helped prevent confrontation over philosophical issues that divided them. He wasn't so enlightened on the humanity of Indians as were the Friends' teachings; he wasn't so quick to abandon the practice of buying and selling humans as some others were; and his personal testimony on peace wasn't so pacific in wartime as the discipline prescribed.

Yet what led to Darby Meeting's disownment of John had nothing to do with the social expression of religious beliefs; it bore no relation to his actions or inactions in the world. The issue that led to over a year of deliberation, of gentle attempts to persuade John of the error of his ways, was heresy, a most unusual charge for the Quakers of his day. John didn't believe in the divinity of Christ.

That wasn't news to those in the Meeting who had known him for decades. Something must have happened to provoke these usually tolerant Friends. Perhaps John stood up in Meeting for Worship and delivered his views, thereby challenging the entire Meeting in a public way that they couldn't ignore. The surviving record doesn't say. It reveals that over the fifteen months following the Overseers' initial complaint against him "for disbelieving in Christ as the Son of God," John didn't show up at meetings called to discuss his beliefs, which was an unfriendly challenge in itself to the hierarchy of the Meeting. When the Overseers visited him at his home to discuss the issue, they "could not prevail upon him to believe in the Divinity of Jesus Christ, but to the contrary," John told them, "that although he [Jesus] was endowed with the power of God he was no more than man." They kept trying, out of love for John, out of concern for their community, out of the habit of gentle deliberation that is the tradition of Friends. Finally, the Overseers reported after one such meeting at John's home that "he did not seem in any disposition of mind to condemn his contrary belief to ours respecting Jesus Christ but still persists therein so far as to say the longer he lives the stronger he is in the disbelief of the Divinity of Jesus Christ."[20]

John was reexamining, rethinking, and finding a greater need to testify to his beliefs as he prepared for the end. Indeed, twelve years after his disownment, John literally carved in stone his testimony to the unitary nature of God: "It is God Alone Almyty Lord the Holy One by Me Adord 1770 John Bartram." What an extraordinary thing to do. Imagine this old man, now seventy-one, hammering out the letters, chip by chip—the sound echoing against the house, outbuildings, and trees as he etched his mortal testament to the Immortal in a medium that would survive far longer than him, and then, with the help of others, sons and/or hired men, setting the monument beneath the second-story window of his library, making it part of his home. It was as if he carved his own tombstone, an act doubly contrary to Quaker tradition.

This monumental endeavor reveals much about the spirit of John Bartram, about the differences between him and William, and about how he confronted his death. After the Darby Meeting disowned him, John continued to attend Meeting for Worship every week with his family. If he had brought his hammer and chisel with him to Meeting, hammered out his message right there in the quiet of the Friends' shared search for the Light, and mounted the words above the front bench where the Overseers sat, his statement couldn't have been more powerful. There he was, week after week, a stony presence among those who judged him, silent and gray, judging them. For a rock he was, of a kind, among men. A daunting, craggy, immovable presence, a hard man to follow as a son.

There's an integrity, a courage, and a stubborn resolve to how John Bartram was facing his end. He confronted his mortality differently than William, less quietly and less peacefully in some ways. There's something desperate about the carving, as well as something inspiring about John's need to challenge others and to memorialize his views. Among other things, John had a sense of legacy that William lacked, a confidence that someone would listen, that his words and actions would survive and influence others, which came from his comparative success in the world and from his role as father and family patriarch.

Embarking, as John did, on his most challenging journey when he was in his mid-sixties says something else about the differences between him and his son. Friends would later remind William, no doubt to his great pain, that his father hadn't used old age as an excuse to remain in the garden. "Come on," a friend chided William when he was in his mid-sixties, "you are not too old. You have sufficient youth, health, and strength for the journey. . . . Remember, that your venerable father continued to make botanical tours long after he had reached your age."[21]

Perhaps William did age more quickly in a physical sense, but that isn't the sole factor that distinguished their actions in old age. John's eyes were also weak, a horse had kicked him in the back, and he, too, had injured his leg. He didn't allow his frailties to stop him because his identity and sense of self-worth were linked to public accomplishments, and he remained woefully insecure about his status as a great man. He needed to go on the Southern tour of 1765, to take the risks, suffer the discomforts, and, hopefully, achieve the fame of discovery upon his return. If he died in the quest, not that he was seeking out death, the greater the glory. He needed the trip just as he needed the praise and recognition that William, too, wanted, but never got. John's successes created a thirst for more fame, for wider recognition by great men, in the same way that one drink leaves an alcoholic yearning for more.

At the same time, John was also becoming more open to exploring things that we can never know. In 1757, the same year that Darby Meeting began its enquiry, John read a book recently acquired by the Library Company of Philadelphia about the life and beliefs of the Chinese philosopher Confucius. This was an unusual choice for John, whose tastes ran more to Thomas Barnes on propagating fruit trees, Philip Miller's *Gardener's Dictionary*, Cadwallader Colden on tar water, Johann Jakob Dillenius on mosses, Nehemiah Grew's *Anatomy of Plants*, and any herbals he could get.

Not only did John read *The Morals of Confucius*, but he took three pages of notes on the book, an uncharacteristic act for this proudly unphilosophical man. The notes aren't quotations drawn directly from the book; they aren't even paraphrases of Confucian teachings. They are, instead, attempts to Bartramize Confucius, to distill from the book wisdom that paralleled what John already believed. Confucius was a man whom John could admire: a man of virtue, who lived a life of "exemplary sobriety . . . [imbued] with every virtue and free from every vice and [who] showed the greatest equableness and magnanimity of temper under most unworthy treatment." This was a man whose teachings restored "human nature to its original dignity, that first purity [and] lustre which it had received from heaven and which had been sullied and corrupted with ignorance and the contagion of vi[ce]."

Confucius taught, in John's reading, obedience to the "Lord of heaven, to honor and fear him, to love our neighbor as ourselves, to subdue irregular inclinations, never to make our passions the rule of our conduct, to sub[mit] to reason, to listen to it in all things." Confucius advised "kings and princes to be fathers to their subjects; to love them as their children. He taught subjects to reverence and obey their kings." In summary, John wrote, the philosopher's "notion of God was that he was the supreme truth and reason or the fountain from whence truth and reason derived and communicated to men . . . that he was the original [and] ultimate end of all things, that he is one supremely holy supremely intelligent and invisible."[22]

The Confucius of John's notes might have been a Quaker, except for one thing. Confucius, just as John Bartram, believed that God "is one," not two or three. Indeed, it may even have been the reading of this book that prompted John to share his views on God's unitary nature with the Darby Quakers, to deliver a message in Meeting for Worship about the parallels between the lives and teachings of Confucius and Jesus, and his estimation that they were comparably great men.

It's unclear whether John read the book before the enquiry started or after it had already begun, or what prompted him to read it, to take such notes, and to what end. The connection between the two events seems more than a coincidence in time, so the story I tell is that John read the book first and his enthusiasm for the wisdom of Confucius is what got him in trouble with Darby Meeting's Overseers. The introduction to *The Morals of Confucius* makes explicit the translators' perception of identities between the teachings of Confucius and Christ. John's notes show that he saw these parallels, too. The Overseers could conduct their enquiry, but it had little to do with the one that John was beginning, a renewed exploration into the meaning of life.

During the same twelve-month cycle in which John read *The Morals of Confucius* and was disowned by the Darby Meeting, he also wrote a long letter to his children, the first of two that he would compose. The epistle, drafted as he neared his sixtieth year, is full of homely advice on everything from table manners to charity and how evening is best spent in the home. He has instructions for his children about eating, dressing, ambition, and industry; he gives his views on the qualities of a good wife, on frugality, jealousy, child rearing, and old age. His children had heard much, if not all, of this before, and quite likely on numerous occasions and in a variety of forms—as fatherly speeches, correction, and table conversation. This was a summary of how the gentle patriarch ruled his home.[23]

Why write it all down? Why remind his children that their father favored "quietude in an evening," which they already knew? Why nag them, in writing, about how they should dress: "let your clothing be plain, strong and neat"? Why give them again his dietary advice about eating "wholesome and plain," on avoiding "high sauces" that excite the appetite "to crave more than nature requires or the stomach can digest," since their meals reflected his views, and which they had heard him explain to dinner guests as an apology for the plain food? "After the luxuries of our cities," J. Hector St. John de Crèvecoeur tells us that John said as the family sat down to its meal, "this plain fare must appear to thee a severe fast."[24]

There was a tradition of writing such letters, which derived from the exalted place of fathers in eighteenth-century homes.[25] John wrote in that tradition because it suited his role. Still, why did he write now? Benjamin was ten, John fifteen, William and Elizabeth nineteen, and the other five "children" were older than that, when John committed his parental advice to paper. It seems a little late for eight out of the nine, but this letter was for all of them, written and then copied eight times. It was also for their children, who would follow in line. He drafted the letter as he approached sixty, a decennial year that symbolized old age in his culture. He wrote now because now seemed the right time; he might not live much longer and these were thoughts he wanted to leave behind. "These, my dear children," he wrote, "are the observations, meditations, and reflections I have made in the course of my travels abroad and I am now in the 59th year of my age."

My wisdom harvested over the course of a lifetime, John was saying, is part of my legacy to you. Here, too, are my fears. If I outlive my reason and my intellectual faculties, please do, "in a loving and tender manner, advise me" should I descend into a "peevish and fretful disposition . . . before it is too habitual." John feared "the pain and uneasiness that our decayed nature will be subject to" and prayed that a pious nature would help alleviate the worst. For his part, John would try, as he advised them also to try, "living today as if we expected to die tomorrow." Perhaps that is where William got the idea that he jotted down in his commonplace book.

John lived. He lived to become the King's Botanist in America, thereby achieving a measure of the recognition he had always craved. He lived to explore the Florida wilderness with Billy, observing, collecting, and chronicling the Empire's botanical fruits and the potential wealth of the land. He lived long enough to retire and turn his budding nursery business over to John Jr., in whose hands it blossomed and grew. He lived to see Elizabeth marry and Billy fail in business again. He lived long enough to lose Billy, his son, his dearest and most difficult child, who fled to the wilderness they had traveled together. He lived and believed Billy was dead, thereby suffering the cruelest of parental losses, the greatest of life's griefs. And then John lived to see Billy alive, his "dear child" again in his house.

Nineteen years after John wrote the letter to his children, as he approached his eighties, he wrote again, this time "The Last Written instructions of John Bartram to his Children." Now they were all grown. Benjamin, the baby, was twenty-nine; Isaac, the eldest, had reached fifty-two. Billy, soon to be William, had come home for good. This letter is even more philosophical than the last, shorter, and without the instructions about clothing and food. Too late for that, and he had said it before. John thought that he had something, though, that warranted saying once more. Seasoned more heavily with biblical quotations than the last one, this letter spoke of the visible presence of God in nature and the connections among all living things. John remained passionate about controlling the passions and soberly instructed his children about temperance again. Moderation, balance, "a sweet calmness and tranquility of mind," gratitude, and patience were the virtues he preached. John was getting calmer, more peaceful in his very last years. His ambition was waning and he was accepting his fate.[26]

The general instructions ended, but the letter continued addressed to just one. I, too, John confessed, once lived in "slavish fear" of lightning, in fear of my own death. As I became an adult, I wanted to live to see my children all grown, so the fear, even as the fear of lightning diminished somewhat, remained in my heart. "But now for several years I have not desired long life, but [am] entirely resigned to the divine will." My greatest fear now is about how I will die. "How many that goeth of this stage by sickness, pains, or old age, by its severity or deficiency rendered invisible both before and at their departure and uncapable of prayer glorifying or praising God." John considered himself fortunate; he thanked God for his fate, because it looked as though he would have his faculties of reason and be relatively free of pain at the end.

"My dear child," the letter goes on, "I should be glad if thee could in a good degree overcome thy slavish fear of thunder. It is a weakness, but who is without a weak side." I have been one of the "fearful mortals" all my life, John confessed, so I know the problem you have, having had it myself. I have known the horror, John might have said. I feared the dark; I feared Indians; I feared snakes; I feared death; and I feared the unknown. I, too, feared thunder that came in the night. I, too, had nightmares, but have them no more. Age, prayer, and the gift of God's grace have given me peace as I die in my bed.[27]

It's unclear to which of the children John addressed his last letter, one of the most endearing he ever wrote. Possibly he began it before Billy's return, then saved it among the papers beside his bed. His son certainly knew all those fears, shared them, and witnessed his father's inability to sleep soundly during their collecting expeditions. Billy suffered from nightmares born of such fear. Imagined alligators and hurricanes would continue to awaken him for decades to come. From what I know, I can envision William screaming out in his sleep, awakening his father, too, during the last nine months that they lived under the same roof. I can picture him startling, perhaps spilling milk, while eating his meal as a thunderstorm began, shuddering at each peal, excusing himself, thoroughly embarrassed and his appetite lost, to suffer alone.

Why would John write a letter to someone living at the time in his house? Perhaps the soul-baring words were difficult to utter out loud. Maybe their relationship was such that what John had to say he feared Billy couldn't hear, having proved deaf to his words many times in the past. Possibly he wanted to leave his son something else, having given the house and garden to Billy's younger brother six years before, having already bestowed, several times over in John's opinion, what financial legacy was rightly his. The other sons all got land. Having helped set up Billy in business and then bailing him out, more than once; having bought him prime slaves, land, and supplies for the failed planting venture, he had already given Billy his share. Still, the generous father left his financially troubled son £200, a considerable sum and twice what he left to Billy's twin sister. Was it enough, though, in John's eyes? In William's? It must have hurt both of them that the beloved garden, filled with the seeds and plants that they had found together, would never be William's.[28]

In a different reverie, I imagine that the letter was intended for Elizabeth, and that a copy was sent along with the longer one that was meant for them all. She probably wasn't there as John's life came to an end. Six years had passed since her marriage; she was off in Lancaster caring for her family now. Perhaps she wrote to her father, shared her fears with him in letters that nobody saved. Maybe her temperament was more like William's than we will ever know.

Billy was there, becoming William, as John breathed his last. My father "never coveted old age," he later would write, "and often observed to his children and friends that he sincerely desired that he might not live longer than he could afford assistance to himself, for he was unwilling to be a burden to his friends, or useless in society." John didn't outlive his worth; he was there to welcome, to cry over, perhaps to forgive, if forgiveness was called for or even sought, and to instruct his large family right up to the end. My father also hoped, William wrote in his own sixty-fifth year, "that when death came to perform his office, there might not be much delay." Blessedly, there was not.

His wishes, in these respects, were gratified in a remarkable manner: for although he lived to be about eighty years of age, yet he was cheerful and active to almost the last hours. His illness was very short. About half an hour before he expired, he seemed, though but for a few moments, to be in considerable agony, and pronounced these words, "I want to die."[29]

CHAPTER TWO

Foundations

FEW PEOPLE'S LIVES begin more sadly than John Bartram's did. Elizah, his mother, died in 1701, after giving birth to his brother, James, when John was not quite two and a half. Ten years later, his father, William, died in North Carolina. These tragic events were certainly life-transforming for the boy and character-defining for the man he would become. John never wrote about them, leaving clues to his feelings only in actions and attitudes across his seventy-eight years.

We can only imagine how the child faced his losses—how he felt about the stepmother who came into his life when he was eight or his father's decision to move his new family from Darby to North Carolina when John was twelve, leaving his brother and him behind in the care of their grandmother. No evidence survives about how he heard, what he knew, and what he imagined about his father's death, how he felt when he learned that his stepmother and her two children, William and Elizabeth, survived, and whether he saw much of them after they returned to Pennsylvania in 1712.

Why John's father was declared "out of unity" with Darby Meeting in 1708 is a mystery, too. That event, whatever its cause, may have influenced his decision to leave the region, but there are no clues as to why William abandoned his sons. John never wrote down what he knew of his father's dispute with Darby's Friends and how that influenced his own disownment much later in life. Whether John harbored some resentment against Darby's Quakers, or the dispute with his father influenced the Meeting's relationship with John, or John learned his controversial views as a child at home is unclear. Perhaps there was no connection at all between the two events, separated as they were by half a century. However, it seems likely that John's stubborn resolve, his willingness to stand alone against the collective wisdom of the Meeting, was a learned trait.

"Abandonment" is not quite the right word to describe William's departure, although that may be how it felt to his sons. Before he went south, the father drafted a will that directed executors to sell his Pennsylvania property. In the event of his death, the proceeds were to be divided equally between John and his brother, James. The boys were financially secure and in the capable hands of their grandmother, who told John what he later remembered about his Quaker ancestors—that they were persecuted in England for their religious beliefs and were among the first to brave the Atlantic for William Penn's experiment here. "I was but young when my father and uncle died, so the best account I could have was from my grandmother who lived some years after," John wrote about the source of what he knew about the Bartrams. No laments, no details, no soul-wrenching pain revealed here, simply an accounting of facts that included deaths in John's youth.[1]

Indians killed John Bartram's father. That's enough to explain the hatred that ran against his grain, a bigotry that he shared with those of his countrymen who had a less personal cause for their racism. What else John knew about his father's death is long ago lost. There were stories associated with the killings of others at the same time, of splinters jammed under fingernails and set ablaze, of skin peeled from bodies that were still alive.[2]

Whether or not John imagined a similar end for his father, he held an unshakable grudge that defined "Indian" as the opposite of anything good. Whether or not his father was tortured, John suffered wounds. He had deep psychological scars, crippling blows to his compassion, and searing burns that blinded him to the positive qualities of Native Americans. The pain of his father's death prevented John from seeing Indians as individuals as well as members of diverse groups, from ever admiring qualities that made "them" different from "us."

John characterized Indians as lazy, jealous, skulking, barbarous, treacherous, and sly. They couldn't be trusted, he said, were habitual liars, drank to inebriation always, and cheated whenever they got the chance. "They won't stir [to work]," John reported, "without one gives them as much a day as they can get in a month." They were "ungrateful"—for what it's not clear. They were "cruel" beyond the comprehension of civilized men. They were "merciless savages," who couldn't be counted on as friends.[3]

Indians' very humanity was suspect. "They skip from tree to tree like monkeys," he wrote; "if in the mountains, like wild goats they leap from rock to rock or hide themselves." Their cruelty was indiscriminate, without consideration of fairness or morality.

O Pennsylvania, you that was the most flourishing and peaceable province in North America is now scourged by the most barbarous creatures in the universe. All ages, sex, and stations have no mercy extended to them. The young man with vigor and activity perhaps with hasty steps, heart filled with raptures of love, is going to visit his intended, is unexpectedly pierced by a silent ball shot by a distant secreted enemy, his active arms unbraced, his vigorous sinews relaxed, his body rouled [rolled?] in blood and exposed to the fouls of the air. Our tender infants have their brains dashed out; our wives big with child have their bellies ripped open. Those killed within their houses [are] mostly burned with them. The beautiful and modest virgin obtains no more mercy than indeed a decrepit.[4]

What a revealing passage this is. Prayerful, almost poetic, the lamentation defines who John is and who Indians are not. The language is lofty, dreamy, and sad, appealing to emotions rather than intellect; it's a morality play scripted with characters who each have a role. The pregnant women and babies are composites based on newspaper accounts of frontier atrocities; the young man and the virgin are fictions designed for effect. Descriptive adjectives heighten the tone, deepen the horror, stir the emotions, inflame the reader's sense of injustice and rage. A "beautiful and modest virgin" and "tender infants" are guiltless, as innocent as persons can be, and yet are brutally murdered without regard for gender or age, logic or cause, justice or mercy. The suitor's only crimes are youth's hasty steps and an enraptured heart. Not so innocent as the infants, maidens, and pregnant wives, the young man is murdered in a manner that's grossly unfair by "a distant secreted enemy" who doesn't engage him in a fair fight and who leaves his so recently vigorous body to rot in the woods.

The Indians are angels (actually John writes "angles") "of death," destroying all life before them. The only way to deal with such "barbarous savages," according to John, "is to bang them stoutly and make them sensible that we are men whom they for many years despised as women." "Unless we bang the Indians stoutly," he wrote on yet another occasion, "and make them fear us, they will never love us nor keep peace long with us." John's wasn't a very Quakerly prescription for healing the wounds of war. He recognized that unscrupulous merchants, speculators, and settlers had done the Indians injustices, which understandably provoked rage. Their "savage" response, though, revealed flaws that called the Indians' humanity into question and justified, indeed required, a violent retaliation from Anglo-Americans.[5]

Also of significance here are John's characterizations of gender and love. His "Indians" are men, unless explicitly qualified as "nymphs," "women," or "girls." Likewise, his "we" refers to Anglo-American men. There's nothing remarkable about this; it's exactly what we'd expect from a man of his time—the linkage of "others" against whom John defines his sense of manhood and self.[6] He's telling us that the Indians—Native American males—aren't really men in the ways that they act both toward white women and children and toward other (white) men. They lack in his eyes the requisite cultural mix of honor, courage, justice, mercy, and paternalism. They are more violent, less logical, more emotional, and less kind than real men should be. The Indians will never love "us"—white men—according to John, unless "we" show "them" that we aren't the women that they believe us to be. "We" must show "them" that we can be violent, too, when justice demands it, but without the barbarity and unfairness that characterize their assaults on "our" women and "us."

One story John told in his sixty-fifth year personified the qualities that he ascribed respectively to Indians and men. "Many years past," he recalled,

> in our most peaceable times far beyond our mountains as I was walking in a path with an Indian guide hired for two dollars, an Indian man met me and pulled off my hat in a great passion and chewed it all round. I suppose to show me that they would eat me if I came in that country again. I stepped up to him and twisted it out of his hands and ran after him . . . 100 yards.[7]

The hat is a symbol, perhaps a more potent signifier for Quakers' traditional refusal to acknowledge authority by baring their heads. The Indian challenges John by grabbing his hat; John asserts his manhood by forcibly taking it back. The Indian reveals his barbarity by chewing the brim as a symbolic threat to eat John, thereby acting out ancient European fears about Natives, the oldest of charges against their humanity—that they were cannibals, not men. The Indian runs, an unmanly act; John pursues, showing that he's the brave one. The role of the Indian guide in this performance is unscripted, unclear. As a culturally liminal figure, perhaps he was unable to act at all. Had John caught the Indian what would he have done in this story about race and manhood, courage and cowardice, and hats with holes in their brims? Perhaps he would have "banged" the fellow, thereby securing his "love."

The love that John lost as a child was of a different kind and left him wounded within. Late in life, John described himself as having been "born with a bad constitution," and remembered "all my younger years being subject to grip, grievous coughs, heartburn, acrimonious looseness, dizziness, and rheumatism." Then there was the "slavish fear of lightning," which he carried with him into adulthood and the sense of himself as "naturally one of the fearful mortals from my infancy." By his own accounting, then, John was a weak, nervous, timid child.[8]

Given the absence of other, more pleasant, childhood reminiscences in his writings, this sounds very sad. There's every reason to suspect that the emotional and perhaps even some of the physical symptoms were related to how and when he lost his parents. What an insecure world he lived in, what a difficult place to find and trust love, to have confidence and hope for the future. Not surprisingly, then, John exhibited signs throughout his adult life of insecurity, fearfulness, and self-doubt. He built with bedrock, carved into stone, craved durable physical symbols of his self-worth, and demanded the sort of validation from others that his parents were unable to give him when he needed it most. John feared the loss of people, of things, of financial security, and of others' esteem. He whined in his writings when he didn't get praise. He was easily offended. He worried about his health, which led to his knowledge of herbal medicine and his eagerness to treat others as well as himself. Throughout his life, John retained childlike qualities that made him endearing and exasperating at the same time.

The "love" that John hoped to evoke by whacking Indians resembles "respect" more than the suitor's romantic love, which is based, at least in part, on sexual attraction. It's something like the "love" that John has for other white males, in the sense that both grow from deference, if not always esteem. Yet this love lacks the warmth that can pass between equals who value each other as friends and is more a product of terror than of trust and mutual regard. In that sense, it's most closely akin to the "love" that an eighteenth-century father hoped to secure from a child he spanked. Even there, though, what John is looking for is the first flush of emotion that a spanked child expresses in tears, not the longer-term warmth that blossoms more from tenderness than fear. Just as most other fathers of his generation, Quaker and non-Quaker alike, John discounts other emotions, such as the frustration, anger, and hurt produced by physical discipline, which have unwanted repercussions even from those who are cowed.[9]

White men also had to change their behavior, according to John—act more like real men—in order to bring about the transformation of Indians to men who love "us," which is the real goal. What's less clear is what "woman" means as an insult to men, although a passage about Indian women in one of John's letters helps isolate race and gender characteristics within his gendered epithets.

I don't remember to have known one English man to have married an Indian nymph. It would [be] reckoned a horrid crime with us, but indeed if they [were] well dressed and as cleanly as our women they would make as handsome, dutiful, industrious, loving, and faithful wives as many of our own women if we could whiten their skin a little and persuade or compel them not to use strong drink. But most of our Indian traders debauch them shamefully, which is one cause of many that have alienated their respect from us. The young girls and women are generally very modest unless debauched by Europeans, then sometimes they throw off all restraint.[10]

The tension in this passage between attraction and repulsion is typical of white men dating back to Columbus's first meeting with Native Americans. John finds Indian "nymphs" sexually alluring, but needing reform to make them almost as acceptable as white women for wives. A good wife is physically attractive, clean, appropriately dressed, complacent, hardworking, tender, devoted, modest, and faithful.

Indian women seem to John capable of possessing all these qualities. Their major failings are racial—their skin is too dark—and biological—they have a weakness for liquor—which leads to a wanton
sexuality that John claims to abhor. Whether or not he personally
engaged in such debauchery with Indian "nymphs," he clearly lusted at
least in his heart and fantasized sexual unions with what seemed to
him alluring Indian women. They may be less suitable as wives for
white men precisely because, in John's eyes, they are more sexually
enticing than white women who dress and act like wives should.

The salacious implications of John's passage about Indian "nymphs"
isn't unique in his writings and raises questions about the nature of
sexuality and the sexuality of nature in John's work. His early, and un-
reserved, attraction to Linnaeus's "sexual system" of plant identification
distinguishes him from others, such as his botanical patron Peter
Collinson, who were at least initially repelled by the new botany's
prurience. John's eagerness to count the male and female parts of plants
provides a clue to his own sexuality and his take on the nature of sex.

Linnaeus's claim to having designed "natural" rather than lascivi-
ous systems for identifying animals and plants belies the culturally
derived presumptions of his science. He named the class of which
humans are members, for example, after mammary glands, which are
prominent in only half of us and only in sexual maturity, not in all
mammals of either gender, and therefore not our most obvious shared
and distinguishing characteristic. As the historian of science Londa
Schiebinger observes, Linnaeus's agenda was as much cultural and
political as it was scientific, and as such is deeply revealing about the
values that he and his disciples brought to their study of nature during
the eighteenth century. "Linnaeus's term *Mammalia*," she writes,

> helped legitimize the sexual division of labor in European society
> by emphasizing how natural it was for females—both human and
> nonhuman—to suckle and rear their own offspring. Linnaean sys-
> tematics had sought to render nature universally comprehensible,
> yet the categories he devised infused nature with middle-class
> European notions of gender.[11]

The same is true of Linnaeus's botanical system, which he based
on purely morphological features—number and mode of union—

those characteristics of plants least important for their sexual function.[12] What Linnaeus was doing, then, was importing cultural notions about gender hierarchy, womanliness, and manliness into the study of nature. That John saw this approach as "natural" reveals only that he shared his culture's presumptions about the place of women relative to men. That he suffered none of the London botanical establishment's embarrassment about the new system reveals a less restrained, more open, earthier sexuality than that of the British gentlemen.[13]

This clue to the nature of John's sexuality is supported by the passages in his writing about actual Indian "nymphs" and the imagined lover murdered by Indians. It's fleshed out a bit more by another clue running through John's correspondence about the plant popularly known as the Venus flytrap. The Latin binomial given the plant, *Dionaea muscipula*, is literally translated as "Aphrodite's mousetrap." The origins of the first term are quite clear. The Greek goddess Dione merged with the more powerful myth of her daughter Aphrodite, who then became Venus in the Roman pantheon. As Venus, she wasn't just goddess of love, but also of sexuality and sexually transmitted disease. The second term clearly means mousetrap and not flytrap, but the translation never caught on in popular nomenclature.[14]

The name suggests some sort of sexual trap, but for what isn't clear except that the trapper is female and the trapped is male. It's also significant in light of the discussion of Linnaeus that the Swedish scientist termed the plant a *miraculum naturae* (miracle of nature) upon his first sighting. Here was a plant that seemed to contradict Linnaeus's presumptions about the "natural" relationship between animals and plants, and by implication between men and women. As a carnivorous plant with rapidly moving parts, the Venus flytrap turned the tables on Linnaeus's understanding of predator and prey in the natural world. A plant that eats meat, a woman who traps men—such things happened in nature; Samson and Delilah, Ulysses and the Sirens were part of the cultural imagination after all, but man-eating women weren't what European men wanted nature to be. They were exceptions to what men saw as natural relations, the world working according to laws of nature and God. Although to Linnaeus female plants were generally "wives" with "husbands," he had to admit that a flower with one pistil and twenty stamens was a wife who slept around.

In the European imagination, men who ate others and women who trapped men with their sexuality were certainly common enough. Cannibals and prostitutes were nothing new, however "unnatural" European men thought them to be. Traditional beliefs about Amazons and cannibals had been exported to America centuries before, and were united in European culture with dreams of Indian women as temptresses, whose sexual "looseness" was both invited and damned. Connections among cannibalism, Indian sexuality, and fellatio were, of course, left to pornographers rather than explicitly revealed in the writings of such men as John Bartram.

The Venus flytrap had a niche to fill; it occupied a place in the sexual system that no other "vegetable" shared. By its very uniqueness, the plant reinforced both a sense of the "natural" and of nature's wonder, which humans could behold but perhaps never fully comprehend in a world created by a God so much greater than them. It's the only species of its genus and a member of a family of meat-eating plants "discovered" in the eighteenth century by European men.[15]

The plant's existence also fit John's sense of how artificial—"unnatural," to use his word—distinctions are between plant and animal life. In his ongoing quest to identify shared traits that beguile assumptions about humans, other animals, and plants, here was a vegetable that acted like an animal in discernible ways. Somewhat akin to natural oddities in the animal kingdom, such as the praying mantis and some species of spiders that consume their mates, here is a specimen that reveals both the incredible variety *and* shared qualities of God's creation.

John wrote to Peter Collinson that "my little tipitiwitchet sensitive stimulates laughter in all the beholders. There was lately a French gentleman from Montreal, which was so agitated that he could hardly stand and said it was enough to make one burst with laughing." When John showed the unusual plant to visiting men, he told a joke about the vulvalike grasper that consumed meat. He saw a resemblance between the trapping mechanism and female anatomy, and saw humor in comparing the fate of the insects it gorged and men's relations with women. The joke was in the plant's shape and movement, the name that he gave it, and the portrayal of men as prey powerless to resist the predatory female trap that ate them.[16]

These shards of literary evidence don't reveal the whole nature of John or even tell the whole story of his relations with women and

Indians. William later recalled that during his childhood Indians were frequent visitors to his father's house. As an adult, John hired them to collect botanical specimens, used them as guides, valued their knowledge of herbal medicine, enquiring about their "recipes" for cures, and considered them authorities on animal habits and the locations of plants. He also saw them as superstitious, a trait he didn't respect. His bigotry, his grudge against Indians as a race, was tempered by a respect for their closeness to nature. If it weren't for the death of his father, John's high estimation of "natural" living may have led him to love Indians in the ways that William did.

As he entered adulthood, John inherited both his Uncle Isaac's estate, which descended through his grandmother, and one quarter of his father's as well, half going to his stepmother and the remaining quarter to his brother, James.[17] Despite his lifelong claim to being a "poor" man, John started off with £100 and a 200-acre farm, including its buildings, livestock, orchards, and equipment. The farm and the cash were a substantial start for any young man in this time and place. In 1728, he also purchased a 112-acre farm in Kingsessing, on the banks of the Schuylkill River, where he rebuilt the existing two-room cabin into the substantial stone house that still stands, established a botanical garden, raised a family, and lived out his life. Tax records list John first among the township's ratables, which means he was the wealthiest man where he lived. In 1769, he owned three horses, sixteen head of cattle, and ten sheep, in addition to his "servant," dwelling house, and 140 cultivated acres. He wasn't rich, but he was a substantial farmer, a solid member of the propertied class. Still, he felt poor; he feared poverty; he needed more.[18]

John suffered more losses: his three-year-old son and his wife Mary within the same year, just before he bought the Kingsessing farm. He didn't mention these tragedies in anything he wrote at the time, perhaps because they rekindled the embers of pain from his youth, stoking an anguish too hot for paper and ink. He suffered the deaths and went on. The new setting was part of a change, a break from sadness for him and his surviving four-year-old son, Isaac, and a home for a new wife, Ann Mendenhall, whom John married in 1729. The new farm was closer to market, had excellent soil of varying types, was a likely spot for a garden, and had good adjoining land that John purchased one tract at a time until the estate had nearly tripled in size.[19]

There is ? telling passage about John's first wife, which I make all the more of because it's all that John ever wrote about her. The occasion that provoked the reminiscence was the death of Peter Collinson's wife, which apparently flooded John with memories and empathy for his friend. The letter begins, "Dear Afflicted friend," and continues for just one deeply felt paragraph.

As I have been once near in some respect in the same gloomy disconsolate circumstances with thine, I believe I am in some measure qualified to sympathize with one of my dearest friends in his close and tender affliction. It seems hard to have one's dearest consort, a loving spouse, an affectionate wife, an object that we love above all terrestrial enjoyment taken from our arms. How grievous is it for one that is thus agreeable to be torn from our hearts! Her dear, sweet bosom is cold. Her tender heart, the center of mutual love is motionless. Her dear arms are no more extended to embrace her beloved, the partner of his cares and sharer of his pleasures must no more sit down with her husband at his table. Oh! my dear friend, let us resign all to God almighty. His will be done! He knows what is best for our ultimate good. We don't know what blessings he may yet bestow upon us. I lost an innocent, loving wife which I lived with above 4 years. I thought my loss could never have been made up. It was.[20]

This was twenty-seven years after Mary's death. The remembrance reveals a romantic tenderness that wasn't typical of John's generation, a passion for which there's a historical tradition in literature, but that isn't often visible in the language of American farmers during the eighteenth century. He really was struck down by the loss, which isn't visible in the surviving records contemporary with Mary's death. John suffered the death of his wife deeply, as he did those of his mother and father at earlier stages in life; he simply didn't often reflect, in writing at least, on the pain that he felt.

John saw his wife as a consort, an "object" of earthly enjoyment, a tender partner who shared intimately his life's trials and triumphs as a best friend. He thought his chance for such joy here on earth, perhaps even his capacity to love in this way, was forever lost with his dear Mary, but his heart recovered with his spirit and he lived to love a good woman again. Since John's second wife, Ann, outlived him by seven years, he never had occasion to write such a tender accounting of her as this.

Other men had more to say about Ann in their letters to John than he said himself. John St. Clair wanted to send her a cow; Thomas Bond offered respects "to your good spouse"; and Peter Collinson appreciated a letter she wrote to him while John was away. John once reported that his traveling plans had to be canceled because his wife and their children were "very sick" with measles. On another occasion, almost twenty years later, he observed in passing that she and one of their sons had "a fever lurking about them, but they mostly keep up." Compared to John, then, Ann had excellent health or, at least, she was able to "keep up" when she didn't feel well, thereby inconveniencing and worrying her husband only twice that he noted in more than forty-five years.[21]

Only one letter from John to Ann survives. There must have been others, though, since the tone and content of this one presumes regular correspondence and promises another soon. The letter is newsy, reporting his safe arrival, troublesome weather and danger overcome, great men he met, and his itinerary. "My dear spouse," John addresses her in the salutation; "My dear love" he calls her in the body of the note.[22]

That's about it. It was a love they both relied on, a tender relationship that no one wrote about. Their passion was private and letters were part of John's public life. She knew his work; he shared with her what was important to him. She not only shouldered the extra burdens of household and farm when he was away, but handled correspondence and shipped seeds to customers who couldn't wait for him to come home. She was strong, healthy, and reliable. She was a good wife and mother, and responsible for the household economy, which is why the gift cow would be hers. Milk, eggs, chickens, and vegetables planted near the house were part of her domain, which John took for granted and Ann probably did, too. Children, cleaning, cooking, and clothes were hers, too; it was her job to make sure all were fed by the dietary rules that her husband set. She was also an amiable hostess for the countless visitors who tramped mud through her house, a member of Darby Meeting even after its members disowned John, a mother, a mistress, a good wife in every way, an almost anonymous presence in the lives of her husband and son.

None of this stopped John from fantasizing about Indian "nymphs" or joking about resemblances between female organs and man-eating plants. At sixty-three years of age, perhaps less secure about his sexuality than he once was, John kidded about how he "fascinated two men's wives." The joke here was in comparing his hypnotic powers over women to those of a snake, an ability to entrap female prey by the look of his eyes. I'm still virile, the joke says; I still have power over women even as I grow old. "I ought not to envy my friend's happiness," Peter Collinson responded in the same vein, "but I should like such a mistress as thou hath got," who sends you curious plants. Women with an interest in botany who intruded on the world of these men were subject to sexual innuendo—speculation about their *real* motives and the *real* nature of their curiosity.[23]

That was the man's world of which John was a part. No worse than most and better than some, his jokes played on gender, nature, and self. They were creations of his mind, and by all indications that's as far as he went. It's how he compensated for insecurities he had; how he measured who he was and wanted to be—one gendered point in a triangulation of self that included Indians and African-American slaves about whom he had fewer kind things to say.

With Ann and his orphaned son, John began his life over again on the banks of the Schuylkill. The house is set in a beautiful place, even today, surrounded though it is by urban blight, oil-storage tanks, an industrially polluted river, and air that no one should breathe. Set back from the road, the house and six-acre garden are an oasis created by the vision of one man and the dedication of other people, which survives an environment hostile to gardens and, when the leaves adorn its huge trees, hides the horror of urban-industrial life from visitors' eyes. It is a place in which to remember, to forget, a site to imagine what was and never can be again. The trees are, of course, larger and different than they were then, especially the ones close to the house that block out the sun's light. The majestic bald cypress is gone; the pond is dried up. The Franklinia tree died, but was replaced, so it still lives. The paths are now paved; the house has aluminum gutters and bathrooms and lights, yet the place wears "improvements" and its shrunken size well.

John Bartram's gardens are dead. Clues to their contents are buried under the ground, where fossilized pollen awaits a curious twenty-first-century archeologist who wants to know more about plants.

Other gardens live in their place, tended by people who honor John's memory, his ambition, his vision, his skill, and who will someday refill the pond and rebuild the dock. From the parking lot on a clear evening, the view of Philadelphia's urban landscape is beautiful in its own way—shimmering, turning night into day and reaching up into the sky like decorated trees or mountains with lights.

A chapter of Crèvecoeur's *Letters from an American Farmer* helps us to see what it all looked like back then. Two pictures of the house drawn at different times provide insights, too. The first drawing is dated 1758, the same year that John read Confucius, was disowned by Darby Meeting, and wrote the first of his long epistles to his children. This helps situate the act of representing the spot within a context of John's contemplation of his place on the earth. The sketch is generally attributed to John, but was actually done by Billy working under his father's guidance. The legend refers to "my" study, which implies John's artistry, but the handwriting is William's, except for the words "1758 Sent to P Collinson," which are in John's hand. The perspective and skill are William's.

Comparison with a crude map drawn by John reveals the artist as plainly as a signature would. There is a romantic quality—typical of William—to the portrayal of the river, with the sailboat and fisherman on the opposite bank. The elevated perspective, slightly off to the left, is a commonplace of eighteenth-century landscape painting and the same one that William later took in his sketches of the Alachua Savanna. As for John's implied claim that it is his, that's typical of the patriarch, who had the habit of casually describing as his work what was done by his children, wife, servants, or other people's slaves.[24]

John's study appears in the sketch as separate from the main house and closer to the river, a place of comparative tranquility away from the bustle of the household, where John could read, write, and think curious thoughts about curious things. Only two small outbuildings are visible in the picture: a springhouse in the shade of the bald cypress tree, not far from the pond, and what's probably a privy up close to the house. No barns or seedhouses are pictured, no animals, wagons, vast fields, or tools. The house, the garden, and their owner are portrayed with no affectations of grandeur. The pond and the springhouse, kitchen and flower gardens, and the long lanes of trees descending gently to the river are featured elements of the garden design.

John Bartram's house and garden (Private collection)

The lone figure in the garden, posed with staff in hand, doesn't dominate the scene, but stakes his claim that the drawing and the vista are his. The patriarchal pose could be William's vision of his father and the fisherman a self-portrait of the artist enjoying nature at leisure and watching from the outside, judging and rejecting his father's role for himself. The picture is more the construction of John, who wanted his European friend to admire the garden for an orderliness that it really lacked, but the picturing is William's and the story it tells is, as always, more complicated than either man's would be by itself. The father sought approval from Europe's great men, who liked formal gardens with plants and trees all in rows, so the perspective is slightly altered from what archeological remains tell us was true, creating a neat line on the left side of the garden, for example, which wasn't really there. The son liked to row in the boat that he drew low on the right and admire the wild irises on the bank that seem taller than the cultivated trees, more natural, more bountiful, and more beautiful, too, than plants bound by the fences he drew.

John built the house with "hewn stone split out of the rock with my own hands." This seems more likely than the claim that he drew the picture, but don't believe for a moment that John, the owner of a slave, who had six sons and hired hands on his farm, hewed alone. "I have split rocks 17 foot long and built five houses," he wrote. "I . . . split rocks to make steps, door sills and large window cases and stone pig troughs. . . . Very easy, pleasant work it is," he recalled the year before the picture was drawn, "but the raising them up is very hard and must be done with iron bars and levers." It must have been slow, careful, skilled, heavy work that John supervised at every step, from choosing to splitting to hauling and lifting the stones into place. "My method is to draw a line upon the rock that I want to split from one end to the other in the middle of which I bore holes according to the depth or toughness thereof," John explained, and he had a formula for calculating how many holes had to be drilled and the number of wedges needed for the size and depth of the natural rock. No stone could resist, he proclaimed, however large, however deep, and whatever mineral it was: "I believe all things considered this method is as cheap as blowing with powder, which bursts the stone all to pieces very irregularly, takes much time in ramming, many times misseth and always [is] dangerous, but by this method you may split the stone to what size and shape you choose. The boring takes the most time; the splitting is soon done." Practical, ingenious, careful, determined, precise, and undeterred by the nature of elements for which he had a use, John took what he found and made what he needed, in this case a house, barns, and sheds for drying seeds.[25]

The house in the 1758 sketch was soon transformed. Several years later it looked much more like the second drawing, which is from the mid-nineteenth century, and the house that still stands today. John's detached study is gone, a south wing balances the north with an addition on each end, the roof is higher and wider with three dormers. In the most eccentric touches, there are four baroque window surrounds (two hidden by vines in the picture), while a Palladian central column and flanking pilasters support the roof and a timbered extension of the second floor. Most of the work was completed between 1758 and 1770, with the right pilaster in place by 1762, when John describes a vine that had already grown thirty feet up its face.[26]

The base of the right pilaster is square, which means it's misrepresented in the drawing, and those of the central column and left pilaster are round. All three are made of large stones, the same Wissahickon schist as the steps and face of the house, but carved round, stacked, and cemented together—which gives a much less elegant impression than the picture represents. The two central doors are still there. Side doors opening onto the veranda remain. The center column blocks the view from and of a first-floor window in the center of the house. The inscription under the second-story window is John's testament to a unitary deity, which he added in 1770 as perhaps his last architectural act.

There is no other house like it standing anywhere. It's the unique expression of John Bartram's design. The free-standing column is perhaps the first on any Philadelphia structure. The melding of elements is a distinctive combination of European influences and local materials as realized through Bartram's planning and supervision. The house, then, provides some clues to a man's mind, to his values, to his ambitions and dreams.

This man in his sixties, who was contemplating his death and the meaning of life, was also building for a future that wouldn't be his. The heaviness of the stone, split in lengths of up to eight feet and four inches thick, lends the house an aura of sturdiness, permanence, and a formidable quality that reflect the man's character and his needs. The

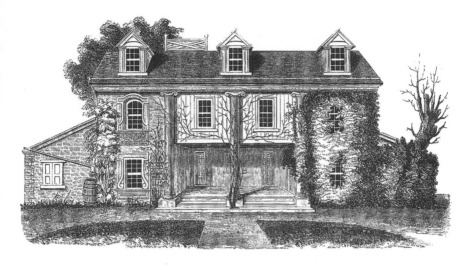

Residence of John Bartram (Darlington's *Memorials*)

Palladian pilasters and column and the baroque window surrounds are expressions of ambition that often got the better of him and make his house look pretentious and a little bizarre. The huge slabs may have split easily by the method that John described, but the rounded rocks in the columns must have put up quite a fight. The shape is achieved against the grain of the schist, as the chisel marks show. What an excruciating challenge to the rock's nature for a purpose that is entirely aesthetic—a very impractical way to hold up a roof. The spherical bases had to be carved one ring at a time, measured against each other and the stones that would sit on their heads.

For all the house's eccentricity, it is not the product of John's whimsy. It was meant to be serious, imposing, an arbor for vines, a shelter against storms, where women could cook and a family would eat, a warm spot to sleep, a secure home for children, a welcoming stop for travelers, a statuesque man-made presence that stands for the ages in a haven for plants. Why did John abandon the square style that he originally planned for the base of his columns, leaving an unmatched set? Why did he build a central column that blocks the view of his beloved garden and the rising sun's light from one of the first-floor windows? I wonder whether these flaws bothered him, too, and whether he ever regretted sacrificing beauty and practicality for an unnatural, contrived botch of European design.

The ambition to die in a great house got the better of him, but that's only the facade of John and his home. It must have been a grand house to live in, as warm and strong, as reliable and sure as John's heart. The principal functional concern, which probably inspired the wholesale renovations, was the creation of the south wing for John and Ann's retirement. The northern half would be inhabited by John Jr., and his new wife, Elizah Howell, after their marriage in 1771.[27]

The large second-floor room on the southwest corner of the house may have been John and Ann's new bedroom; the much smaller room on the southeast corner was John's library, with the carved testament under its window. The functions of the other second-floor rooms are not known, but there would be children and guests to fill them; and beginning in 1777, one would be for William, returned from his travels and needing a place to sleep for the next forty-six years. Perhaps his father's library, overlooking the garden, facing the first rays of morning sun, would be William's room or maybe he moved around to accommodate changes—the deaths of his father and mother, the birth of his brother's children, the arrival and departure of guests. The room directly below the library may have been where John kept his collections of rocks, shells, petrified wood, Indian pottery, and fossils. It was almost certainly the room where William wrote his book, essays, and letters, and drew pictures of animals and plants after his father's death, the same room from which he walked from the house to the garden on his last day.[28]

Crèvecoeur tells a story that idealizes the place that John built. The narrator is a "Russian gentleman," not the author himself or Farmer James, the principal narrator of *Letters from an American Farmer*, published five years after John Bartram's death. The chapter devoted to "Mr. John Bertram" is the most delightful, sentimental, and affirming of the twelve "letters" that make up the book and is based on visits that Crèvecoeur made himself to the Kingsessing farm. The fictional narrator and the misspelling of the real John's last name are the first clues that the farm and the farmer are being transformed, that the story is a source for what John Bartram could be in Crèvecoeur's hands, but not always reliable for what the man or the home ever was.

As the gentleman enters the front door, he gives us a metaphorical description of the builder as represented in his work—simple, decent, modest, unique, guileless, strong, practical, and towering in the way that a plain staircase can be. Crèvecoeur's visit was in the spring of 1765, before the major expansion took place, so the house he describes is "small but decent" and unremarkable from the outside. Upon entering the front door, the gentleman sees "something peculiar in its first appearance which seemed to distinguish it from those of his neighbours: a small tower in the middle of it not only helped to strengthen it but afforded convenient room for a staircase." The "small tower" isn't there anymore, so we can only imagine the structure inside the house.[29]

Bertram isn't at home when the gentleman arrives, so the visitor decides to search the fields rather than waiting for him to return.

After a little time I perceived the Schuylkill, winding through delightful meadows, and soon cast my eyes on a new-made bank, which seemed greatly to confine its stream. After having walked on its top a considerable way, I at last reached the place where ten men were at work. I asked, if any of them could tell me where Mr. Bertram was. An elderly looking man with wide trousers and a large leather apron on, looking at me, said, "My name is Bertram; dost thee want me?" "Sir, I am come on purpose to converse with you, if you can be spared from your labour." "Very easily," he answered; "I direct and advise more than I work."

Here we have another perspective on the nature of John Bartram at work altering nature's course, making the river more useful by confining its stream, challenging the elements more boldly than when he split rocks, but not hewing or shoveling alone. Indeed, Crèvecoeur's Bertram is, by his own testimony, thrilled to stop supervising the other men's toil. This sounds more like John Bartram than the portrait he drew of himself.[30]

The physical description rings true as well—the practical clothes, the old man deep in the mud, congenial, always willing to talk. The drainage project that John oversaw was really a community endeavor and the workers were drawn from other farms, too, adjacent to his, which leads to a mistaken impression about the relationship between Bartram and the laborers that has long survived Crèvecoeur's account.

After returning to the house, where John changed his clothes, it was time for a meal.

> We entered into a large hall, where there was a long table full of victuals; at the lowest part sat his Negroes; his hired men were next, then the family and myself; and at the head, the venerable father and his wife presided. Each reclined his head and said his prayers, divested of the tedious cant of some and of the ostentatious style of others.[31]

Let's suppose that the scene occurred much as Crèvecoeur's gentleman tells us—that there was a party supervised by John building a drainage bank, which could have taken place while Crèvecoeur was visiting the farm, and that upon their return to the house a meal was served to the workers seated in ranks. Crèvecoeur is struck by the interracial harmony, the patriarchal presence, and the Quaker simplicity of the scene. The "Negroes" wouldn't have been John's in the sense that Crèvecoeur means. Bartram owned just one slave, whose name, family tradition tells us, was Harvey. This would be the slave whom William says, in the published eulogy to his father, "had been raised up in the family almost from his infancy" and then was freed "in the prime of his life." Perhaps there were other African-Americans who worked on the farm or possibly those seated at John's table were slaves owned by neighbors, who sent them to help with the community project; we simply can't know.[32]

Over the course of his visit, the Russian gentleman is greatly impressed by the demeanor of the patriarch and the behavior of African-Americans who work on the farm. Ultimately, he credits Bertram with altering the nature of slaves by granting them freedom and treating them well. "In the first settlement of this province," Bertram informs his guest, "we employed them as slaves, I acknowledge; but when we found that good example, gentle admonition, and religious principles could lead them to subordination and sobriety, we relinquished a method so contrary to the profession of Christianity." In other words, it was appropriate that they were slaves in the beginning, but "we"—by which he means Quakers—educated the slaves to be something else, to be sober and subordinate, and to accept a place at the bottom of a great chain of freedom with their former masters still on the top.[33]

There may be no literal connection at all between this story and John Bartram, but such a benign view of slavery within a philosophy of nature is utterly consistent with his son William's views later in life. This leads me to wonder whether the foundation for such beliefs may be visible in the Russian gentleman's tale. What can be known, though, is that John Bartram expressed views about the education of slaves very different from the ones that Crèvecoeur put in his mouth. In a letter critical of George Whitefield, the famous evangelical minister who preached to huge crowds during the Great Awakening, John expressed utter disdain for both Whitefield's Calvinism and his ambition to educate slaves. What was the point, Bartram asked, of teaching young Negroes and then returning them to their masters?

> If they was elected so long ago [i.e., if they were among God's elect], what need he to trouble his head about them? If they was damned what signifieth his tutoring? However this, we may be sure he will teach them to think themselves as good or better then their masters and too good for servants.

If John Bartram favored any education at all for slaves, which it sounds as though he did not, it would have been a less ambitious curriculum than Whitefield's, one that emphasized distinctions and subordination rather than the equality of all in God's eyes. In other words, John wasn't the exemplar of Quaker liberalism that Crèvecoeur portrays him to be.[34]

Neither John nor William wrote much about slavery, which is in itself revealing about two men who bought, sold, and owned more than one. John "zealously testified against slavery," William tells us;

> and, that his philanthropic precepts, on this subject, might have their due weight and force, he gave liberty to a most valuable male slave, then in the prime of his life, who had been bred up in the family almost from his infancy.[35]

There is no reason to disbelieve this, but other words and behavior belie the moral simplicity of this story. The language William uses here, too, suggests both more and less than he intends to tell us. The slave was "bred up" in the household "almost" from birth. In other words, John

43

somehow acquired a small child, almost literally tearing the boy from his mother's breast, whatever John's precise role in the transaction. We lose in this telling the pain of her loss, any sympathy that John had for a child who must have been emotionally crushed. Didn't it remind John of his own mother's death, when he was about the same tender age? If it didn't, why not? Where was his compassion, his empathy? Where was his rage at a labor system that was so cruel, so unjust?

John freed Harvey at a financial loss to himself, so we might give him some credit for becoming enlightened about the immorality of owning another man and acting against his own pecuniary interest in the name of what's right. Even that is hard to do, though, since he bought and sold slaves for Billy when his son wanted to try his hand as a Florida planter. These transactions in people take the Bartram family almost up to John's death, and there's not a word in his correspondence that testifies to the enlightenment with which William credited him. On the contrary, what few words survive show John in a different light.[36]

Throughout his journals of Southern trips, John notes in passing that slaves are "lent" or their labor sold to him as guides, to "row and cook for us," to swim horses across rain-swollen rivers, and to provide other menial services. In none of these situations does John comment critically on the servitude of these people or decline, as at least some other Quakers of his day would, to profit from the labor of slaves. He discusses improvements wrought in the landscape by slave labor, without comment on the institution of slavery, but in praise of the change. The silence speaks volumes.[37]

Crèvecoeur's chapter on Bertram is a reverie, an oasis in his parched indictment of the nature of man, but consistent with his belief that our nature and nature itself must be transformed if we are to survive. Here, in letter eleven, he offers a model that dictates abandoning the lessons, texts, and manners of the past for a new way out of the violence that threatens to destroy civilization. Bertram, the good Quaker, is an ideal of the way humans could live in harmony with each other and with the earth. "Every disposition of the fields, fences, and trees seemed to bear the marks of perfect order and regularity," Crèvecoeur's gentleman reports. The meal he's served is an "honest country dinner," free of insincere ceremonies and the "polite expressions" of the civilized world. This isn't the forest or the city, but an idyllic garden somewhere between, where there is peace. Philadelphia's streets remind the gentleman of Pompeii, the ancient dead city, which represents his indictment of urban life. The wilderness of previous letters is a horror more deadening still.

The garden is a treasure of nature transformed. Fields drained by honest labor become pastures where cattle graze, "deep-bellied, short-legged, having udders ready to burst." The fields produce bounties commensurate with Bertram's labor, where he has thrown lime, ashes, and horse dung two times a week. "By these simple means I mow, one year with another, fifty-three hundreds of excellent hay per acre from a soil which scarcely produced five-fingers [a small plant resembling strawberries] some years before." Bertram rotates his crops according to the best scientific advice and reaps astonishing crops of wheat, flax, oats, and Indian corn, "a miracle in husbandry" inspired by God.[38]

All of this is more or less true. John had his fields drained and manured, and he directed the rotation of crops. He was an extremely successful farmer. He read books on agricultural methods, including such works as Robert Maxwell's *Treatise Concerning the Manner of Fallowing the Ground* and Jethro Tull's *Horse Hoeing Husbandry*, and culled them for what worked in this climate and soil, with these crops and the animals that he raised.[39] He experimented, exchanging information with other agricultural innovators who visited his farm and whom he met on his searches for new plants.

All of this led Crèvecoeur's gentleman to wonder when Bertram imbibed his "first wish to cultivate the science of botany," to wonder why and how he became the curious man of nature that he was. Bertram's reply tells us something about John and more about the plot of Crèvecoeur's story. These are the lines that he needed his character of Bertram to say:

I have never received any other education than barely reading and writing; this small farm was all the patrimony my father left me; certain debts and the want of meadows kept me rather low in the beginning of my life; my wife brought me nothing in money; all her riches consisted in her good temper and great knowledge of housewifery. I scarcely know how to trace my steps in the botanical career; they appear to me now like unto a dream, but thee mayest rely on what I shall relate, though I know that some of our friends have laughed at it.[40]

This has a ring of the real John—the claim to an impoverished beginning, which we know isn't true, and the portrayal of himself as an uneducated man, which is just a bit closer to fact. He didn't attend college or receive formal training in Latin or Greek as a gentleman would, but he had a solid Quaker education that was probably superior to graduating from a good high school today. The Darby School was a short walk from John's childhood home and students typically attended twelve months a year, eight hours a day for five days a week, with four more hours on Saturday. It was a practical curriculum that suited John's social class, stressing reading, writing, "casting accounts," and arithmetic. Books probably included George Fox's *Primer* and speller, as well as texts on grammar, geometry, and keeping accounts. There would have been religious instruction, too, taught in a catechetical method that employed rote.[41]

John was neither uneducated nor entirely self-educated as he claimed in the letters he wrote to great men, some of whom were no more formally trained than he was. The story that John told about himself, and apparently shared with Crèvecoeur, has in common with his friend Benjamin Franklin's *Autobiography* an exaggerated sense of how low he began and how high he rose by the sweat of his brow. John was painfully conscious of the distance between his own education and that of men he knew, botanical scholars who wrote books and letters to him that he couldn't entirely comprehend. He wasn't a gentleman, nor was he university trained, which created a gulf that no amount of hard work, recognition, and accomplishment could fill for John. He feared, sometimes quite rightly, that the great men were laughing at him, making fun of his lack of manners, plain dress, and simple prose. He would have liked to turn his rusticity into a badge of superiority, as Franklin did so brilliantly in Europe's royal courts, but John lacked the confidence, genius, accomplishment, and rhetorical skill that enabled Franklin to make himself into a joke.

How, then, wondered Crèvecoeur's gentleman, had this impoverished farmer become America's preeminent authority on the nature of plants? What led him to put down his plow, study botanical nomenclature in a language foreign to him, and wander off into the wilderness in search of flowers previously unknown to curious men?

> ... one day I was very busy in holding my plough (for thee see'st that I am but a ploughman), and being weary, I ran under the

shade of a tree to repose myself. I cast my eyes on a daisy; I plucked it mechanically and viewed it with more curiosity than common country farmers are wont to do, and observed therein very many distinct parts, some perpendicular, some horizontal. "What a shame," said my mind, or something that inspired my mind, "that thee shouldest have employed so many years in tilling the earth and destroying so many flowers and plants without being acquainted with their structures and their uses!"[42]

This tale may be true in the sense that John told it to Crèvecoeur, but it makes a claim for an interest in botany blooming fairly late in life that is unlikely and contrary to what John told other men. In one letter he says that his interest in botany began at age ten; in another he says he was twelve, which would have been the same year that his father was killed.[43] In the sadness he suffered, in the fields where he cried by himself, perhaps John began to feel what was around him in ways other sons of farmers did not. Through his tears John may have seen more clearly the wildflowers that others thoughtlessly plowed. The story begs the question of inspiration when it acknowledges a Lockean sense that ideas aren't innate without speculating on the source for John's curiosity. In any event, formal Quaker education included the study of botany, so John's fascination undoubtedly preceded the purchase of the Kingsessing farm and his second marriage.

The Russian gentleman's story does reveal, though, the distinctive combination of qualities that made up the true man about whom Crèvecoeur is writing. For all its bucolic efflorescence, the story also reeks of the practical, "mechanical" farmer who gazes at a daisy and sees the structure of its parts. Bertram ponders, not the beauty of the flower, but the possible "use" to which it could be put. That isn't how John Bartram's son William would see or the kind of story that he would tell about himself. The focus on structure and use captures part of John well, whether he told the story in a similar way or Crèvecoeur just made it up.

This seeming inspiration suddenly awakened my curiosity, for these were not thoughts to which I had been accustomed. I returned to my team, but this new desire did not quit my mind; I mentioned it to my wife, who greatly discouraged me from prosecuting my new scheme, as she called it; I was not opulent enough, she said, to dedicate much of my time to studies and labours which might rob me of that portion of it which is the only wealth of the American farmer. However, her prudent caution did not discourage me; I thought about it continually, at supper, in bed, and wherever I went. At last I could not resist the impulse; for on the fourth day of the following week, I hired a man to plough for me and went to Philadelphia.[44]

If there is any truth to this part of the story, the wife who discouraged John's impulse was his first wife, not the one who opened the door when the Russian gentleman knocked or who cooked for Crèvecoeur when he visited the Bartrams' farm. John had already embarked on his "scheme" when his second wife, Ann, came to live in the Kingsessing house, so the story conflates the two wives into one, when it would have been Mary whose entreaties fell on her husband's deaf ears. The concerns Crèvecoeur describes are financial and they are also about class. Act appropriately to your station, the conflated wife pleads; you aren't a gentleman with the leisure for curious habits; farmers don't indulge themselves in books. Whether it was a wife or John's conscience or Crèvecoeur's fertile imagination that gives this story truth, it captures the nature of the leap that John Bartram took.

As Bertram tells the story, and as John Bartram told it, too, books were the foundation upon which his study of nature was built. He borrowed from James Logan, who had the largest personal library in colonial Pennsylvania, and who patronized promising young men such as Bartram and Franklin. Later in life John would also borrow from the Library Company of Philadelphia, the paid subscription library that Franklin helped found, but only after its members granted him a free share. He was grateful for the gift of membership, because he couldn't see laying out the "six pounds to purchase a share and ten shillings yearly (they having few books of botany or natural history)." His reading was focused and he watched where his money was spent.[45]

John ordered books from London, which he asked Peter Collinson to send as partial payment in kind for the seeds and specimens that he shipped to aristocratic customers. Collinson thought that John needed only two botanical books, Philip Miller's *Gardener's Dictionary* and John Parkinson's *Herbal,* which by their indexes would enable John to find the Latin name of any plant his customers could want. Eventually, these volumes arrived as "presents" from wealthy patrons. Although Collinson played an essential facilitating role in the building of John's personal library and his education as a botanist, he also served as a censor and unwelcome guide to the knowledge obtainable from books. John had requested a copy of Joseph Tournefort's *Elements of Botany;* Collinson replied that it cost too much, wasn't necessary for a collector of plants, and, anyway, John read too many books. You already have Miller and Parkinson, Collinson pointed out, and "I would not have you puzzle with others for they contain the ancient and modern knowledge of botany. Remember Solomon's advice, in reading of books there is no end." Collinson didn't send Linnaeus's *Systema Naturae,* as John had asked, because "his coining a set of new names for plants tends but to embarrass and perplex the study of botany as to his system on which they are founded. Botanists are not agreed about it. Very few like it, be that as it will." Besides, the book wasn't in English and John's Latin wasn't very good.[46]

The attraction to Linnaean classification was more than a passing fancy of John's and he didn't allow Collinson to dismiss his interest so lightly. In a relatively short period of time, Linnaeus's system swept aside all before it and even Collinson succumbed to its lure. It reduced names of animals and plants to two Latin words, binomials, one placing an organism within a group that shared characteristics, the other labeling its uniqueness from any other on earth. Linnaeus had a strong sense of order, a practical and concrete way of thought; he was visually oriented and focused on detail. John Bartram thought the same way and was attracted to the simplicity and clarity of Linnaeus's system. He also shared with Linnaeus a naturalistic view of mankind and an anthropocentric understanding of plants, thereby integrating mankind and nature in a holistic philosophy of nature and God. From the first time he heard about the work of the Swedish philosopher, John wanted to master enough botanical Latin (which wasn't at all the same as the classical Latin that gentlemen knew) to read Linnaeus's *Systema Naturae* and apply the system to his search for new plants.[47]

"I take thy advice about books very kindly," John replied to Collinson, his patronizing friend, "although I love reading such dearly and I believe if Solomon had loved women less and books more he would have been a wiser and happier man than he was." Eventually, John got Linnaeus, Tournefort, and many more books about travel and plants, which he adored, and a few others that he never asked Collinson for and didn't want. "Barclay's *Apology* I shall take care of for thy sake," he wrote to his friend, "it answers thy advice much better than if thee had sent me one of natural history or botany which I should have spent ten time[s] the hours in reading of while I might have laboured for the maintenance of my family."[48] Here we see John's delightful good humor in play, his endearing wit gently chiding Collinson, and an expression of interests clearly expressed—no religion, no philosophy, no disputes about silly things. John wanted the facts about nature written by men who knew what they were talking about. He was grateful for Henry Baker's *The Microscope Made Easy* and Samuel Purchas's *Hakluytus Posthumus or Purchas his Pilgrimes.* And he cherished Mark Catesby's *History of American Birds* and *Natural History of Carolina, Florida, and the Bahama Islands,* Sir Hans Sloane's *Catalogus Plantarum,* Johann Jakob Dillenius's *Historia Muscorum,* Johann Friedrich Gronovius's *Flora Virginica* and *Index Supellectilis Lapidaea,* and Thomas François D'Alibard's *Florae Parisiensis Prodromus,* all sent by the authors, which made them more special still.

These were John's books, and there were many more, too: his tools, his bibles, his foundation of knowledge for the research he would do. He built a place of honor to keep them—with his own hands, he'd say, which wasn't quite true, but a special place, "my little library or chapel as I call it"—where he could quietly worship the truth. The equation of library and chapel reveals John Bartram as a man of his time, one who neither saw nor feared contradiction between his science and his God, a man of the early Enlightenment, who found the Bible an authoritative source for most truths that he sought. "The book of Nature" revealed God just as surely as the Bible; Linnaeus's *Systema Naturae* helped him comprehend the meaning of the specimens he found in the wilderness "temple" where he worshiped and studied. He lived at a post-Copernican, pre-Darwinian moment in time, when all systems of thought were mutually supporting, when the "truth" that bound experience—social, spiritual, and biological—in a system of natural laws was within reach, if not grasp. John hewed and built upon theological foundations that could support his observations of nature without fear of crumbling; and he found the assurance in nature that eluded the Puritans before him and most Euro-Americans born since his death.[49]

The New World provided the perfect setting for amateur botanists to make contributions recognized and appreciated by European "philosophers," men who would be called "scientists" beginning in the nineteenth century. The need was for identification, collection, domestic nurturing, and classification of "new" plants. Identification and collection of previously unknown (to Europeans) and recognized plants of medicinal value was a job for colonial amateurs, who then shipped specimens—seeds, drawings, inked leaf prints, and live root cultures—to European merchants who served as botanical middlemen in the business of nature for the philosophers, who classified and named the "new" finds, and for the gentleman gardeners, who tried to nurture the most novel, useful, and beautiful of the New World flora in their formal gardens. Of the 8000 species of plants that grew in eastern North America, only 6 reached Europe before 1600, another 50 in the next half-century, and by 1734, when John Bartram began collecting, about 300 had already been sent. Between 1734 and 1776, when the American Revolution interrupted this lucrative trade in plants, the number of "new" finds doubled to about 600 and John Bartram was personally responsible for about half of this increase, or one quarter of all the plants identified and sent to Europe during the colonial period.[50]

It would be difficult to overstate the significance of this one man's accomplishment in his life's endeavor. In sheer volume—a measure of the kind that mattered to him and the great men whom he knew—John's contribution surely earned him Linnaeus's praise as the greatest botanist of his day and the King of England's stipended recognition as a Royal Botanist for the mainland North American colonies. In terms of the scientific significance of John's finds, the achievement was equally vast. And not least, in terms of the praise that he craved and the financial rewards that he reaped for his labors, were the aesthetic consequences of John's shipments of beautiful plants to British patrons. For nature was not just a science and a business in the world where John lived, and the eyes through which he saw nature were not those of a farmer with manure on his boots and flakes of chiseled rock in his hair. John envisioned his library as a "chapel," after all, and imagined the wilderness as a

> grand and spacious temple amongst the lofty chains of mountains, the craggy precipices of elevated rock embellished with various

shrubs, pliant evergreens out of their uneven surfaces and the gloomy shaded vails with the variety of the ferny tribe or various shrubs and plants of quiet recess. The purling streams and glittering cascades, the level plains, the concealed humid bosoms discharging numerous pearly drops perpetually trickling down, or the shore of the mighty ocean, the great metropolis of the finny tribe, where we view the rolling waves dashing against the shore and breaking into steam, rising up in vapour which is collected in humid fleeces in the vast expanse. All the objects, all these variety of situations, demonstrate the power and wisdom of an almighty power, the contemplation of which with humble adoration we sincerely resign our will to his.[51]

Where does this come from? What was the inspiration for these images inside John's head? What led this "simple ploughman," as Crèvecoeur calls him, to see "humid fleeces" up in the sky and "glittering cascades," "purling streams," and "pearly drops" down here on earth, where other farmers would notice the potential for rain and water for their animals and crops? How did he perceive "craggy precipices" and "lofty chains" rather than monstrous mountains that got in the way of development and where you couldn't grow wheat? Why did he feel the gloom of "shaded vails" instead of seeing rich soil and trees that hid Indians, rattlers, and wolves, trees to be chopped down and fields to be plowed, whose worth could be gauged as acres and lumber? Was it the books that he read in his "chapel" or the daisy that Crèvecoeur says John found in his field? Was it religion or science or a sensitive soul that heartened his mind?

These are difficult questions to answer, as they would be for anyone living or dead, even when you can reconstruct his life's reading, when you have seen what he built, read what he wrote, and know the books that he touched and that touched him. Questions about influence are much more complex than that; our minds are both more and less than what's in the books that we own or say that we've read. They are, perhaps first, questions about what we can see.

CHAPTER THREE

Visions

T O ASK WHAT JOHN BARTRAM SAW when he botanized the wilderness is to enquire about all his senses; for sound, smell, taste, and touch all fashion perceptions of our environment. No less are questions about John's sight also about his mind, because imagination is the most powerful tool used in constructing experience from the elements around us. Finally, and not least significantly, questions about John's vision are about the culture that shaped his expectations, thereby influencing what he would see and how he would report it to others who shared his curiosity about nature.

What we can see, any of us, is usually not much more than we're prepared to see and is often quite a bit less. Preparation is no guarantee that images can be fully comprehended within the scope of our vision, but knowing what we are looking for is certainly an aid in finding it—whether "it" is there in any objectifiable sense—and is also a barrier to seeing something we don't expect. Just as our eyesight is limited by distance, in the sense that objects can be too close or too far away for us to see, and is subject to cognitive, environmental, and physiological distortions, so, too, do our culturally shaped expectations and the ability of our imaginations to sort myriad and novel images define our visual capacity. None of us sees everything; all of us see something; few of us see the same thing.

Others have pondered the implications of subjectivity in the writings of explorers, who, like John Bartram, sought to objectify nature in their reports. From geographers to literary and art critics, all are fascinated by the combination of the objective and highly personal in depictions of landscape; and they see such descriptions, whether written or drawn, as rich sources for contemplating the cultural and personal dimensions of exploration. Accounts of engagements with nature often contain idealized notions of habitat, with moral, aesthetic, economic, and political features that are much more revealing than the narrators intend. The critics alert us to motion and pause, foreground and background, and conceptions of time in explorers' reports. They posit connections between seeing and words, persons and things. The writer or artist is always situated in the landscape, whether he presents himself as a central figure or attempts to minimize the impact of his presence. "We never look at just one thing," John Berger writes; "we are always looking at the relation between things and ourselves." The culture, the self, the imaginative, and the real combine for each explorer into a landscape imbued with personal meaning. "What is most striking in conceptions of nature," Clarence J. Glacken proclaims, "is the yearning for purpose and order." John Bartram's writings are no exception.[1]

The most visually striking display of John's yearning for order is his map of the East Coast from New York south to the Carolinas. Maps are a quintessential attempt to order space, to control by naming, to fix location as a way to avoid feeling lost. This one is crude in the extreme, ignoring coastal features and lacking a sense of scale. It has a riparian focus, with rivers labeled and oriented in relation to one another. The origins of rivers are imagined, inaccurately as it turns out. The map could be useful to a traveler only in the limited sense of revealing the name of a feature *if* he could fix it in relationship to others on the same page. For example, if you know that you are standing on the west bank of the Delaware River and walking south, the map identifies the next major waterway encountered as the Susquehanna. The map inaccurately portrays all the rivers as running due west to east, proportionately understates the size of the Chesapeake Bay, and would be an unreliable guide to distances between features in any direction.

What these limitations tell us is that John's ambition was confined to naming and ordering. The map was not intended as a travelers' guide; indeed, it was meant for Peter Collinson, the London merchant, who never planned to cross the Atlantic. The map would help orient across space the information that John shared with his friend in

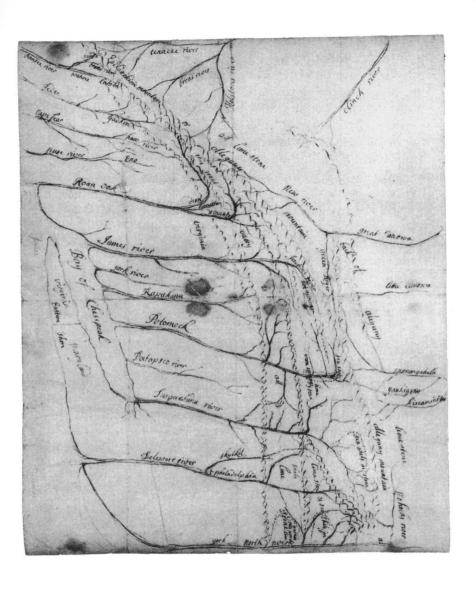

John Bartram's map (American Philosophical Society)

other written forms, details about where a particular plant grew in the wild, where John had traveled in relation to the features represented here. Curiously, the map names no political boundaries, which commonly help fix Euro-Americans' place on the landscape. It's a natural map into which humans intrude as the namers and John as the draftsman who records where the land ends, where water flows, and the ocean and mountain barriers that defined Anglo-Americans' space.

Philadelphia is the only city, the only unnatural feature identified by the map. The intrusion of this one human construction is a self-referential gesture by which John situates himself in relation to the natural landscape he draws. This is the home base by which readers can calculate the orientation of John's mind to the rest of the map. In this regard, it's significant that the sketch is principally focused on features south of Philadelphia. When John drew the map, which was sometime between 1738 and 1742, he had yet to travel south of Virginia and had made several trips farther north, to areas that he doesn't even include.[2] John was drawn southward, to the place where his father died, where his half-brother now lived, where there were more plants to discover and a more enticing wilderness to explore, to a simply "ravishing place for a curious botanist."[3]

John's method of labeling dictates that the map be inverted from the standard north at the top. The reader faces south to read the names of the rivers and west for the remaining features, away from the population centers of British North America, toward the regions where nature was least affected by the "improvements" of man, where plants had yet to be named by Europeans. This introduces an element of time to the drawing, almost certainly unintended, with the New England and European pasts behind the reader, who faces the wilderness future with its large blank spaces. Again, though, let us not be deceived about the empty spots on the map; we can be sure that John had expectations that would help fill them in.[4]

Within these parameters of selection and representation, the map is artless to a fault. There's no embellishment by color, no expression of any river's grandeur compared to the rest. There's no estimation of any peak's character in relation to others in the Appalachian chain. John hadn't traveled to either the southern or western extremities, so the map's frontiers are based on a combination of secondhand knowledge and imagination.

One additional detail suggests the cast of John's curious mind. He plots an area on the banks of the Schuylkill River, at the foot of the Allegheny Mountains, where there are "sea shells in stone." This is an observation of no significance for its developmental potential or practical use. He might better have plotted the locales where iron was mined or medicinal plants could be found. It isn't a feature that helps the reader fix himself in space, but rather one that addresses questions about time, which identifies a conjunction between the science and faith that guided John Bartram's travels.

What John asks of these seashells is their relationship to biblical events. The shells in the mountains reveal to him that the entire area east and north of the chain was once beneath the ocean, but that by itself doesn't date the change. He's left with the question of the relationship between the nature he observes and the deluge from which God saved Noah.

> As for the vast body of sea shells, some petrified, some not, which are found beyond our blue mountains, included in rocks, I take them to be of an earlier date than the Noachin deluge itself. These I rather suppose to have been deposited where we now find them, after the spirit of God had moved on the face of the waters, and light was separate from darkness; before beasts lived on dry land, or fowls flew in the air. Moses does not particularly mention shell-fish, or when the sea produced them, but I take this to be the likeliest time. For when the terrestrial particles of matter began to subside and coalesce, might not those shells be fixed and tumbled together in various directions in the confused manner they are found.[5]

The evidence John marshals to date the shells from before the great flood meld a scientist's—he would say philosopher's—interpretation of the Bible with observed fact. "I don't deny the Noachin flood," he explains to a correspondent, "but I believe by the account we have of it being mixed with so much fresh water those shells were neither bred in it nor was it natural for such prodigious numbers to be then formed in such masses of rocks all over the back country."[6]

The Bible helps John fix the meaning of what he can see. Viewed through this prism, his map depicts the present and past of the region that he explores, just as he unintentionally portrays the origins and future of the culture whose empire spreads beyond the space that he draws. Nature and the Bible are both open books, to use one of John's favorite metaphors, open to those curious enough to examine the evidence for themselves. He's impatient with men who lack the courage to read nature and with those who, without the experience of nature to guide their reading, dictate the Bible's meaning for other folks. This man, who tried so hard to judge others tolerantly, had little good to say about ministers and armchair philosophers. He thought ministers were the principal barrier to people's understanding of the Bible, which seemed to him accessible to anyone with common sense who could read. George Whitefield's Calvinism, for example, struck John as unnatural, with its images of

> such favorites as was elected before they were born or begot or before the foundations of the worlds was laid, and then when they get up into heaven they are to witness against us at the great day of judgment when our bodies must rise again after they have been wonderfully dissolved and transformed in elemental and vegetable and often animal species.[7]

John's view of nature limited what he could imagine about the hereafter. He didn't believe the laws of nature would be broken, in this case reversed, to conform with what somebody without common sense and a firsthand knowledge of nature read in a book, even the Bible. That's not to say that John challenged the Bible in any systematic sense—although, as we know, he didn't believe in the image of Christ as God presented in the New Testament, not because he didn't think Christ's teaching wiser than that of most men, but because miracles that defy the laws of nature simply couldn't be true. He found stories about water turning to wine, loaves and fishes multiplying by the hundreds, and corpses coming to life and ascending to the heavens impossible to believe in any literal sense. Rather than dismissing the Bible, though, John explored it for truths that conformed with what he "knew" about how nature works and disputed only "unnatural" interpretations. The Bible shaped his view of nature—the meaning of shells found in the mountains, for instance—just as surely as his firsthand knowledge of nature limited what he could believe about God.

John's disdain for paid, professional clergy is the standard Quaker critique with a naturalist's twist. Even the labeling of professional ministers as unnatural has its roots in the writings of George Fox and his seventeenth-century followers in the Society of Friends. So, too, is John's ambivalent relationship with the Bible typical of Quakers, who see it as only one source of Divine Revelation, and no more privileged than the continuing revelation of those Friends inspired by the Light. Likewise, John's love of books and his suspicion of book learning present an innate tension that is unremarkable for an eighteenth-century Quaker farmer from Pennsylvania.[8]

What makes John's perspective distinct from its obvious cultural influences is the extreme to which he carries his views and the degree to which he uses nature as the test against which all else, including the Bible and the divinity of Christ, is measured. If Quakerism partly explains John's naturalism, nature explains his unique personal form of Quakerism, which ultimately gets him disowned by Darby Meeting. In other words, John is a Quaker naturalist and a naturalistic Quaker at the same time and sorting out the direction and nature of the influence any more precisely than that would distort a complex web of interaction.

A search for "Quaker texts" that account for the perspective John brought to the forest would be a mistake, both because he explicitly rejected such disputatious books, as when he declined to read the copy of Barclay's *Apology* that Peter Collinson sent him, and because, for all the surviving discussion of books in his correspondence, he never mentions, quotes from, or paraphrases a single one. Furthermore, a reconstruction of his family's library reveals that the Bartrams owned none of the classic Quaker texts, not even George Fox's *Journal* or any of the writings by William Penn. That's not to say that John hadn't read such books, probably as a student; it's simply to observe that they had no visible, demonstrable effect on the way that he saw what he saw or wrote what he wrote.

There were, of course, books that profoundly influenced John. Any man whose library is a "chapel," as John's was to him, is a man who reveres the printed word. He borrowed books, bought them, and received them gratefully as gifts. "So earnest was he in the pursuit of learning," according to a posthumous biographical sketch, "that he seldom sat at his meals without his book; often his victuals in one hand, and his book in the other." John devoured books along with his food, worshiped them in his library, and, as his eyes weakened over the course of his life, pulled his chair ever closer to the light of the fire and buried his face deeper into the pages that nourished, enlightened, and sometimes inflamed him. His reading was focused on nature, on what helped him to see, to interpret, to use, and to profit from what he found in the woods and nurtured in the gardens adjacent to his house.[9]

With the exception of the Bible, John favored new books over old, because "ancient books, whether sacred or profane, mostly contain truth mixed with (I was going to say error) which is to be discovered only by an unprejudiced and experienced reader." There was also danger in books, which could lead one astray, down a path toward ignorance and lies. He saw experience and objectivity as the foundations for knowledge supplemented by books.[10]

Thomas Burnet's *The Sacred Theory of the Earth* was an important supplement to John's experience and reflects a perspective similar to John's on knowledge, nature, and God. "Reason is to be our first guide," Burnet maintains, and the philosopher of nature "should be of an ingenuous and unprejudiced temper," which does not "so much require book-learning and scholarship, as good natural sense to distinguish true and false, and to discern what is well proved, and what is not." John liked to see himself this way.

As for the relationship between revealed religion and science, Burnet's ideas are again echoed by John. "We are not to suppose that any truth concerning the natural world can be an enemy to religion," Burnet writes, "for Truth cannot be an enemy to Truth, God is not divided against himself." Finally, Burnet advocates using the Bible as a natural history manual in the way that John does. "It seems to be very reasonable to believe," says Burnet,

> that besides the precepts of religion, which are the principal subject and design of the books of Holy Scripture, there may be providentially conserved in them the memory of things and time so remote, as could not be retrieved, either by History, or by the Light of Nature. . . . These I always looked upon as the seeds of great

knowledge, or head of theories fixed on purpose to give us aim and direction how to pursue the rest that depend upon them.

According to Burnet, then, if we take the Bible to nature it can help us comprehend what we see. John also reverses this process, though, when he takes his experience in nature to the Bible as a test of what he reads there. Burnet is not the source for that sort of thinking, which he would find heresy, but it's a logical inversion of the ideas in his book.[11]

Similarly, John Ray's *The Wisdom of God Manifested in the Works of the Creation* complemented John's experience of nature and helped him describe what he saw. Ray found God reflected in nature, for

there is no greater, at least no more palpable and convincing argument of the existence of a deity, than the admirable art and wisdom that discovers itself in the make and constitution, the order and disposition, the ends and uses of all the parts and members of this stately fabric of heaven and earth.

Ray rejected Descartes's vision of animals as machines, substituting a sense of brutes as sharing, in varying degrees, the same emotions and skills as humans. His equation of talents across species lines is neither so developed nor as extreme as John Bartram's, but it's a kind of thinking that John could build upon.

Ray was also among those who saw mountains differently than others had described them before, in a way that John saw them, too. "Because mountains have been looked upon by some as warts, and superfluous excrescences, of no use or benefit," Ray begins, "nay rather as signs and proofs, that the present earth is nothing else but a heap of rubbish and ruins, I shall reduce and demonstrate in particulars, the great use, benefit, and necessity, of them." That's John's kind of thinking, which links appreciation to "use," even though Ray stops short of seeing the beauty that John, the new pastoral poets, and advocates of the sublime found in mountain ranges during the generations that follow Ray's life.[12]

Despite such clear influences on John's philosophy, he maintained that his theology and science were principally inspired by nature that he saw for himself. "I hope," he wrote to Benjamin Rush, that "a more diligent search will lead you into the knowledge of more certain truths than all the pretended revelations of our mystery mongers and their inspirations." In other words, let observation of the workings of nature, rather than professional clergy, be your guide to God, and you will get closer to the spiritual truths that you seek. For the truth is right there before our eyes, John believed, if we have the wisdom and courage to see it; and the fundamental truth that nature reveals is in the order to which all conforms. "I shall now beg leave to make some remarks on these observations," he wrote to Peter Collinson, "as first the wonderful order and balance that is maintained between the vegetable and animal economy, that the animal should not be too numerous to be supported by the vegetable, nor the vegetable production be lost for want of gathering by the animal." Order and balance were nature's way, what God intended for all. "I have been the subject of many misfortunes in my lifetime," John wrote later in life, "but as many has had worse and many better than I, so I praise our God in leading me about the middle way." The middle way, order, and balance were the natural path for a man to take in his life. Where suffering and happiness about balance out, a life is in tune with the natural forces inspired by God.[13]

No less than man, animals, and plants, such lower life-forms as wasps were subject to the same destiny. "The order of Providence is remarkable," John believed, "in prescribing the different ways and means for this noxious tribe of insects to perpetuate their several species, no doubt for such good ends and purposes with which we may not be well acquainted, but most likely for the prey and food of other animals." There's a plan even where we cannot comprehend it; the plan works even when we don't know how. The plan is God's and it's visible in the workings of nature.

The very means by which the number of wasps is limited reflects God's design. "The wisdom of Providence is admirable by giving annually a check to this prolific brood of noxious insects in suffering all the males to die, which are the most numerous in the family and only reserving a few impregnated females of each species to continue their race into another year." Whether or not we see God's design, we can be sure that it's all for the best.[14]

Nature, according to John, can be read in two directions: down, as in the passages just quoted, as an expression of God's plan for us all, and up, as a means through which to know God. It was through the "telescope" of nature that John saw "God in his glory." The telescope metaphor, fixed as it is on the sky, needs to be brought down to earth, parallel to the ground, to see another of John's views of nature. God's plan can also be read across species, by using humans as the model for comprehending other life-forms and by employing insects, animals, and plants as guides to understanding us. This turning of the Great Chain of Being on its side is one of the most significant innovations in early-modern religious thought, for not only does it provide, in the imagination of a man such as John Bartram, new ways to conceive mankind's relationship with nature, but it opens the door to deistic visions that eventually bring God to earth, too.

The suggestion that the study of inferior life-forms could shed light on superior ones was new to the late seventeenth century; the remarkable innovation of the eighteenth century was reversing this expectation to use higher life-forms as models for comprehending lower ones. The consequence of these inversions was to raise plants to a higher dignity in relationship to animals and to diminish the place of humans in relation to the rest of the natural world. Since humans and other animals have a circulatory system, for example, as first theorized in the early seventeenth century and universally accepted during John's life, the expectation that plants had a parallel system only made sense. Sexuality, too, could now be seen as a universal means of procreation, which led to Linnaeus's new method for identifying plants by their sexual organs. John Bartram didn't invent these conventions, but he was among the earliest Euro-Americans to be affected by this line of reasoning and to play out its implications in a natural philosophy that was both derivative and distinctive to him.[15]

Although John didn't reject a hierarchical chain as another metaphor for natural relationships, including that between nature and God, he was more absorbed in the search for what species shared even across what seemed to him an arbitrary line between animals and plants. "It's certain," he wrote to Benjamin Rush, that

> many animals hath a large degree of cunning and [are] endowed with most of our faculties and passions and several particular beyond many of our species, but I have been many years upon the enquiry after the operation of plants and wrote to curious persons upon the subject, that if they had not absolute sense yet they [had]

such faculties as came so near to it that we wanted a proper epithet or explanation.

Order, balance, and similarities across the spectrum of living organisms are what John saw and what he sought out in nature. In these connections he found evidence of a "universal intellect" shared by animals and plants.[16]

Humans are prone, in John's estimation, to elevate ourselves unnaturally above the rest of creation. He saw the gap between the lowest and highest life-forms as narrower than generally conceived, and, in some cases, he thought the hierarchy totally misconstrued. As a botanist with a spiritually inspired vision of nature, he witnessed qualities in plants that defied commonplace distinctions between what he termed the animal and vegetable kingdoms. Name any characteristic that seems to distinguish humans from other living things and John could cite an example where the same characteristic is shared or surpassed in a particular animal or plant. He saw courage, cunning, curiosity, generosity, loyalty, and connubial and parental affection manifested throughout nature. He believed that plants have volition, which suggests the "sense" that he discussed in his letter to Rush. John reported to Alexander Garden a story that he heard and believed about "a plant much like a daisy that if a person looked at the flower when open it would immediately shut up. This surely must be a very modest flower and a great curiosity."[17]

Modesty, simplicity, beauty, passivity, and moderation were also spread throughout creation, and all reflected back on the Creator himself. "The more we search," John maintained, and examine God's

works in nature, the more wisdom we discover whether we observe either the mineral, vegetable, or animal kingdom, but as I am chiefly employed with the vegetable I shall enlarge more upon it. What charming colors appear in the various tribes in the regular succession of the vernal and autumnal flowers, these so nobly bold, those so delicately languid. What a glow is kindled in some; what a gloss shines in others; with what a masterly skill is every one of the varying tints disposed. Here they seem to be thrown on with an easy dash of security and freedom, there they are adjusted by the nicest touches.

The sheer variety of colors and blends testifies, in John's eyes, to the Divine inspiration.

> The verdure of the impalement of the shadings of the petals impart new liveliness to the whole, whether they are blended or arranged. Some are intersected with elegant stripes or studded with radiant spots. Others affect to be genteelly powdered or neatly fringed. Others are plain in their aspect and pleaseth with their naked simplicity. Some are arrayed in purple. Some charm with the virgin's white. Others are dashed with crimson while others are robed in scarlet. Some glitter like silver lace; others shine as if embroidered with gold.

Color, then, is one aspect of beauty, but shape, smell, function, and size also contribute to the variety, which pleases or affronts all our senses.

> Some rise with curious cups or pendulent bells. Some are disposed in spreading umbels; others crowd in spiked clusters. Some are dispersed on spreading branches of lofty trees, on dangling catkins; others sit contented on the humble shrub. Some [are] seated on high on the twining vine and wafted to and fro; others garnish the prostrate creeping plant. All these have their particular excellencies, some for the beauty of their flowers, others their sweet scent, many [for] the elegance of their foliage or the goodness of their fruit, some [for] the nourishment that their roots afford us, others please the fancy with their regular growth. Some [are] admired for their odd appearance and many that offend the taste, smell, and sight, too, [are] of virtue in physic.

Plants bring us unique beauty, occupy niches of practical and/or aesthetic significance, but share characteristics with us. "When we nearly examine the various motions of plants and flowers," John continues in this long flowery passage,

> in their evening contraction and morning expansion, they seem to be operated upon by something superior to only heat and cold or shade and sunshine, such as the surprising tribes of the sensitive plants and the petals of many flowers shutting close up in rainy

weather or in the evening until the female part is fully impregnated; and if we won't allow them real feeling or what we call sense, it must be some action next degree inferior to it for which we want a proper epithet or the immediate finger of God to whom be all glory and praise.[18]

Whether waxing poetic on the varieties of beauty in plants or singing the praises of animal life, it was the connections among all, the similarities, and the need for greater species modesty among humans that he emphasized. "As for the animals and insects," he observed,

it is very few that I touch of choice and most with uneasiness. Neither can I behold any of them that have not done me a manifest injury in their agonizing mortal pains without pity. I also am of opinion that the creatures commonly called brutes possess higher qualifications and more exalted ideas than our traditional mystery mongers [are] willing to allow them.[19]

Such a sensitivity to the suffering of animals, which derived from a view of the connectedness of nature and of nature to God, led John Bartram to take unique stands, for his place and time, against sport hunting and the wanton killing of rattlesnakes. Other chapters take up these themes and their influence on William's bolder articulation of the same views, but it is important to note here that John was the principal source for an eccentric combination of ideas, some of them new to his culture and his century and some of them commonplace among Quakers and naturalists of his day. The Bartrams saw nature differently than other eighteenth-century Euro-Americans, but all the elements were present in their time for what we tend either to assume are "modern" sensibilities or to romanticize as survivals of more primitive, non-European cultures and pasts.

John Bartram's identification of a shared intellect among all living things enticed him to romanticize nature in a way generally believed to have originated with the next century's Romantics and Transcendentalists. Inverting relations among species and seeing similarities that seemed divinely inspired led John to portray nature as good and label as "unnatural" all behavior that offended his sensibilities. "Unnatural" corresponded in John's mind with evil, thereby reversing the medieval fear of wilderness, which the Puritans shared, as the haunt of the devil and his familiars. The critique of ministers imbedded in John's writings is also later embodied in deistic and humanistic assaults on organized religion, but those future developments shouldn't blind us to the origins of such ideas among Quakers and naturalists or to the demonstrable influence of such writers as the Bartrams on the Romantic poets and nature writers of the nineteenth century.

Just as John Bartram viewed ministers as barriers to clear readings of God's plan, so, too, did he have little patience for those who theorized without taking the risks of exploration themselves. His countrymen lacked curiosity, John complained: "I can't find one that will bear the fatigues to accompany me in my peregrinations."[20] Anglo-Americans, he thought, "may be ranked in three classes," none of which shared his curious nature.

> The first class are those whose thought and study is entirely upon getting and laying up large estates, and any other attainment that doesn't turn immediately upon that hinge they think it not worth their notice. The second class are those that are for spending in luxury all they can come at and are often the children of avaricious parents. . . . The third class are those that necessity obliges to hard labour and cares for a moderate and happy maintenance of their family and these are many times the most curious, though deprived mostly of time and material to pursue their natural inclinations.[21]

Imbedded in John's complaint about his fellow subjects of King George is a critique of Anglo-America's economic culture. On the one hand, this denunciation of avariciousness and high living is typical Quaker fare; on the other, it's clear that over the course of the century some Quakers began to live pretty ostentatiously themselves. Without discounting the sincerity of the economic aspect of John's lament, it's difficult to take him too seriously here, both because of the exterior design of his house and his own pursuit of wealth beyond what seems necessary to ensure the competence of his family. By all accounts, he was frugal in his personal habits, although he did discard an old hat that Peter Collinson sent him, which, Collinson said, he would have continued to wear himself if he had known that his "poor" friend would dispose of it so ungratefully. Others, including Crèvecoeur, described John's appearance as that of a "plain country man," in keeping with Quaker tradition.[22]

In John's critique of American economic culture, as in his complaints about professional clergy, there's a strong dissent from the cultural mainstream and one that has its origins in John's naturalism as much as it does in his Quaker heritage. The problem, he says, with Americans' pursuit of the main chance is that it undermines the fabric of the family, which is a commonplace Quaker observation,[23] and saps the curiosity that emboldens men to risk wilderness travel for the sake of the common good. This second concern is both personal, because the absence of curious others necessitates that he confront the dangers alone, and social at the same time. John thus takes on the trail with him the social burden of finding in nature what is of "use" to his fellow man; and, for John, the concept of "use" has strong moral and economic dimensions that are mutually supportive. John's search for objectifiable meaning, for "reality" and "truth" in nature is itself an important part of what he carried with him into the forests and swamps, and is intimately connected to his practical interest in nature's "use."

During the first half of the eighteenth century, when John grew to adulthood and began his explorations, it was more difficult to achieve the sort of certainty that Francis Bacon, the English theorist who most influenced the new science, envisioned a hundred years earlier. Descartes, Hobbes, and Locke, among others, had intervened between the observer and truth to suggest that sight is a subjective experience conditioned by the mind of the beholder. The origins of modern subjectivity posed no immediate threat to the observational focus of the new science, though, as the Royal Society sought truth in a "probabilism" that replicated experience with multiple observations and confirmations. The philosophers of John Bartram's day thus wedded Baconian faith in the individual experimenter with a belief that universal order would eventually be revealed at the end of an investigation. A confident empiricism remained at the heart of exploration, saving observers such as John from bewilderment and inarticulateness.[24]

This scientific way of seeing focuses on objects rather than landscapes. The philosophical observer of the late seventeenth and eighteenth centuries looks *at* rather than over things, which unintentionally introduces a tendency to isolate individual subjects of study from their surrounding visual contexts. This can be seen in art as well as writing, where specimens are often pictured either in total isolation or in juxtaposition with features that aren't present in the objects' native environment. Scientific sight differs, then, from that of poets and later artists, whose vision glides over landscapes to locate truth in mirrored images that connect the viewer and the viewed. The scientific gaze is also quite penetrating, exploring strata and internal features not visible to more superficial looks, sometimes engaging the senses of touch, taste, and smell in combination with visual perception. The poet aims for penetration, as well, but less in a biological or geological sense than in an emotional one. Unlike the poetic view, the scientific shuns reverie; it attempts to elude idiosyncratic observation and tries to suppress the self. Philosophers intended to see differently than poets, to supplement and surpass poetic visions in ways that we may see as self-delusive, but which they saw as heroic.

Another book that John read describes a version of scientific sight. Robert Boyle's *General Heads for the Natural History of a Country* is a detailed guide to the method and content of scientific reporting. Boyle instructs the philosophical traveler on what to look at, what questions to ask, and the order and manner in which to record all that he sees. Fix longitude and latitude, Boyle advises, to make sure where you are for others who follow and attempt to replicate sightings.

> Secondly, about the air is to be considered, its temperature as to heat, dryness and moisture, and the measures of them, its weight, clearness, refractive power, its subtlety or grossness, its abounding with or wanting an estuarine salt; its variation according to the several seasons of the year, and the times of the day: How long the several kinds of weather continue, what sort of meteors it breeds and [are] most commonly generated, and how long they usually last: Especially what winds 'tis liable to; whether any of them be stated, and ordinary, &c. What diseases are epidemical, that are supposed to flow from the air: What other diseases the country is subject to, wherein that had a share, e.g. the plague and contagious sicknesses. What is the usual salubrity or insalubrity of the air. And with what constitutions it agrees better or worse than others.

Then, test the water depth—useful knowledge for invasion and trade—its contents of useful animals and plants, tides, currents, and taste. Next, the traveler should examine the soil, its texture, type, and vegetative productions, "and, moreover, how all these are or may be further improved for the benefit of man." Inhabitants are to be observed and measured in the same fashion as the plants and animals for their potential threat, value, and use. Boyle blends the goals of science and empire into mutually supportive enterprises and enlists the traveler to curious environs as a spy and a naturalist at the same time. He searches for what's novel and can be "improved" to serve British culture, but not for God in nature, the nature of God, or the beauty that inspires poetry.[25]

In fact, John's natural history defied any strict division between science and poetry, producing a literature that combines both ways of seeing. It makes more sense to locate the writings of such eighteenth-century naturalists as the Bartrams on a spectrum of ambition and accomplishment that runs from the new science, with its focus on objectivity and the suppression of self, to the new pastoral poetry beginning with James Thomson's *The Seasons,* which aimed, as Richard Holmes puts it, at "a new truth of feeling through its very harshness and 'romantic' melancholy."[26] John lacked the emotional vocabulary of the sublime and the picturesque, and if he read the new pastoral poets he never mentioned their work, but he shared the emotions expressed by the new aesthetics. He lacked the panoramic view of the new poets and nature artists, but he saw associations across what we call ecosystems, noting relationships among land, weather, animals, and plants that share a landscape. His natural religion, his personal experience in nature, and the nature of his life shaped the emotional character of his observations in ways that readers of only his published journals are likely to miss.

John Bartram is generally portrayed as an exemplar of the scientific view, a man of simple, plain prose, whose nature writings are catalogues of observed phenomena. As one scholar phrased what so many others have said, "John Bartram left the esthetic appreciation of the . . . wilderness to his son William."[27] There is some truth in such a contrast, but the contention that John was exclusively a measurer, counter, and chronicler of nature, who lacked an appreciation of its beauty, necessarily ignores passages such as those discussed above, where he indulges in eloquent reveries about "purling streams," "glittering cascades," "humid fleeces," and the colors of flowers, and ponders the celestial connections among all living things. He was clearly in awe of nature, shared his reverence in writing, and had an aesthetic appreciation that was an integral part of his reveries.

The characterization of John as a simply numerate man is generally sustained by a consideration of his two published journals in isolation from the larger body of his lifetime of writings. The journals of his 1743 trip to Canada and his 1765–1766 journey to Florida are fascinating texts that most fully embody John's ambitions to conform with standards for scientific observation set by the Royal Society in the 1660s and refined by Boyle's *General Heads*. The spareness of the prose, the desire to keep himself out of the story, and the new science's passion for measuring and counting reveal John as a proponent of this model and also show how far short he fell of the goal of objectivity that he set for himself.

The first journal begins on July 3, 1743, with John's horse already saddled, his food prepared, and his bedroll packed for a journey to Canada. He would travel with fellow Pennsylvanians headed for Onondaga to negotiate a peace treaty with the Iroquois. The day he left home was "exceeding hot," he tells us, and he and his friend Lewis Evans, who was along to make maps, traveled beyond Perkiomen Creek. That's all he has to say about the first day. He writes nothing about his anticipation of what was ahead or his feelings for those he left behind. If he was worried about his family or farm, about Indians, snakes, or getting lost in the woods, he doesn't share his doubts or his dreams here. He doesn't want to intrude into the narrative, which wasn't meant to be about him.

The next day may have been hot, too, but John drops the weather report now that he has curiosities to record. He and Evans rode up the west bank of the Schuylkill River, passing Flying Hills, "so called from the great number of wild turkeys that used to fly from them to the plains." The travelers next reach "a fine prospect of the Blue Mountains, and over the rich Vale of Tulpehocken; the descent into which is steep and stoney." As they move from the valley, through the steep, rocky incline, to the foothills and mountains beyond, they cross both space and time: from a land that once was a wilderness abundant with wild animals, but no longer is; from a valley with soil that now richly repays the labors of farmers, to the mountain frontier between domesticated nature and landscape not yet transformed.[28]

Here, in the spare notations of a journey scarcely begun, we can see the pattern to which the rest of the journal adheres, the ways of seeing and reporting for a public audience that remain essentially unchanged throughout John Bartram's life. Identifying the model is an important step toward exploring its sources, the influences that shaped how and what John would report. It helps place him within a culture of seeing that influenced his methods directly and in ways that he didn't know. The pattern is also a guide to John's departures from the model, thereby revealing circumstances under which he and his culture weren't in control; times when he was afraid, awestruck, or confused; those moments when his heart and soul overwhelmed his culture and mind.

The model to which John's journals conform is, indeed, highly quantitative, constantly measuring distance and size, and focused on the potential usefulness of improved wilderness for a farming economy. A great ridge is "a mile steep"; good soil measures "three feet deep"; a grove of trees is "half a mile broad"; a grassy plain is "20 acres"; a creek is "big enough to turn two mills"; a swamp is so thick with spruce trees that "a bullet must hit one before it could fly 100 yards"; a grassy patch of bottom land is "40 rods wide"; and Lake Ontario is "120 miles broad and near 200 long." The principal qualitative measure is the usefulness of natural features. Soil is "middling," "very poor," "good low land," "poor and stoney," "good level rich land," "fertile," "exceeding rich," "rare," "boggy," "very good," and "most excellent level ground than which nothing can be more fruitful." John measures creeks by their capacity to turn mills, values soil by its fruitfulness, and reports the quality, quantity, and size of timber that grows naturally in the forests that he rode through.

In all these ways, John's vision is typical of Enlightenment values and perceptions of nature. The Renaissance science of the two and a half centuries before his birth brought with it a rejection of antiquity and "superstitions" associated with the past, an emphasis on observation and a concomitant impatience with theory, an appreciation of carefully designed and repeatable experimentation, a mathematical and quantitative approach to nature, and a focus on botany for its practical contributions to medical knowledge.[29] John embodied all these values; they defined who he was as an architect, a farmer, a herbalist who treated illness and injury with natural recipes, and a philosopher of plants who sought new ones out and used his garden as an experimental nursery. The same practical, confident, rock-solid approach to the world shaped his character as a husband, father, businessman, and friend in ways that are more elusive, but nonetheless real.

There's another side to John, though, and it, too, is revealed even in this spare journal of his Canadian trip, just as it is in the more emotive passages of his correspondence. It's there in the adjectives he uses to describe "lofty" and "noble" pines, "charming" country, "pleasant" creeks and vales, "truly charming" weather, an "enchanting" prospect, a "lovely" mountain, across which he rode "under the grateful shade of those lofty trees that every way adorn it," and the "musical howling" of a wolf. It's an aesthetic appreciation of nature unimproved by the hand of man. This way of seeing wasn't in conflict with John's dominantly practical side, but it was independent of the useful qualities attached to some features. In other words, John's most ecstatic praise of nature wasn't for the beauty of rich soil or the majestic stature of oaks (which he elsewhere describes as the most useful of trees), perhaps precisely because he saw oaks as lumber and fruitful bottom land as acres to be plowed rather than in relation to their natural surroundings.

Although we may see tension between John's practical and aesthetic appreciations of nature, he didn't feel it as modern naturalists would. His ways of seeing weren't alternative visions at war in his culture as they are in ours. John's imagery of creeks dammed for mills, trees felled for lumber, and vales fenced for cattle, on the one hand, and his appreciation of the musical quality of a wolf's howl, which, as a farmer from a settled region with long-standing bounties on wolves, he "had not heard for many years," fit comfortably together in his mind. They were simply two ways of seeing and he had the capacity for both.

A comparison of this journal, kept when John was forty-four, with that of his 1765–1766 Florida trip adds the dimension of time to this analysis of his observational self. Now at sixty-six, having become more introspective, more philosophical, and more frail than he was in his forties, John keeps a much more detailed journal that shares many qualities with his earlier notes. In a counting frenzy replicated throughout the later journal, John measures a marketplace in paces and feet, a grapevine "seven inches in circumference, [which] bore 216 clusters, one of which measure[s] eleven inches in length and sixteen and a quarter in circumference," an olive tree, a new church, and a nectarine, all in one day. In the same entry, he also gives the nectarine's dimensions (for it was, indeed, a prodigious fruit at 15¼ inches in circumference and weighing 19 ounces), calculates the local productivity of rice fields in quantity and cash realized for the crop, and estimates the population, the number of houses, and the size of the militia.[30]

The quality of John's descriptive phrasing is, in many ways, similar to that of twenty years past. Again, the principal qualitative measure is use. Land is "piney and poor," "very poor sandy soil," "a sandy virgin mould," "a very tenacious clay," "poorish," or "exceeding black deep soil," evaluated for its farming potential. "The land is good," John wrote at one point, "but the cultivation of it is too expensive to produce any considerable profit." Rice seemed to him "a very profitable grain." Creeks worth mentioning were "big enough to turn a mill" or "deep enough for a large boat to swim loaded to its head."

None of this is new; it reflects how John generally perceived nature, by size, quantity, weight, and potential for "improvement" by careful husbandry. Good soil could "be improved by culture"; a "large fountain" was one "big enough to turn a mill"; a remarkable oak was one that "measured 105 foot [in] diameter in the spreading of the boughs and 20 foot round above a foot from the ground." Rather than seeing what was already there, John imagined nature transformed by axes, plows, and oxen to clear stumps and haul away rocks. This was how John traveled through savannas and swamps: weighing, measuring, digging, and planning for change. "I measured one pine," John writes in his journal, "81 foot high to the first limb, thence 54 foot to the top; another 2 foot and a half diameter and 90 to the first branch, thence 28 to the top and very straight." The pines must have been the tallest and straightest that he saw, and he valued them for their uniqueness, for curiosity's sake, and for their potential use as lumber rather than as trees. Rocks were impediments, so he weighed them, perhaps to calculate the size of a farmer's job in clearing them from what could be "improved" to a "profitable" field.

As a farmer, John was not content with a superficial view of nature; he dug below the surface to examine strata of earth. How deep was the first layer, he wanted to know; what was beneath it and under that, too. How productive would the soil be, he wondered, not just in the first planting, but over time. As a philosopher, John was also curious about the history of the earth that he trod. He poked among the ruins of Indian and Spanish settlements for clues. His curiosity was limited, though, to practical questions. He saw the ruins as a guide to choice sites for development and wondered as well about why others failed in apparently fruitful locales. He didn't see ruins and burial mounds as occasions for contemplating mortality or the fragility of human endeavors. At least, if such thoughts engaged him as he burrowed through old bones looking for pots that still could be used, he didn't record his reveries in the journal he wrote.

While soil required digging to supplement sight, John enlisted his other senses for exploring beneath the surface of water. "One of these streams was so warm," he writes, "that although I was in a sweat yet it seemed warm to my hand." "The water," he says about another creek, "is loathsome and warm, but not so hot as one's blood." He had a thermometer for measuring the temperature of water and air, so taste and touch enhance, without supplanting, descriptions of warmth measured precisely in degrees. He encounters a fountain that "smelled like bilge water" and "tastes more loathsome than the others before mentioned," but he still doesn't abandon his method of full sensory engagement with a natural world that assaults his nose, his tongue, and ultimately, as he reports in the journal, his bowels as well.

There were days and weeks when this sixty-six-year-old man suffered from malarial fever, intestinal distress, and an overwhelming fatigue. He watched his diet, stayed in his tent and rested, wrote in his journal, prepared his specimens, and treated himself with purges and other herbal remedies that he concocted from the environment in which he contracted these ills. One day the strain got the best of him and he shared, in a weak moment, that "this was the longest journey and had the most effect on me of any I ever rode." Still he went on, feeling quite ill, but suffering bravely the small, debilitating scourges of exploration in a tropical clime, revealing in the journal when he felt overwhelmed just how much courage it took to endure. And triumph he did, in his own way, for as the weather cooled through the fall into Florida's winter, John's strength returned and with it his enthusiasm for the natural world.

John not only tasted nature; he was touched by it, too. As in the first journal, John saw beauty even without imagining fences, orchards, and fields. He recorded the "finest lofty pines I ever saw," "a pretty little shrub," "delicate flowers," "a lovely oak," and "the loveliest spring of clear water I saw in all this journey." Even a snake could be "beautiful" in its own way, with its colorful skin shimmering in the warm light. But it was curiosities that he was after, things remarkable for their uniqueness as well as their use, objects that others hadn't seen and reported before. "We found a very curious evergreen shrub and a very odd large plant," on a good day. He and his party "found several curious species of plants and an odd dwarf oak," which also marked a success. On a bad day, "we found no curiosities" or anything of potential value.

The best observations combined aesthetics and use. One such locale so enchanted John that he named it for himself. "This situation pleased me so much," he explained, "we called it Bartram's bluff, and for an industrious planter with a few hands may be a pretty estate." A "pretty estate" could be created from a plain with a beautiful view by an industrious husbandman with some laborers, perhaps slaves, and some profitable grain. The party rode, shortly thereafter,

> over the most extensive savannas I ever saw, and meadows producing good grass middle high and as thick as it grows in our best meadows. Here one may ride 6 miles in the open savannas amongst lofty pines 100 foot high and 60 without a limb, exceeding straight, and see deer running a quarter mile round.

The savannas were pretty, idyllic, and productive, as was Bartram's bluff, which reflects the scope and the limit of what John reported. Although he still appreciated the howling of wolves when he heard them in Florida, just as he had on his Canadian trip, his most effusive language is reserved for locations that are beautiful in some measure because of their fruitful potential in a nature transformed.

John in this way reflected a fusion of aesthetic and utilitarian attitudes in Anglo-American culture dating back at least to the mid-seventeenth century, which enabled even a colonial farmer such as him to see beauty where a short time before European poets were capable of perceiving only "warts, wens, blisters, [and] imposthumes." In a period of about fifty years, shortly before John's birth, the conventions of natural beauty were utterly transformed.[31] As John's odes to the beauty of nature amply display, his was a romanticized nature, affected by these aesthetic changes even when he tried to conform with the utilitarian models of the new science for nature reporting.

It's no coincidence that John's most extended reveries come in correspondence rather than in the journals, both of which were published, and that John drafted with a wider public in mind than the single good friend for whose eyes he intended the dreamier letters. The Board of Trade and Plantations published a long extract from the Florida journal as part of William Stork's promotional tract on East Florida. In this form it went through three editions before the American Revolution.[32]

If John was calculating the "use" to which his journal would be put, he measured correctly. The king didn't favor John with a stipend for him to go off into the wilderness and contemplate the relationship between nature and God. As the King's Botanist in the colonies, his job was to be of use to the Empire, to discover curious plants and provide information that would help extract value from the American "possessions." As the practical farmer, mason, architect, herbalist, gardener, botanist, and Enlightenment explorer that he was, John welcomed the job and the recognition of his work that it represented. There was no conflict between the Empire's ambitions and John's desire to exploit the wilderness for its use.

What John shared in the journals was not all that he saw, dreamed, or hoped as he traveled to places that few others had seen and written about. We know this from his correspondence and the journal passages where he steps outside the models of science and empire and reveals more of his soul. The journals were true to a significant part of John's self, though: to experiences, books, and people that influenced him. They reflect part of his ambition and give hints of a system of thought that blended concepts of value and use, religion and nature, science and empire into visions of profit from wilderness experience in more ways than one.

CHAPTER FOUR

Business

NTIL THE END OF THE EIGHTEENTH CENTURY, gardening was the model pastime, gardens the idyllic setting, and the gardener/farmer was the moral exemplar of eighteenth-century Anglo-American culture. The nature of the gardener's gaze, as discussed in the last chapter, was earthy and deep—digging beneath surface soil to explore strata and type; tactile—employing all the other senses in conjunction with sight; and wide-ranging—reaching beyond the rootedness of herbage and the borders of gardens to explore, to collect, and to dream.[1]

None of these qualities necessarily conflicted with others; science, religion, and aesthetics were colors on a gardener's palette, which could be blended into various subtle hues without clashing as they do in the nineteenth and twentieth centuries. They also combined, sometimes less attractively, with personal qualities that define in their eccentric mix who we are as individuals. In John Bartram's case, spirituality, numeracy, an appreciation of natural beauty, sensitivity, ambition, insecurity, and practicality shaped his views.

John's business was nature, and he had economic ambitions that complemented his quests for scientific discovery and personal fulfillment. This Anglo-American gardener fixed his gaze on use and profit; his practical, market-oriented view harmonized with other ways—aesthetic, scientific, religious—in which he saw the world. The terms "use" and "profit" are best understood here in their broader and overlapping senses, for he viewed usefulness as profitable to mankind in any number of ways.

In John Bartram's eyes, a flower's beauty profits us by revealing the nature of God. The study of plants' internal structure also gives useful insights to connections among species. Most obviously, plants that could be usefully employed in herbal remedies, as dyes or construction materials, or consumed as food by humans or domestic animals are potentially profitable in social and pecuniary senses. John especially valued books on the more profitable uses of the vegetable kingdom. Samuel Hartlib's *Legacy of Husbandry*, for example, is a practical how-to book that encouraged experimental farming. "He that will have profit," Hartlib advises,

> must use the means, they must not sit and give aim, and wish, and repine at other[s'] increase: There must be observation to mark how others thrive, inclination and imitation to do the like by endeavour and change; and if one experiment fail, try a second, a third, and many. . . . We have indeed a kind of plodding and common course of husbandry, and a kind of peevish imitation of the most, who (as wise men note) are the worst husbands, who only try what the earth will do of its self, and seek not to help it with such means as Nature hath provided, whereas if men were careful and industrious, they should find that the earth would yield in recompense for a good husband's travail . . . an hundred for one.[2]

Experiment, be careful and industrious, and nature will repay your investment generously. These were the lessons, from a variety of perspectives, that such books as Thomas Barnes's *A New Method of Propagating Fruit-Trees* and James Justice's *The Scots Gardiners Director* provided to John, and these were the kinds of books that he generally read. It was a literature that reflected his values, his ambitions, and his sense of nature as a business in which he "invested" labor and measured "profit" financially. Barnes's method was "founded in the most plain manner on reason and the nature of things." It was a natural approach to nature that appealed to John's businesslike sense of propagating plants. "We do not enough regard the uniformity of nature," Barnes wrote, which teaches lessons about seeds that can be applied to grafting fruit trees, as well as across lines between animals and plants. Justice advises those who, like John, make "the culture of flowers their business." The book explores practical methods for growing "what is useful to furnish a good garden with." Plant your kitchen garden between your house and stables, Justice suggests, "for the conveniency of wheeling in dung," and he has recommendations about watering, soil type, and other details of planting and caring for a "curious garden."[3]

When John wrote advice to fellow gardeners, it combined the same practical focus on detail; the same folksy wisdom about dung, water, and sun; the same experimental approach to gardening; and an eye focused keenly on the relationship between labor, profit, and use. The point was to improve nature in ways that profited man. So John wrote an essay on reforestation, which recognized the limits of chopping nature down and the need to cultivate trees just as any other crop. Here we can get yet another view of the connections between John's developmental ethic and his appreciation of the earth's rhythms, and see the articulation of his ambition to maximize profit from agrarian labor in a domesticated "natural" setting.

"Diligent observation" brought John to his view that "timber will soon be very much destroyed" in the settled areas of Anglo-America. This unfortunate circumstance resulted from farmers' "necessity" in clearing land for tillage and pasture, and from their need for fuel and fencing. The preferred wood for fences was oak, which is slow-growing and deteriorates quickly in use. John recommended reforesting with red cedar, which seemed to him the most likely choice for the region in which he lived,

> considering how easily it can be raised from the seed; its readiness to grow on most kinds of soil; its quick growth; the profits it will afford while it is arriving to maturity; and the long duration of the wood when grown to a proper size for the materials we want for our several occasions in husbandry or building.

Any farmer who had a worn-out ten-acre field could grow 1600 trees in twenty years, each of which would yield seven posts and a rail; if husbanded for forty or fifty years, they would "make good boards for floors, or planks for naval uses." What's more, "a field thus planted, will yield good pasture while the trees are growing; for either grass or corn will grow very well near the cedars . . . and when cut down will be fresh land for tillage." Finally, if the farmer plants 100 trees each year, after twenty-four years he can cut down 100 trees a year without threatening his stock,

> allowing every tree to yield eight posts, every post to fetch one shilling, which they will now readily do (and hereafter may be more), which amounts to forty pounds; a fine yearly profit, considering we lose so little ground from tillage, and the trouble and expense of raising them is but little, and the profits so great, that I believe we can't generally fall into a method that will afford the farmer more profit with less expense, and more sure to hit.[4]

John didn't rest content, though, exploiting domesticated nature. He harvested the wilderness, too, using his farm and the surrounding countryside as a borderless botanical garden for the domestic production of previously "wild" plants. John's garden was a commercial nursery in which vegetation was situated without regard for aesthetic design. He planted his finds with an eye toward their respective needs for sun, water, and soil type, not in "artificial" juxtaposition by color, size, and the season of their bloom. "His garden is a perfect portraiture of himself," Alexander Garden observed; "here you meet with a row of rare plants almost covered with weeds, here with a beautiful shrub, even luxuriant amongst briars, and in another corner an elegant and lofty tree lost in common thicket." What surprised the visitor even more was that John's nurturing of plants wasn't confined to the garden or the fields that he owned. "On our way from town to his house," Garden continued,

> he carried me to several rocks and dens where he showed me some of his rare plants, which he had brought from the mountains, etc. In a word he disdains to have a garden less than Pennsylvania and every den is an arbor, every run of water, a canal, and every small level spot a parterre, where he nurses up some of his idol flowers and cultivates his darling productions.[5]

The phrase "darling productions" captures John's nurturing manner, his tender affection, his paternal care for the plants that he raised. The visitor's image of the garden as "a perfect portraiture of himself" isn't intended as an entirely flattering description of John or his grounds. The depiction captures John as rare, weedy, beautiful, luxuriant, thorny, elegant, lofty, and common. Not a bad rendering, although a little ungenerous. He was a complicated man with dark corners, crannies, and dens, whose idols were flowers, whose nature roamed unconfined by fences that define property lines or the social conventions about how gardens or people should look. After all, nature was a business as well as a science to John, a personal philosophy, a religion, and a way of life. He had already torn the plants from their natural setting and his goal was to make them grow.

There were, of course, problems at each stage of the process, from obtaining the specimens, to nurturing, marketing, packing, shipping, and sale. The business of nature was a risky one, with the dangers of wilderness travel, the fragility of the product, and tenuous connections across great distances, including the vagaries of Atlantic shipping, between the producer and his customers. Profits were elusive, clients fickle, perils great and, John lamented, unappreciated by those who casually requested seeds obtainable only at great cost and offered a parsimonious "gift" in return.

There were direct sales, in which a potential customer would visit the garden, write with specific requests, or, later in the garden's life, respond to broadside advertisements that listed hundreds of available plants. By one of these means the customer identified specimens that he wished to purchase and placed an order for shipment to his plantation or farm. George Washington and Thomas Jefferson, among other men drawn to Philadelphia by Revolutionary-era politics, became customers in this way. There were domestic mail orders for seeds and plants from across England's North American colonies—from Jared Eliot in Connecticut, Cadwallader Colden in New York, William Byrd II in Virginia, and Alexander Garden in South Carolina, among other American gardeners who heard of Bartram's curiosities and who helped him locate more. From a financial perspective, though, the principal market was England, and the main clients were British gentlemen who craved "curious" plants for their elaborate formal gardens.

Critical to this transatlantic business was the mercantile middleman, the London merchant who could be relied upon to receive shipments, market the product, keep accounts, advise on future shipments, and forward payments in cash or goods back across the Atlantic in a timely fashion. The American producer was entirely dependent on the integrity, good will, and business acumen of his London contact, and John's connection with Peter Collinson was fortuitous and essential. The introduction, via mail, of Collinson and Bartram came in 1733, when Collinson enquired of an American correspondent whether he knew of anyone in the colonies who might be interested in a mutually advantageous exchange of botanical specimens.

Collinson's ambition wasn't of a business nature, which he tried to make clear a number of times. "I only bear mention these plants," Collinson wrote, "not that I expect thee to send them. I don't expect or desire them, but as they happen to be found accidentally and what is not to be met with one year, may be another." In other words, don't go out of your way or expect that I value them highly, because I can't repay your expenditure of much time or energy searching for them. "This year, pray, rest a little from thy labours," he wrote in the same vein. "We expect no unreasonable and hard things and will not have thee exert thyself out of reason to serve us," Collinson explained once again.[6]

From trades conducted at leisure, the relationship quickly moved to "gifts" in exchange for John's shipments, as aristocratic gardeners of Collinson's acquaintance asked if he could procure curiosities for their gardens, too. A suit of clothes crossed the Atlantic as a "present," but please don't tell others I sent it, Collinson insisted, because "there may be some with you may think they deserve something of that nature." "I hope this year to send thee something as a reward for thy trouble," Collinson wrote the following year; "I hope thee will not fail to find some gratitude in us." There were books, a magnifying glass, watches, a compass, and other "gifts" sent as expressions of "gratitude" by Collinson. Sometimes Collinson chose the presents and sometimes they were selected by aristocratic patrons who appreciated John's seeds.[7]

It was John who pushed for a more formal business relationship that recognized cost and value in setting a price rather than relying on the haphazard system of "gifts" for seeds and plants that suited aristocratic patrons just fine. He wanted to be paid; he wanted a role in setting the value of what he sent; and he wanted to choose the form of compensation that would be remitted to him. Collinson complied with John's wishes, soliciting a subscription that garnered twenty guineas to support John's travels each year.[8]

Still, there were tensions based on what Collinson described as John's ingratitude, on what John thought was an undervaluation of his work. After all his labors on John's behalf, Collinson was angry that "by the sequel of thy letter thee thinks thy self not amply rewarded. . . . Pray, let me hear no more of it; if thee canst not afford to go on with this business tell us so and it will be at an end." John's response reflected both wounded pride and a businessman's negotiating stance. "In thy letter," he wrote,

> thee supposed me to spend 5 or 6 weeks in collections for you and that ten pounds will defray all my annual expenses, but I assure thee I spend more than twice that time annually and ten pounds will not, at a moderate expense defray my charges abroad, beside my neglect of business at home in fallowing, harvest, and seed time. . . . I don't begrudge my labour, but would do anything reasonable to serve you but by the sequel of thy letter you are not sensible of the fourth part of the pains I take to oblige you.[9]

The strains continued over the three decades of their dealings. Bartram accused his friend of sloppy accounting, inattention, and bad faith. Collinson mocked John's class pretensions, ignorance, ingratitude, and carelessness. They both had their points. Collinson's accounts were a mess; he threw John's letters away after reading them, often forgetting significant details; and he surreptitiously handled seeds of other procurers, while telling John that there wasn't a market for more than he already sent. For his part, John gave mixed and misleading messages about his "poverty" while pursuing his botany in a fashion more appropriate to a "leisured" than a "working" life, knew little about international commerce, made incessant demands, and lost a number of shipments through careless packing and labeling.

Some of these stresses were inherent in the business enterprise, but they also reflected the personal idiosyncrasies of the two men. There can be no mistake about it, Bartram and Collinson were more than business associates, more than correspondents who shared a passion for plants. They were friends whose strong feelings for each other, some of them warm, some of them hot, survived good times and bad for more than thirty-five years.

It's difficult for us to appreciate a friendship planted by letters alone, especially one that blossomed amid torrential demands and blistering insults and survived icy silences for seasons on end. In an age without phones, faxes, e-mail, or planes, these two men sustained a closeness that was more intense than face-to-face encounters generally are in our time. Perhaps Collinson's and Bartram's relationship was unusual for their day—male intimacy during the eighteenth century hasn't yet received adequate study—but it reveals, nonetheless, the possible strength of friendships, the conceivable intimacy of social relations, and the unguarded emotionality of some eighteenth-century men.

Collinson took a fatherly interest in Bartram, although he was John's senior by only five years. The paternal pose could be condescending, an expression of class superiority, perhaps, and a reflection of metropolitan prejudices against a less educated, more rural man, who was also a colonist. Not that Collinson was unkind or haughty; on the contrary, he closely identified with his fellow Quaker, held him in high esteem, and wished the best for John's botanical endeavors. John, the orphan always in search of parental substitutes, generally accepted the inferior position in the relationship, but there were limits that offer insights to the natures of the two men.

As any good eighteenth-century father, Collinson worried about John's appearance in public and pictured his protégé, right from the start, as a sartorial embarrassment. "Dress thyself neatly in thy best habits," the merchant advised, before presenting yourself to a great man, "for I have in a particular manner recommended thee to him." "One thing I must desire of thee, and do insist that thee oblige me therein," Collinson wrote on another occasion,

> that thou make up [a suit of] clothes [from the cloth that I sent you] to go to Virginia in and not appear to disgrace thyself or me, for tho I would not esteem thee the less to come to me in what dress thou will, yet these Virginians are a very gentle, well dressed people and look perhaps more at a man's outside than his inside. For these and other reasons pray go very clean, neat and handsomely dressed to Virginia.[10]

Collinson recognized that sensitivity was called for here. It's your best interest I'm looking out for, he instructs John; not that I judge you by the clothes I picture you in, but you would embarrass us both if you presented yourself to a great planter in your normal state of dishevelment. Hence their disagreement about the hat sent along with other cast-offs from Collinson's wardrobe: clothing that was no longer appropriate for a London merchant to wear in public, but that Collinson imagined as an improvement over what his friend generally wore.

"There was an old fine velvet cap," John wrote to his patron, among the used clothes that you sent, "which was so rotten that I never brought it home. Had this been [w]hole I should endeavoured to have worn it at particular times for thy sake many years." Now it's John trying to be sensitive, rejecting the present while valuing the presenter. As for the other clothes, which John kept, he would find "particular times" to wear them, perhaps when their shabbiness compared to his usual dress permitted the indulgence of his affection for Collinson without belittling himself in public. A farmer, gardener, and explorer certainly had occasions when the appearance of his clothing was of little concern. Having cast himself as a "poor" man in his relationship with Collinson, John now had the burden of playing that role and perhaps sometime even dressing the part.[11]

"My cap," Collinson wrote back, showing that the castoff was more significant than its ragged appearance implied, "it's true, had a small hole or two on the border, but the lining was new. Instead of giving it away, I wish thee had sent it me back again. It would have served me two or three years to have worn in the country in rainy weather." Collinson was offended, and he rejected John's conciliatory gesture. The hat was good enough for me, he fumed, clearly implying that it was good enough for Bartram, too. Small holes on the border wouldn't affect the hat's utility for keeping off rain. What, indeed, was the business of this "poor" man, this plain Quaker farmer, who found no use for a fine velvet cap?[12]

Again, John apologized, extending over the course of an entire year the correspondence about an old cap that he now described as "rotten, mouldy, and eat[en] full of holes." "I never did believe it was thine," he continued, "[you] not having mentioned it in thy letter. . . . I thought some sorry fellow had thrown it." Now John was changing his story, revealing in yet another way that this moldy old hat has a value far greater than its condition suggests. In the previous letter, John said that, had the hat been in better condition, he would have worn it for Collinson's sake. Now, he says that he hadn't realized that Collinson sent it, implying both that it seemed unworthy of his friend ("I thought some sorry fellow had thrown it") *and* that, had he known, he would have worn the cap, mold, holes, and all, out of affection and respect for the man who sent it to him. But he also has Collinson dead to rights; if the cap was valued by its sender why didn't he even mention it when listing the other clothes in the box? Why was Collinson making so much of an item of clothing for which he had no use and that he stuffed inside another, less battered, hat?[13]

The cap is a marker that identifies more far-reaching tensions in the two men's relationship. Its lack of material worth may have made it even a more potent symbol of the issues over which the men struggled. Each felt undervalued by the other; and the hat, because of its holes, allowed them to talk around the problem without the sort of head-on confrontation that might have threatened their complex interaction as businessmen, botanical enthusiasts, and friends. Was the hat an appropriate gift? Was its presentation or rejection an insult? Was John as "poor" as he claimed? Did Collinson treat John with disrespect? Did the incident reveal conflicting values or simply reflect different valuations each had of himself and/or the other? The cap sat uncomfortably on either man's head, raising such questions, perhaps unintentionally and unconsciously, but nonetheless meaningfully for the two friends.

It is difficult to say how much of Collinson's vision of John as a man who needed an old cap was purely imagined and how much was based on John's portrayal of himself as impoverished. Collinson told others that he served as Bartram's agent "for the pleasure of assisting a poor man," which suggests that his picture of John is more tattered than true. His criticism of John's clothes and his apologies in letters of introduction aren't reflected in the comments of those who met John for the first time. Perhaps Collinson had the British class system in mind when he wrote to such colonial "aristocrats" as Cadwallader Colden and John Custis, imagining his American correspondents as comparable, albeit inferior, to British nobility, and John as a member of the English working class. Possibly he didn't have a clear sense of the less stratified society that Bartram lived in. "Don't be surprised,"

Collinson wrote to John Custis, "if a down right plain country man" shows up at your house. "I so much persuaded myself of such an interest in your friendship [that] you'll not look at the man, but at his mind for my sake. His conversation, I dare say you'll find compensate[s] for his appearance."[14]

Although John was neither so plain nor so poor as he portrayed himself, he was by all accounts "a plain country man" in his dress. Collinson had that part right. But such an appearance was not so inappropriate in the colonies as it would have been in the drawing room of an English lord. As for the physical attributes of John's appearance, he was described in his early twenties as a "tall thin spare" young man. Crèvecoeur helps a little to flesh out what John looked like later in life, with the distinct advantage over Collinson of actually having seen the man. He portrays John at about sixty-six years of age as "an elderly looking man with wide trousers and a large leather apron," at work in his fields. Crèvecoeur's description—plain but appropriately dressed—harbors no criticism of John's clothes, showing only the surprise of a "Russian gentleman," who wasn't used to patriarchs laboring shoulder to shoulder with their serfs in the fields.[15]

William Bartram is more helpful than Crèvecoeur or Collinson, even though working from memories half a century and more old. William portrays his father's stature as "above the middle size, and upright. His visage was long, and his countenance expressive of a degree of dignity, with a happy mixture of animation and sensibility." A man somewhat taller than average, with a long nose and a distinguished face, but not formal and grim; expressive, bright, animated, cheerful, kind, that's what the son remembered about his father's face.[16]

This is all useful information, but how reliable is unclear. The rest of William's sketch romanticizes his father's character, so we might suspect the physical delineation as well. Indeed, it isn't really all that descriptive, except for the nose and the height. William himself was a small man with an aquiline nose, which might lead us to suppose that he got that feature right. As for his father's stature, John seemed huge to his son, but that may not be an accurate reflection of John's size.

It would be nice to have a portrait; the problem is there are two and reasons to suspect that neither is the life-rendering that each claims to be. John never mentions posing for an artist. William is silent on the question, but is quoted long after John's death as saying

J. Bartram/Wollaston (National Portrait Gallery, Smithsonian Institution)

John Bartram [?] (Pennsylvania Horticultural Society)

that no "likeness" of his father was ever made. Neither John's silence nor the assertion of his granddaughter's husband seventy-nine years after John's death (and more than thirty years after William's) is definitive; nor would the two stand against a portrait that can be authenticated by other means. Although questions about provenance are interesting, they aren't crucial for deciding whether either or both of the extant pictures shed light on John's visage. I would like to know whether one was painted by the portraitist Gustavus Hesselius, as a modern owner was told; by John Wollaston, as a curator of the National Portrait Gallery believes; or by somebody else. It would be interesting if the other painting was one of Charles Willson Peale's, as the attribution on its back attests. However, both paintings are unsigned and each claim has authoritative challengers.[17]

What no one disputes is that these are eighteenth-century portraits of someone. There is no alternative claimant to John Bartram as the subject. And it is possible that neither was drawn from life, but that both represent a fair likeness of the same man. The notation on the back of the "Peale" portrait makes a stronger case than arguments by inference or absence of evidence ever could. "Portrait of John Bartram of Darby died 1777," the inscription reads in an eighteenth-century hand, "C.W. Peale Artist. Property of Isaac Bartram 1795." Isaac (1725–1801) was John Bartram's eldest son and the only surviving child from his first marriage. Perhaps family members commissioned the posthumous portrait as a gift for Isaac, now the patriarch of the Bartram clan—possibly even in commemoration of his seventieth birthday.

Maybe the artist had the other portrait to work from, the advice of family members, and even his own memories of the deceased subject. Since the Peales were friends of the Bartrams—Charles Willson was in his midthirties at the time of John's death—and the portrait could have been executed any time during the quarter century preceding 1795, there are a number of plausible scenarios that conform with the inscription. Again, though, the critical issue here isn't who painted the pictures or when, but what they tell us about John.

The portraits are fascinating for their differences as well as for the physical similarities between the subjects. Indeed, in a number of senses the men are mirror images of each other, one facing left, the other right, one wigless and plainly dressed, the other bewigged and more formally attired. Since the poses represent two sides of John's character—the plain Quaker farmer and the self-conscious aspirant to a place in the world—together they provide the sort of insight that one portrayal never could. A man as complex as John in exactly these ways could never be captured in one suit of clothes.

If one wasn't painted with the other in mind, the coincidence of the contrasts is quite remarkable. Let's imagine that the portrait of the man in the wig was commissioned by a gentleman botanist, one of John's colleagues, customers, and curious friends. This is what the modern scholar and curator of the portrait guesses, although there's no reason to believe, as he does, that John actually sat for John Wollaston, who painted Cadwallader Colden and his wife. The circumstantial evidence also includes Wollaston's presence in the British North American colonies during the 1750s and 1760s, when Bartram's prized Petre pear tree first bore fruit, which could help date the portrait and explain the prominent place of a pear in the picture.[18]

The wig, green velvet coat, lace handkerchief protruding from the pocket, and fine linen shirt suggest an accomplished man, whose public persona is somehow linked to the fruit. John, whether or not the painting is really of him, would have liked to see himself portrayed in this way. Like the elaborate facade of his house and the testament that he chiseled in stone, a portrait of John as a great man would display his life's meaning long after he died.

That is a nice story. It's comforting to imagine that the portrait helped John find peace. Surely, though, he would have bragged about posing or shared his reactions to the artist's rendering of him. It seems more likely that if the portrait is of John, he never saw it and didn't know it was done. The fact that the pear is greatly oversized and bears little resemblance to a real Petre pear may also speak to the artist's reliance on imagination rather than posing John with his fruit or it may be further evidence that the modern attribution is wrong.

If the painting is of John, his family might not have liked it; it wasn't the way they remembered the man or wanted others to commemorate him. Indeed, this bewigged figure isn't the father described by William and quite likely would be something of an embarrassment to this Quaker family, which maintained the style of simplicity even when the spiritual content was gone. Maybe they had the second portrait commissioned as a response to the first or, at least, so they would have an alternative vision that was more consistent with who John really was—at least with who he was to them.

Possibly the man in green velvet helps explain the one dressed in brown: the gentle, modest subject, who shares a balding pate with the wigged figure, a prominent nose, brown eyes, a round face, and hair that was once also brown, but now is predominantly gray. The bare head and plain brown coat evoke the simplicity that they intend and, along with the shoulder-length halo of hair, resonate working-class values that are easily pictured in rural environs even without the artificial presence of fructified nature close to the man's hand. The simple man is older than the better-dressed one, which suits my story about the paintings' sequence and also my sense of the man. As he got older, John got simpler, too; but both men are John Bartram, even if neither of them really is.

We also know that John was a physically active man until very late in his life—climbing trees, hiking, riding, and rowing across a wilderness landscape, participating in the rebuilding of his house and chiseling his philosophy in stone. He was a substantial farmer and a botanist of larger than average stature, but probably not corpulent given his strictures on eating, drinking, and exercise. Temperate in spirit, John's "common drink," William tells us, "was pure water, small-beer, or cider mixed with milk." His food was "wholesome and plain," as John reminded his children, and without "high sauces to excite the appetite to crave more than nature requires or the stomach can digest to suitable nourishment." Even without the assistance of an authentic life rendering, we can imagine John as "erect and slender, [with] a sandy complexion, cheerful countenance . . . [and] an air of solemnity," as one posthumous rendering describes.[19]

Then, of course, there's what went on inside John's head, the qualities of mind discussed in the last chapter that few artists can paint: cheerful and solemn at the same time, says the entry in Rees's *Cyclopedia*. It would take a talented portraitist to capture that look on a face. "Modest and gentle," with "an amiable disposition and liberal mind"; again, subtle qualities that might be read in his eyes and the turn of his mouth, but difficult to freeze in a still-life. He was "a lover of charity and social order," which apparently means that John favored assisting the poor in their place. You couldn't discern such values by looking at him unless you guessed from his class, his house, and his clothes. "Active and temperate," the portrayal continues, "but always maintained a plentiful table"; in other words, he didn't begrudge his guests a more substantial meal than he ate; "and annually, on new-year's day, he made an entertainment of his own house, consecrated to friendship and philosophy." A character right out of a Washington Irving or Charles Dickens novel, a generous squire who knew how to keep the holidays well.[20]

John's knowledge was vast but untutored, informed by experience and limited by ignorance of Latin and a lack of aptitude for classification schemes. His acquaintance with wild plants was intimate and, unlike that of most gentleman correspondents, firsthand. He knew where to find the specimens and the conditions under which they prospered and grew. Not only could he, among fewer than a handful of men, procure a rare plant from its natural setting, he could instruct curious gardeners on how to keep it alive. "You desire me to recommend some person to you that is curious," Alexander Garden wrote to a correspondent of his.

> This is the hardest task that ever you gave me. I really know of none such nearer than Mr. De Brahm to the southward, or Mr. John Bartram to the northward. If any other exist, I really know them not, nor have yet heard of them.[21]

Such men were in short supply. William Gerard De Brahm was a cartographer, and as such no competition for a curious botanist. No, if you wanted to know about North American flora, if you wanted a curious specimen for yourself, everyone knew the right man in the business of selling plants.

Those who made John's acquaintance valued him as a procurer, a man full of useful information, and a warmhearted guest who lit up a parlor with his stories and jokes. He was an entertaining conversationalist, full of curious anecdotes about nature. "He stayed with me 2 nights and a day," John Custis reported to Collinson, "and [I] could by no persuasions keep him longer. . . . never was [I] so much delighted with a stranger in all my life." John shared information generously, trusted instinctively, and lacked pretense and affect, which charmed his hosts, his friends, and his family, too. "How grateful was such a meeting to me!" Garden effused upon first making John's acquaintance,

> and how unusual in this part of the world! . . . How happy should I be to pass my life with men so distinguished by genius, acuteness, and liberality, as well as by eminent botanical learning and experience!—men in whom the greatest knowledge and skill are united to the most amiable candour.

His humor was earthy, could be deadpan, and sometimes even a little bit mean, as Peter Kalm never quite figured out. "Mr. Bartram told me," reported the Swedish botanist,

> that when a bear catches a cow he kills her in the following manner: he bites a hole into the hide and blows with all his power into it till the animal swells excessively and dies, for the air expands greatly between the flesh and the hide.

John's victimization of the credulous Kalm, who recorded the bear and cow story in his *Travels,* shows just how dependent Linnaeus's student was on his American source for information and how irritated John became with Kalm's persistent questioning, arrogance, and lack of gratitude for the information that he gave the younger man. The story reveals John's quick wit, creative mind, and ability to appear solemn and be cheerful at the same time, as the posthumous entry in Rees's *Cyclopedia* describes. It also demonstrates that John had a sense of humor about himself and his work, although I wonder whether he was embarrassed or just amused that Kalm cited him as the source for this incredible story.[22]

Although John's personality was, with the possible exception of Kalm, universally admired, not everyone appreciated his wisdom or even his knowledge of nature's curious facts. From the beginning of their correspondence, Peter Collinson made it insultingly clear that he valued John's ability to find plants in the wilderness, but not his mind. "The box of seeds came very safe and in good order," Collinson wrote; "thy remarks on them are very curious, but, I think, take up too much of thy time and thought." I find your "histories of nature" entertaining, Collinson told John on another occasion, "but this I must tell thee as a friend I am afraid thou takes up too much of your time. . . . Indeed, when thou art collecting thou are paid for it." Be practical, Collinson says; I don't have time to read the long commentaries you send and you won't get paid for them in any event.[23]

John certainly shared Collinson's valuation of the practical and was also self-conscious about his education. "If thee see mistakes," John wrote to James Logan, "I hope thee will consider that I am at the best but a learning." The letters from Gronovius, John lamented to Cadwallader Colden, are "so mixed with Latin I can't read many of his words, altho I can understand his English pretty well." John was also sensitive, though, as is clear in a defensive response to Collinson's criticism of his writing—which is, in fact, pretty bad.

> Good grammar & good spelling may please those that are more taken with a fine superficial flourish than real truth, but my chief aim was to inform my readers of the true real distinguishing characters of each genus.

If I've made substantive mistakes, he continued, please let me know so that I can correct them. John didn't want the "superficial" concerns that Collinson burdened him with, such as those about the cut of his clothes or the slant of his pen. He was a man of business who dealt in "truth" and didn't have time for the style and flourishes that occupy wealthier but less substantial leisured folks.[24]

Even John's critics found much to admire. Despite his lack of skill in classifying plants, Garden found him

> alert, active, industrious, and indefatigable in his pursuits, and will collect many rare specimens, which, from their being sent home, will give you a good idea of the country productions. He is well acquainted with soils and timber, and will be able to give you much light on these heads. He appears to me not very credulous, which is one great matter.

Collinson introduced John to Cadwallader Colden in a letter that described the botanist as "an ingenious man and a great teacher unto nature," which is a higher estimation than he generally shared with John himself. "I hear often from our friend Mr. Bartram," Colden reported to Gronovius. "It is very extraordinary that a man of the lowest education without the advantage of any kind of learning should have such a taste for knowledge & acquires so great a share of it." Even such a compliment as this is couched in a description of John's limitations, as Colden continued, "the good man was obliged to send to me your letters to him to translate the Latin parts of them." "He is naturally a wonderful observer," Colden explained to Collinson, "but when I saw him had not acquired sufficient knowledge of the principles of botany as a science." "I find he knows nothing of the generic characters of plants," Garden agreed,

> and can neither class them nor describe them; but I see that from great natural strength of mind and long practice, he has much acquaintance with the specific characters; though this knowledge is rude, inaccurate, indistinct, and confused, seldom determining well between species and varieties.[25]

John could be counted on as a collector, for his knowledge of soil and trees, and for his incredulity, all of which made him a valuable asset in the European-American botanical community, and he sought to capitalize on his worth. It was John's personality and natural talents that the great men valued, describing him as ingenious, industrious, shrewd, entertaining, and in some measure wise, as well as a man of unparalleled experience as a collector and gardener. As Alexander Garden put what the others said, too, John was "a most accurate observer of nature." No one knew the botanical nature of North America's forests better than him. Nobody could deliver more specimens than he could. When Benjamin Franklin sent John a list of ninety-nine plants that he wanted to purchase for a London friend, John had all but ten ready for immediate shipment. For five guineas, John sent subscribers a box containing the seeds of 105 trees and shrubs, each of which he identified for them.[26]

Others were more impressed with John's knowledge than Garden or Collinson. Collinson informed John that he read part of one of his letters before the Royal Society, whose members received it well and wanted him to send more observations on nature. Now this is what John was eager to hear—that great men were taking him seriously as a "philosopher," not just as a collector of seeds. "I shall have the greatest pleasure if I can be a means of persuading you to make your knowledge more public," Colden wrote to his curious friend; "I likewise hope that you'll find a private advantage in it." What Colden had in mind was a monthly newsletter on natural history. "I make no doubt you'll find several [men] forward to encourage and assist you where it may be necessary," Colden continued, "especially in such parts where you may be under difficulties by your not having had in your youth the advantages of learning." Twenty-five years later, Benjamin Franklin encouraged John to write "a natural history of our country. I imagine it would prove profitable to you, and I am sure it would do you honour."[27]

Both Colden and Franklin linked John's knowledge with prospects for profit in ways that indicate their own turns of mind and their knowledge that John was in the business of nature. Each recognized profit as a fundamental consideration for any undertaking of John's. Perhaps it was John's self-consciousness about the limitations of his prose, a lack of confidence in the products of his mind, or a more active temperament than suited the writing life, but he continued to indulge in long letters and wrote precious few monographs. He was certainly gratified when Collinson read parts of such letters to the Royal Society, which saw fit on several occasions to publish his comments in their *Transactions*, but he may also have felt burned by his experience publishing the journal of his southern trip in the mid-1760s.

Although the journal went through several editions during John's lifetime, it's unlikely that he profited financially from the venture. Collinson, offended that John hadn't yet sent him a copy, thought that "few will buy so dear a book." Collinson was also angry that John published the journal without his advice or patronage. In fact, it was forwarded to the Board of Trade and added without John's knowledge to the second edition of William Stork's *Account of East Florida*. In light of this route to publication and the subsequent lack of correspondence on the subject, it appears that John's compensation wasn't of the kind he could spend. The journal was likely considered public property, a product already paid for by the monarch's annual stipend to his colonial botanist.[28]

If John wasn't going to profit financially from his writings, then he had to pursue other avenues of compensation as vigorously as he could. He sought payment in goods that he could easily resell or in British coin that circulated at double its face value in his neighborhood. He had pursued an annual salary that would add predictability to his financial condition, one that he eventually got. And John insisted that he couldn't afford to continue the business unless he realized profits from his wilderness labors that compensated him for time away from his cattle and fields.

John's business wasn't just about money, though; it was about accomplishment, recognition, and fulfillment, too. So he must have been gratified, when Collinson finally received a copy of the published journal, that he described it generously as a "laborious entertaining journal full of fine discoveries, useful reflections and pertinent observations." Sometimes practical and emotional needs for financial profit were secondary concerns. On several occasions, he gratified his ego at the expense of hard cash. He was so thrilled, for example, by the "gift" of five guineas paid by Sir Hans Sloane, President of the Royal Society, that he asked Collinson to take the money and "send me a silver can or cup as big and good as thee can get for that sum, which I or mine may keep to entertain our friends withal in remembrance of my noble benefactor." John was thrilled by the cup that eventually arrived, with his connection to the great man engraved on its face: "The Gift of S. Hans Sloane Bart to his Frd John Bartram Anno 1742."[29]

After complaining for years that "gifts" didn't feed or clothe his family, that a "poor" man such as he needed to be paid, here was John's insecurity, his ambition, his need to be validated by great men turning cash into a goblet useful mainly for bragging. He was thrilled that Sloane's name was large enough on the cup "that when my friends drink out of it they may see who was my benefactor."[30] John's need didn't stop at a lie, which is what this vessel was. The idea for the cup wasn't Sloane's and the sentiments that Collinson had etched on its side weren't of the great man's devising. The engraving was even ante-dated to memorialize a friendship that never existed, as if Sloane had really bought a chalice and inscribed personal sentiments instead of passing along cash for plants to a merchant representing the colonist who found them in the woods.

This need for evidence of his life's meaning superseded others that John had; challenged his modesty, integrity, and plain style; and altered his focus on the useful and natural. John's request for an engraved chalice wasn't the only time he preferred a material tribute over cash. He gratefully accepted a gold medal struck in his honor in lieu of a £7 10s.

seed debt from a Scottish customer. The cup was not the sole case where we catch John in a lie that bolstered his fragile ego. Alexander Garden was outraged that John claimed as his find a tree that Garden gave him. "You tell me you are surprised that I overlooked a new species of the live oak, which John Bartram found near Charleston," Garden stormed at a friend. "Let me assure you that John Bartram received from me these very specimens . . . of which he has, it seems, made a different use from what I apprehended." Here again rears John's ugly habit, a product of ambition and insecurity run amok, of claiming as his work what somebody else did. And the cup wasn't the unique example of John exaggerating a patronage connection. The published edition of John's Florida journal also made a declaration that, as Collinson pointed out to his friend, was untrue and dangerous: "To publish the . . . [journal] as King's Botanist to the World, which by the way is a title which thou assumes without the king's leave or license . . . is making very free with majesty. It is possible for this undue liberty thy annuity may be withdrawn, but I hope not."[31]

Exaggerating the scope of his Royal appointment—John was King's Botanist in the North American colonies, not *the* botanist there or *a* botanist elsewhere in the Empire—is an understandable expression of pride. It's even the sort of authorial puff that may have been his editor's idea rather than his, a proclamation of authority that could help sell books. The claim is consistent with John's insecurity and ambition for public recognition, though, and he didn't deny that the posturing was his. His bragging certainly wasn't confined to quenching his friends' thirst and his ego at the same time; his letters often drop famous names and an intimate detail about their lives for no reason but to establish the connections between great men and him. "When I came [home]," John wrote to a friend, "I had the pleasure of receiving many entertaining letters from my correspondents in Europe, and Sir Hans Sloane, [who] was constituted president of the Royal Society after Sir Isaac Newton's decease, hath in particular desired my assistance."[32]

I am linked to Newton, John suggests in this passage, through a great man who is my friend and who needs me to help him. Drink from my cup, John might later have said, and join the direct line from Newton; imbibe an immortal association that includes me. There's a generosity to this boasting, a desire to share his good fortune with friends. The bragging is also pathetic, blowing tenuous third-party business connections into false claims of friendships with men John never met.

John ached for acceptance by the great men, for the sort of recognition that his orphaned childhood lacked. He was prepared to play son to them as father figures, was easily hurt by their slights, and displayed sibling rivalry with others seeking adoption by royal and aristocratic patrons. When William Young, Jr., received the good fortune of Royal preferment by Queen Charlotte in 1764, John was beside himself with jealousy.

While John labored into his old age with neither royal stipend nor title to recognize his contributions to science and empire, the Queen called John's much less accomplished neighbor to London to study botany and made Young her botanist in the colonies. At first John tried to hide or suppress the competitive feelings, expressing the view that Young "will make a botanist as he is very industrious and hath a good share of ingenuity." In the very next line, though, John's emotions begin to leak out. "I hope thee will find some way to forward the box I sent to thee for the king," he casually adds in this letter to Collinson, "not that I depend on having any such preferment as Young, but chiefly as a curiosity." It's difficult to imagine that John fooled even himself here, because the letter proceeds with a plea that runs directly counter to the denial of wounded pride and personal ambition: "My dear old friend, I am well assured that thee is well acquainted with many of the nobility, some of whom no doubt [are] men of curiosity. Could not they be prevailed upon," he implores, to support my travels, my work, my contributions to botanical science before "I must yield to the infirmities of age or death?" I'm older, wiser, ever so much more accomplished as a botanist than Young, John tries to say without revealing his wounds, so please help me get what I deserve. Young is a fraud, a liar, a fop, and there are rumors that he has been in jail. How can such a thing happen, John wonders; "it's a pity but the truth was known and the lying partly snubbed."[33]

John's appointment as botanist to King George III, which came in 1765, helped fill the hole in John's soul. It helped him forget the slights from such men as Professor Dillenius at Oxford, who neglected to answer John's letters for years at a time, and Philip Miller, author of the *Gardener's Dictionary*, who failed to credit John as the first to identify a new plant. It helped put behind him the condescension of Peter Kalm, the Swedish botanist whom John helped with his research, and the petty insults to his ideas, his manners, his spelling, and his clothes that Peter Collinson delivered over the years.[34]

The appointment, secured through the good offices of Collinson, made all the difference in the world; indeed, John would have had a far more difficult time reconciling accounts late in life without this evidence of his contributions to the Empire and his fellow man. The King gave John a title *and* a stipend that enabled him to go south, to explore, to discover, and to profit from nature's bounty in all the ways that were important to him. Now his science was recognized, too. Now he could travel to the wilderness again, one more time, with his son.

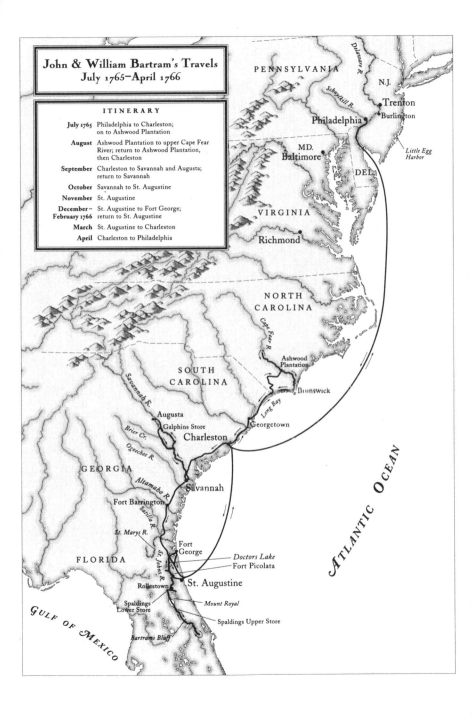

John & William Bartram's Travels
July 1765–April 1766

ITINERARY

July 1765   Philadelphia to Charleston;
             on to Ashwood Plantation

August   Ashwood Plantation to upper Cape Fear
             River; return to Ashwood Plantation,
             then Charleston

September   Charleston to Savannah and Augusta;
             return to Savannah

October   Savannah to St. Augustine

November   St. Augustine

December–   St. Augustine to Fort George;
February 1766 return to St. Augustine

March   St. Augustine to Charleston

April   Charleston to Philadelphia

PENNSYLVANIA
N.J.
Delaware R.
Schuylkill R.
Trenton
Burlington
Philadelphia
Little Egg
Harbor
MD.
Baltimore
DEL.
VIRGINIA
Richmond
NORTH
CAROLINA
Cape Fear R.
Ashwood
Plantation
SOUTH
CAROLINA
Brunswick
Long Bay
Savannah R.
Augusta
Galphins Store
Georgetown
Brier Cr.
Charleston
Oconee R.
GEORGIA
Altamaha R.
Savannah
Fort Barrington
Satilla R.
St. Marys R.
FLORIDA
Fort
George
Doctors Lake
Fort Picolata
St. Johns R.
Rollestown
St. Augustine
Spaldings
Lower Store
Mount Royal
Spaldings Upper Store
Bartrams Bluff
GULF OF MEXICO
ATLANTIC OCEAN

CHAPTER FIVE

Beginnings

LEXANDER GARDEN JUST COULDN'T BELIEVE IT. "Is it really so?" he asked. Has the King named John Bartram royal botanist? "Surely John is a worthy man," Garden remarked with a dash of admiration and a cup of condescension, "but yet to give the title of King's Botanist to a man who can scarcely spell, much less make out the characters of any one genus of plants, appears rather hyperbolical. Pray how is this matter?" How in a well-ordered universe, in a kingdom ably ruled, could such a thing happen?[1]

It's the title that irked Garden, not the stipend. The appointment was a deflation of honors royally bestowed, a devaluation of Garden's own knowledge, his training in Latin, his education at the University of Edinburgh's famed medical school, and his status as a Fellow of the Royal Society. John Bartram was no more of a botanist in his eyes than were the laborers who actually dug holes where he told them to dig in his Charleston garden.

All praise was due to the King for sponsoring John's expedition to the Florida wilderness in search of new plants. "The very idea of ordering such a search is noble, grand, royal," Garden wrote. "It may be attended with much use to mankind, much honour to the Royal Patron; and it will be a further illustration of the power, wisdom, and goodness of our great Heavenly Father." John deserved a reward in addition to his expenses for risking the elements, Indians, poisonous plants, and venomous snakes that endangered his life. But a title seemed to Garden too much.

It would be difficult to say which John valued most, the honor or the cash, for he "needed" them both. He would have undertaken the expedition as he began his sixty-seventh year without the title, but would have demurred on the grounds of poverty without the reward. Now, though, he could embark on his greatest beginning with both an enhanced self-esteem and a first payment of the £50 annual stipend as Royal estimations of his worth.

John's Bible, claimed in his hand as "John Bartram his Book 1761," unpacks part of the emotional baggage that John carried with him as he started each of his trips. The inscription on the first page, which testifies to the beliefs he would later carve into stone, also prays to the God in whom "I put my trust" for some relief "in times of deep distressings." John was still distressed when he etched those words in the beginning of his book. "I believe misfortune will pursue me to the grave," he wrote about his botanical business when he was sixty-one years of age, "let my intention and care be ever so good."[2]

Fear remained one of John's distresses, but it didn't immobilize him. "I am afraid of mortal sickness," he wrote the same year that he signed the Bible; "two of my neighbors [are] to be buried today, by 2 or 3 days sickness." Fear of Indians, wild animals, and the unknown kept him from sleeping soundly on any of his trips. "Slept but little," he wrote in letters and journals time and again.[3]

Injuries distressed him, but he continued to farm, garden, and travel, finding inaction more excruciating than working with pain.

> I have had a sore blow on my back by a horse which drove one or more of my ribs out of joint and bruised me inwardly grievously so that I was not able to turn myself in bed nor suffer any person to help me, so that I was forced to lie upon my back, which was a great affliction to me who can't rest long without action and who cannot endure confinement.

Then at sixty-two he fell from a tree, a fall that left his arm "so weak that I can hardly pull off my clothes, so that climbing trees is over with me in this world and in the next I rather choose to fly like an angel to search for vegetables in realms unknown to mortals."[4]

The tumble was from the top of a tree where he was gathering berries. "My little son Benjamin was not able to help me up. My pain was grievous. [A]fter [I was] very sick, then in a wet sweat in a dark thicket. No house near and a very cold sharp wind and above 20 miles to ride home." In the throes of describing this recent event, while his arm still hurt every time that he raised it and he couldn't roll over in bed without the pain waking him up, even as he considered a near future with wings, John still moved ahead. "I have a great mind to go next fall to Pittsburgh in hope to find some curious plants there," he concluded the passage describing his injury. And then he went.[5]

John continued to start over again, straining his hip while lifting a large box packed with soil and plants in the same year that he fell from the tree, which "I did not get over 'til spring." Traveling was never easy, and got more difficult with each passing year, over "deserts of sand and such miry swamps that sometimes both we and our horses had much ado to get out." He had to contend with impatient guides who helped him find his way to remote places and then wanted to go home before John had thoroughly botanized the locale. On one trip his horse disappeared—was stolen, he thought—and after searching three days he had to buy a replacement in order to get home. On another occasion, a "fit of sickness seized me . . . so that I was constrained to return home while I had a little strength left to support me."[6]

Still, this indomitable spirit in an increasingly frail body endured. Exposure to the elements always took its toll. When he was in his mid-forties, John had traveled across New Jersey in two feet of snow and climbed trees in a driving rain that lasted all day to get a particular kind of pine cone for an English customer. During his Florida trip, in his mid-sixties as the King's botanist, conditions were sometimes equally bad.

> This day it rained all day and most of the night. The roads extreme bad, the causeways covered with water belly deep and forced in others to swim our horses, the bridges being drove away. We reached Savannah town before night in miserable wet order, our clothes in our bags and papers being wet by plunging in water.

Not surprisingly, John became ill during the expedition. "Was very bad of ague and fever," one journal entry reads; "I was very sick," says another; "a vomit worked both ways," he writes with relief. "This day kept my bed"; "kept my bed all day, being much tired"; "I am so very weak can hardly stand without reeling"; "took a vomit"; "I took a purge of Glaubers salts which work well"; "I had no fever last night," he finally can say when he emerges from a malarial fog. John must have prayed often for relief from such miseries, of illness, the weather, and insects distressing his body as well as from the fear plaguing his soul.[7]

The bookplate in the front of John's Bible is as revealing of his spirit as the prayer and dated signature are. A poor, plain Quaker farmer with a coat of arms! Again, John's ego and ambition complicate the simple self-portrait he drew. It's unclear how he came by this heraldry, which presents a front, a visage, that was not really John Bartram, a claim to connections that simply aren't true. Perhaps he bought this honor, which was surely manufactured for him. "J'AVANCE" over a ram is an aggressive presentation of self, a bannered proclamation of leadership that has a martial tone. It can also be read as an endorsement of forward movement, a refusal to get stuck in the past. In this sense, the banner represents John's temperament well, as he kept charging right into old age. The Maltese crosses also trumpet a crusade; John was certainly a crusader undeterred by the forces of nature arrayed against him, nor was he easily dissuaded from a lost cause. The banner draped across the bottom of the plate, with its celebration of faith in God, is even closer to home, to the religious values that he espoused in the two letters he wrote to his children when he reached an old age, and to the way that he lived throughout his long life. The linkage of God, family, and home is typical of John, who redesigned and rebuilt right into his seventies and chiseled his religious beliefs in the stone that he quarried and laid.

The French is an affectation not easy to explain—like the pilasters and column on the front of John's house—of a man who didn't speak the language, which someone else wrote. Surely, he wished he could speak French like more educated men, but since he couldn't someone must have translated his message to give it a cosmopolitan style that John clearly lacked. Sometimes he would say that he knew enough botanical Latin to get by as a philosopher, but the testimony of friends suggests otherwise. What John told Crèvecoeur and others about his knowledge and educational past, he told Peter Kalm, too: "In his youth he had no opportunity of going to school, but by his own diligence and indefatigable application he got, without instruction, so far in Latin as to understand all books in that language and even those which were filled with botanical terms." French was not, however, part of his personal myth. Here again we see John trying to be more

John Bartram's coat of arms (College of Physicians of Philadelphia)

than he was and coming up short of his true and much more remarkable self.[8]

Why French? I wonder. Was the design John's idea? Crèvecoeur's Russian gentleman provides a few clues.

> I was no sooner entered [John's study], than I observed a coat of arms in a gilt frame with the name of John Bertram. The novelty of such a decoration in such a place struck me; I could not avoid asking, "Does the Society of Friends take any pride in those armorial bearings, which sometimes serve as marks of distinction between families, and much oftener as food for pride and ostenta-

tion?" "Thee must know," said he, "that my father was a Frenchman; he brought this piece of painting over with him; I keep it as a piece of family furniture, and as a memorial of his removal hither."[9]

Since John's father emigrated from England, not France, and since his name was William, not John, there are problems with Crèvecoeur's story that need working out. As Crèvecoeur recognizes, it is also difficult to reconcile the heraldry with the portrayal of John Bartram that the Russian gentleman gives us. Crèvecoeur could, of course, have left this information out of the story, thereby avoiding the question that his gentleman asks about John's Quaker values, but that's not what he chooses to do. Crèvecoeur lets us know that all, even here, may not be what it seems—what it claims that it is.

As for the explanation that the gilt-framed "furniture" means little, is simply a filial reminder of the family's past, we're left to wonder whether John or Crèvecoeur made this part of the story up. Surely John would be embarrassed by such a challenge to his presentation of self as the Russian gentleman made. Just as certainly, the truth wouldn't have suited Crèvecoeur if John offered it to him. I had it drawn for myself, perhaps John would say, to decorate my wall and enhance my self-image, to honor my most precious books, to record my reverence for the printed words that I worship, to commemorate my spirit long after I'm gone. Or maybe the story would be that the drawing was made by his artistic son, as a gift, as a bestowal of affection and respect for the noble spirit that John represented to William. Possibly, John told Billy what he wanted drawn, as he did for trees, turtles, and other natural things (and as I imagine he did with the sketch of his house), and then the artist took over from there, adding his own flourishes, perhaps even the French, to enhance the chivalric imagery that inspired him.

Part of the story is true: John owned the coat of arms and it very well may have hung in his den as well as adorning some of his books. As for the explanation, the garbled lineage doesn't seem like John's lie. It's too bald, too obviously untrue for John to deceive himself about his own character in this way. It's a denial of a heritage about which he wasn't ashamed. Nor does it seem likely that John created this past as a joke to amuse himself at the expense of his guest, as he did with the story he told Kalm about bears blowing up cows like balloons. This just wasn't his kind of fun.

Perhaps John was more dissembling than I think, but this tale of French ancestry is a grosser lie than any I know that he told. The French words and heraldic design more likely suggested their origin to Crèvecoeur's fertile mind and he created for John a story better than the one that the Quaker patriarch told, if he told one at all. The Frenchman gave the Kingsessing farmer a past closer to his own, a connection of culture or even blood to complement their closeness of soul, for Bertram is the most heroic figure in the whole book. In any event, the two drawings of a fictional past—the coat of arms and Crèvecoeur's lengthier sketch—aren't true representations of John's beginnings no matter what either man said.

Which is not to say that John had stopped dreaming, that his imagination had dried up like an old and overused spring. As he began his last long journey on earth, he saw a future aloft, where he no longer struggled against the elements or suffered injury and ill health in pursuit of his "beloved amusement." This "curious gardener," as he still called himself, "delighted most to dream of flying from the top of one mountain to another. . . . now every few nights I dream of seeing and gathering the finest flowers and roots to plant in my garden." He expected this dream to come true when he died, when he began the life of his spirit with wings.[10]

John continued to enjoy being the first to a place, a botanic philosopher discovering new plants, a prophet reaching the new promised land, a missionary to the forest sent by mankind, an ambassador to flora appointed by God.

When I am travelling sometimes on the mountains or in the valleys and the most desolate craggy dismal places I can find where no mortal ever trod, I chiefly search out, not that I naturally delight in such solitudes, but entirely to observe the wonderful production in nature of transformations and transmutations.

He celebrated changes across the different climates, altitudes, and soil conditions that he explored. He loved to watch nature begin over and over again as the changing seasons brought death, birth, and growth. The newness always amazed him; he never lost a sense of wonder about nature transformed.[11]

The 1765 journey to John's "eden," to that "ravishing place for a curious botanist," was also a chance to start over again with his son, to stoke the cooled embers of their troubled relationship in an environment where they both thrived.[12] The trick was to warm their relations without engulfing the forest in flames, for their passionate natures were like dry kindling that could ignite with a word, a look, even a breath of old air. The trip was also an opportunity for Billy to start his life over again, to find himself in the wilderness desert and then return to his place in the world, wherever that was—because he hadn't found it at the age of twenty-six years. He was still Billy in his father's eyes, as he knew perfectly well. Though the editor of John's journal would change the entries to "William" from what John really wrote, that wasn't nearly enough. William wanted to be a man in the eyes of his father, whose opinion mattered to him as much as his own.

Between the notice of William's birth and his fourteenth birthday, there is no surviving record of him at all. We're left to imagine good times and bad, the love that his family bestowed on the boy, childhood illness and play, his earliest chores, interaction with siblings, his first years in school, and the distinction of being a twin. Someone taught him to read, but who taught him to draw? Billy's father had once drawn a map, and Peter Collinson expressed admiration for another of John's drawings, "a beautiful draught on a sheet of paper of the falls of Mohocks [Mohawk] River." There's also a sketch of the town of Oswego on the title page of John's *Observations*, which is probably recast from a drawing by him. A crude "figur" of a blossom and stem is with his papers. And that's about it. The "figur" and map are both crude in the extreme, so it is unlikely that he was Billy's tutor.[13]

Then, in the summer of 1753, William's name first appears in the correspondence of his father that still survives. "There is a little token in a box for Billey," Peter Collinson writes, "whose pretty performances please me much." "Pretty performances" for which Billy was paid—a compliment and a reward. Perhaps it was cash, but whatever Collinson sent him it must have seemed grand. What a profound reinforcement for a sensitive, artistic lad. The word "performance" is an interesting choice, and all the more significant because that is how Billy himself described what he sent. A small brown bird—perhaps a creeper, but the beak isn't right, or a sparrow with the markings and colors a bit off—signed "Wm. Bartram His performance" tells us a number of things about the artist. "William" is what he calls himself; a "performance" is what his drawing was. He drew for others, although he often wrote for himself; he performed for an audience and craved applause.

The birds from this first batch are crude, but already surpass the talent and skill displayed by his father's map; and quickly, with practice and encouragement, William improves in great leaps. The tit in a tree is lifeless, awkward, in an unnatural position, with leg and tail set at unlikely angles, the colors not true to life; it was just a beginning—not his best work. Already, though, we can see John's influence in at least a couple of ways. Right from the start, William places his subjects in environs natural to them—in a tree where they really light, with insects that they really eat. His sanderling, for example, is pictured on a beach, surrounded by shells and plants that are part of the world the bird actually inhabits.

William's subject is nature, in all of its parts, and the connections across species lines are already drawn. Having seen the same connections made in John's writing this shouldn't be a surprise, but it's unusual among the nature drawings made at the time. Different from Mark Catesby, a transitional figure in the history of naturalist art and William's principal early model, who often represented the variety of nature in his prints without regard for natural connections across all forms of life. In this sense, Catesby's art is less "natural" than William's first drawings; his flamingo, for example, stands next to a coral that grows under the ocean surrounding the Bahamas. The bird and plant are out of proportion, with no sense of respective size or their actual relationship in nature, which is difficult to discern from any perspective. Later in life, William would sometimes draw this way too.[14]

"My little botanist" is what John called the boy with whom he traveled north to the Catskill Mountains and Cadwallader Colden's estate in that same year. "There is a little token to my pretty artist Billey," Collinson wrote again that same summer before John and William departed; "his drawings [have] been much admired and better than could be expected for his first trials." The merchant intended to show the pictures to George Edwards, the famed English botanist and artist, whose opinion counted for much.[15]

William Bartram, tit, brown bird (Private collection)

When father and son set off in early September on their botanical trip, William already had a reputation as a promising botanist, a boy who drew birds that Catesby had missed. Forty miles the first day, followed by fifty the next, reaching the mountains during the third sweep of the sun, a stiff pace for the boy to keep up with the man. They stopped in the mountains on the Jersey side of the Delaware River at about noon, according to John,

> to rest ourselves and observe the vegetables that grew thereon. . . .
> my son spied a large rattle snake quoiled up in the compass of one's
> hat. . . . I wished my son had brought his box of paints with him
> (which a Switzer gentleman made him a present of with a quire of
> fine drawing paper) to have drawn him in his greatest beauty for
> he was a yellow one such as Catesby drew, but I believe he drew
> him dead, but we could not make him offer to bite so we merci-
> fully let him go without harm.[16]

William Bartram, sanderling (Private collection)

An opportunity to surpass Catesby missed, but there would be others on different days. John was encouraging the boy to bring color and vibrancy, not death, to the page, to make a flat picture radiate life. Such images would be closer to nature than what other talented artists drew; and we might suspect, given the context and the tone, they would be more humane in the sense that the subject didn't always have to die. The boy who lived in nature as his father did could see what others, like Edwards and Georg Ehret—the other great nature artist then living in England—could only guess from the corpses that served as their models.

Already the boy had, in addition to his father, two patrons—Collinson, who had twice sent him gifts in return for some sketches, and the anonymous "Switzer" gentleman, who must have admired

Billy's drawings in a visit to the Bartrams' home and made a very prac‑ tical present to encourage the young artist's work. Perhaps John got the gentleman's nationality wrong and it was the Swedish artist Gustavus Hesselius, who we know brought Peter Kalm to the Bartrams' for the first time. How did Hesselius come to know the Bartrams and why did he visit on more occasions than one, knowing the family well enough to furnish an introduction for his countryman?

Recall that the last modern owner of the portrait of the man with a pear believed that Hesselius was the portraitist and that the subject was John. Who, more likely than an artist, would encourage Billy in this way, by purchasing for him better supplies than the ones that he used? Whose opinion would John be more likely to solicit than that of an artist about the work of his talented son? Maybe Billy watched the adult artist at work; perhaps the man gave some lessons, or at least pointers, to the promising boy. And, then again, perhaps not. Imagine John showing off his son's pictures to a famous artist with the boy in the room, giving Billy the sort of paternal boost that John didn't get at that age, the very same age at which John's father left him and then died.[17]

Collinson touted William as "an admirable painter of plants. He soon will be another Ehret, his performances are so elegant." That was the highest compliment that John's friend and patron could give, a favorable comparison to the artist who set the standard, a plotting for William of a potentially brilliant career. To Cadwallader Colden he wrote,

> I wish your fair daughter was near Wm. Bartram. He would much assist her at first setting out. John's son [is] a very ingenious lad, who without any instructor has not only attained to the drawing of plants and birds, but he paints them in their natural colours, so ele‑ gantly, so masterly that the best judges here think they come the nearest to Mr. Ehret's of any they have seen.[18]

There was no instructor that Collinson knew about; so William was a natural artist whose colors were natural, too. Elegant, masterly, a boy with a future and a good family past. If Jane wasn't fifteen years older than Billy, I'd imagine some matchmaking going on here. As it was, they could hope to be like-minded friends.

Then, of course, there is John's take on his boy, a pride that holds back just a bit, but that's unmistakable, touching, and identifies closely with him. To Collinson, who criticized John's spelling and grammar, the father wrote in defense of himself as well as his son.

My son William hath drawn most of our real species of oaks and all our real species of birches with an exact description of their particular characters, not according to grammar rule, or science, but nature.

The boy now is "William," for the moment at least, praised by his father for following nature rather than anyone's rules. The William drawn here is a colleague as well as a son, a boy who knows what's important and what's not. The primary influence, John was teaching him, must always be nature rather than books. Paint what you see; see what is there. The artistic problem seemed simple, obvious, to John. The goal of art was the same objective gaze that he aimed for in looking at nature with a philosopher's eyes.[19]

In one of their trips together, through the Catskills in 1753, John and William braved a wilderness that challenged them both. The only accommodation they could find one night was with eight other people who lived together in a cottage "hardly big enough for a hen roost," John complained; "I and Billy on the ground after a piece of a musty supper slept but little in this lousy hut which we left as soon as we could well see our path in the morning." The next day they reached Colden's, but the doctor wasn't at home. They admired his daughter's "botanical curious observations," according to John, and botanized the region surrounding the house. John suffered from a fever, which weakened him for the rest of the trip. Walking up a mountain with provisions on his back made "heavy climbing" for John, who couldn't eat when they got to the top. The guide helped by carrying his bags, but John still lagged behind and Billy almost stepped on a snake. Later, the fever struck Billy, too. "I wanted much to climb again," John wrote to Collinson after they got home, "but the bushes being very wet and Billy now as well as myself being weak, and afraid he would be worse, made us post home as fast as possible, while he had strength."[20]

Danger, discomfort, disappointment, and illness plagued both of them, yet they reveled in this life. John worried about Billy but still encouraged him in the wilderness travels they shared. "I have a little son about fifteen years of age," John wrote to Gronovius the next year,

> that has travelled with me now three years and readily knows most of the plants that grows in our four governments. He hath drawn most of our oaks and birches with a draught of the drowned lands and several of the adjacent mountains and rivers as they appeared to him in his journey by them; this is his first essay in drawing plants and a map. He hath drawn several birds before, when he could find a little time from school where he learns Latin. I now send these draughts to our friend Peter Collinson. . . . I design next spring to set my son to draw some of our flowering trees and shrubs in their flourishing state.

Billy was drawing the nature he saw, when he could spare the time, and his father wanted him to draw more. He was also learning the Latin that hindered his father so much. John clearly delighted in Billy's accomplishments as an artist and scholar and had ambitions for his son that drew them together in the work they both loved. "It gives me great satisfaction," John wrote to Collinson the following year, "that Billy's drawings [are] so well received." A week later, John wrote, "I design to set Billy to draw all our turtles . . . as he has time, which is only seventh days [Saturdays] in the afternoon and first day [Sunday] mornings, for he is constantly kept to school to learn Latin and French."[21]

So the coat of arms, and even the French, could be Billy's work. The pride in his father, which the bookplate reflects, could mirror the encouragement that John had given to him. Admiration of others comes most easily from those who admire themselves, and Billy had every reason to believe, as far as we know, that the world already thought a great deal of him. John taught his son the most important things. William also studied French and Latin, thereby attaining skills that the older man lacked. Drawing he apparently was teaching himself.

In 1754, at the age of fifteen, Billy began his studies at the new Philadelphia Academy, precursor to the University of Pennsylvania. The school had existed for only three years; the "philosophical school," which instituted college-level classes, began in 1752, just two years before William enrolled. Now his son could get the sort of education

John sorely lacked; the kind, more or less, that the gentleman botanists had. William would read Virgil in Latin; he would study logic, Euclidean geometry, algebra, and trigonometry in his first year; Juvenal, Cicero, Livy, and Thucydides, along with Locke's *Essay on Human Understanding*, and the "*Spectators, Ramblers*, and monthly magazines for the improvement of style and knowledge of life." Then he would add moral philosophy and science, Longinus, Pope, Horace, Aristotle, and Newton's philosophy. Finally, on top of it all, would be Hutcheson's ethics, Burlamaqui's natural law, Bacon on science, and Locke on government.[22]

Here we can glimpse Billy and his father growing apart, as the classics hidden from John are now found by his son. Virgil's *Georgics* and *Eclogues* were now in William's head, with their bucolic perspective, which he already shared, and a poetic language to celebrate nature in ways different from those of his father. The new aesthetics was revealed here to William, perhaps for the first time, by Charles Thomson, the tutor he adored. William Hogarth's *Analysis of Beauty* and Edmund Burke on the sublime provided a sweeping new concept, a way of seeing nature that John never possessed. James Thomson's *Seasons* gave poetic expression to these ideas, even before the theorists wrote them down, as did Mark Akenside's *The Pleasures of Imagination*. This was the imaginative, philosophical world that opened to William so many new things, that gave voice and vision to what he would see, write, and draw for the rest of his life. These were the books and the poems, the essays and thoughts, that William carried with him wherever he went—not in his hand, not always even in his head, but in his heart, where his science and art shared the same spot.

Then his childhood came to an end. It was the spring of 1755 when the world as William knew it fell down around him. Was it a misunderstanding? Did John change his mind? Were the father and son now at odds for the first time? At this point, there was a real crisis, not just a fork in life's road, but a catastrophe from William's point of view. "My son William is just turned of sixteen," John wrote to Collinson;

> it is now time to propose some way for him to get his living by. I don't want him to be what is commonly called a gentleman. I want to put him to some business by which he may with care and industry get a temperate, reasonable living. I am afraid botany and

drawing will not afford him one and hard labour does not agree with him. I designed several years to put him to a doctor to learn Physick and surgery, but that will take him from his drawing, which he takes particular delight in. Pray my dear Peter, let me have thy opinion about it.[23]

There can be no doubt about what William wanted and that there was a serious disagreement between father and son. John didn't envision Billy as a gentleman, but he doesn't say why he had encouraged the boy down a path that led him to become a university-trained artist whose subject was nature in all of its parts. Apparently John had always seen botany and drawing as a hobby for Billy when he became a man, never as a means for the boy to make his way in the world. That may seem inconsistent, since John himself had stubbornly rejected advice from his first wife and his patron-friend, too, pursuing his beloved pastime as a career. John's perspective clearly perplexed his son. William flat-out refused to apprentice as a physician, perhaps at least in part because a medical practice would keep him with people and away from the woods. It was more than "delight" that William took in his art, but the language of the poets and philosophers that influenced him wasn't one that his father spoke.

What about a career as a surveyor, a printer, or an engraver for the boy? "I am well pleased that Billy gives you such satisfaction in his drawing," John wrote to Collinson later that year;

> I wish he could get a handsome livelihood by it. Botany and draw-ing are his darling delight. [I] am afraid he can't settle to any busi-ness. Also, indeed, surveying may afford an opportunity to exercise his botany, but we have five times more surveyors already than can get half employ[ed].

John's fears were rightly placed; the boy was resisting all good advice. "By all means make Billy a printer," came Collinson's reply; "it is a pretty ingenious employ[ment]—never let him reproach thee and say, Father if thou had put me to some business by which I might get my bread I should have by my industry lived in life as well as other people. Let the fault be his, not thine, if he does not." Already, the issue is blame for failure that these practical men see ahead. The same patrons who had encouraged the boy in his "darling delight" now believe that he must put aside toys and take his place in the world as a man.[24]

"He is now come to years of understanding," Collinson continued in a subsequent letter in the same vein, "and therefore it is time for him to consider how he must live in the world and give up his darling amusements in some degree that he may attain a knowledge in some art or business by which he may with care and industry support himself in life." Why don't you accept our kind friend Benjamin Franklin's offer to take him as an apprentice, Collinson asked; who better to teach that profession than the most successful printer the colonies had known? "Last night I was with our friend Benjamin," John explained to Collinson,

> and desired his further advice about Billy and reasoned with him about the difficulty of falling into good business and that as he well observed he was the only printer that did ever make a good livelihood by it in this place, though many had set up both before and since he did and that was by his extraordinary and superior abilities and close application and merchandizing, was very precarious and extreme[ly] difficult to make remittances to Europe. He sat and paused awhile, then said there was a profitable business, which he thought was now upon the increase; that there was a very ingenious man in town who had more business than he could well manage himself and that was engraving, and which he thought would suit Billy well.[25]

It was John who rejected Franklin's offer to take Billy in, on the grounds that printing wasn't a very promising life for a boy less ingenious than the American genius who was his friend. It must have been William, though, who declined to consider engraving as a career.

Alexander Garden also proposed training Billy as a physician and surgeon. Few boys get two opportunities like this, but neither appealed to John's son. "I am much obliged to thee for thy kindness to my son William," John wrote to Garden;

> he longs to be with thee, but it is more for the sake of botany than physic or surgery, neither of which he seems to have any delight in. I have several books of both, but can't persuade him to read a page

of either. Botany and drawing are his delight, but I'm afraid won't get him his living. I have some thoughts of putting him to a merchant. I have wrote to Peter Collinson about him and expect an answer by the first ships.[26]

From John's perspective, Billy was being stubborn, unreasonable, and unrealistic about life. Colden and Garden were physicians, although Colden had long ago given up his practice to pursue surveying, land speculation, and politics, all with great success; Collinson had his woolen drapery business and John had his farm. Nobody, except a man of independent means or one with a wealthy patron who paid his way, pursued botany as an occupation. There was no place for a man to make his way in the world by drawing flowers and birds as he reclined under a tree. In the next century others would have this problem, too. Thoreau had to make pencils and sometimes teach school. Audubon failed in business a number of times, and sketched in impoverishment for years, unable to support his family or sometimes to feed himself. He borrowed, defaulted, and some said he stole; this wasn't the sort of life that a responsible father would want for his son.[27] Billy needed a career, a way to pay for his bread, and he had to face this reality, as his father told him time and again.

From William's viewpoint, we can picture a sense of betrayal by a disloyal father and his traitorous friends. All this insistence on a regular job seemed vile treachery to the boy that William was. What a perfidious world, where a man couldn't pursue his passions, his talents, the life that the poets and forests had prepared him to live. George Edwards, after all, highly valued his work, using his bird drawings as models for his massive books, *Gleanings of Natural History* and *A Natural History of Uncommon Birds*, praising his talents, generously acknowledging his debts, sending him copies of these expensive, multivolume tomes, paying for William's sketches and asking for more. "The marsh hawk," as Edwards told his readers,

is engraved from a drawing done from the life in Pennsylvania, and sent to me by my obliging friend Mr. William Bartram, a native of that country. . . . Tho' I have not seen the bird itself, I have great reason to think Mr. Bartram very correct in his drawing, and exact in his colouring, having compared many of his drawings with the natural subjects and found a very good agreement between them.

The white-throated sparrow and the yellow butterfly were also his, as were other drawings, models, and descriptions from which Edwards worked. Of the black-throated green flycatcher and the black and white creeper, Edwards wrote that

> these two rare and beautiful birds (which I believe to be nondescripts) were altogether unknown to me, till I had the pleasure of receiving them from Mr. Bartram, who obliged me at one time with fourteen American birds, mostly non-descripts, with some short accounts and observations concerning them, in a letter dated Pennsylvania, June 1756. All [of] which birds are figured in the second part of my Gleanings &c.[28]

William sent the fourteen drawings and descriptions as his college studies were coming to an end, in the year when his adulthood, as defined by his father, was to begin. Before 1756 came to a close, John apprenticed Billy to a successful Philadelphia merchant, where he remained until 1761 when William turned twenty-two. From this period of William's life, there survives a small piece of writing in his hand: "Received Augt. 9th, 1759 of Jain Nichols five pounds sixteen shillings in full to my Master James Child. William Bartram." The receipt says so little that it means a great deal about how he now lived—how he spent his days and what his hands and his mind now did in a warehouse, a store, sometimes on a wharf, in the city rather than the garden or wilderness that he adored. He wielded a quill, not a brush, in his work; the drawings of birds and flowers were for his free time.[29]

During this same stretch of years, Peter Collinson purchased Billy a book, *A New Introduction to Trade and Business*, which was a primer on drawing receipts, promissory notes, bills of exchange, and keeping book debts, and which defines terms and instructs on their use. On the title page, in William's handwriting it says, "William Bartram's Book"; it is his and he claims it, perhaps values it now in his work. The overleaf reads in another recognizable hand, "The GIFT of Mr. PETER COLLINSON F.R.S. To his Friend Wm. BARTRAM." "F.R.S.," Fellow of the Royal Society—Collinson's honorific self-reference may have stung William, recalling dreams turned to resentments. Though a far cry from Virgil, Thomson, Hogarth, and Burke, the book is what his father's friend Peter thought he should read now that he was a man.[30]

There's no need to take sides in the father-son dispute that provoked William's crisis. There's no point in judging harshly the battles that each fought within himself and with the other, too. What John asked of Billy was not unreasonable—to choose or have chosen for him a path with a clear future, with the financial security that John always craved. John had friends who were eager to help his son, great men in a position to ease the boy's way into their world, the public world of eighteenth-century men. If Billy showed any interest in a reasonably promising career, his father, with the help of Colden, Collinson, Franklin, or Garden, would do what he could to make sure that it worked. What more could a son reasonably ask? What more could he expect his father to do?

We have to imagine William's point of view from the way that he acted and the things that he couldn't do. He was temperamentally unfit for the world of great men, perhaps for working with people at all. Wasn't there some way, he wondered, to make a go of it in the woods; wasn't there a place where he could live his own life and be by himself, where he could indulge his passions for drawing and writing about animals and plants, where he could battle his ambition and conquer himself? The guilt that he felt was compounded by his love for his father—his sense that John must know what was best. All the logic of money was on his father's side. William didn't really have an alternative plan. His father accused him of ingratitude, a lack of common sense, perhaps even laziness, which to an eighteenth-century Protestant was still one of the gravest of sins. To all of these accusations, William pleaded guilty in the way that he acted or in what he wrote. He felt evil, believed himself bad, fulfilled his own sense of who he was by failing time and again. He was cursed by ambition, or so he believed; he had no recourse but penance, atonement in the desert, and a return to the life of a saint. Lured from the garden by a biblical snake, who promised him more than a good man rightly should want, William believed himself snakelike and at the same time sought to make his peace with the snakes he stumbled upon—in nature, his nature, in his heart and his soul.

First, though, William tried to make it his father's way. John, it appears, was conflicted, too. "I am in a poor state of health," he wrote to Collinson, "and hath been so for a month. My son William is apprenticed to a merchant and I have only a couple little boys to help me." He missed Billy, felt poorly, and pitied himself, but sometimes a father has to do the hard thing for the good of his child no matter what the child might think. John must have gotten some comfort from the support of his friend. Collinson had, after all, advised Billy "to leave off his Darling Delights to qualify himself to live in the world." When he knew that Billy, at John's insistence, had taken his advice, Collinson wrote again about the relationship between art and "the world." "Our friend Neve carefully delivered Billy's drawings," Collinson reported, "which are very elegant and much admired. I am glad he has found out that he may be in a way to rise in the world. Probably there may be at times some leisure hours in which he may divert himself in his favourite amusement."[31]

Collinson sent William another book to draw in and a primer on drawing to complement the one that he sent on keeping accounts. The idea wasn't to discourage the boy from practicing his art, but to help him gain a perspective on its rightful place in the lives of grown men. "My Billy comes on finely with Captain Child," John was relieved to report, "who is very kind to him and keeps him very close to his business. He hath sent thee a letter and acknowledges thy kind present of the drawing book." Collinson got the letter and, always eager to improve the Bartrams, critiqued it for John: "I received Billy's letter. I am pleased to see him improved in his writing. I wish I could say as much in his spelling, which will be easily attained with application. I send him 2 books to assist him." Whatever their merit, the books didn't help.[32]

Then came the time for William to strike out on his own. No written account helps us to see how he felt, whether the day came too fast or not soon enough. It is not even clear who chose the Cape Fear region of North Carolina for him to set up shop. John's half-brother, also named William, was living there, near the place where Billy's grandfather had died, so there would be relatives to watch over him, to help him make the connections that a businessman needs in the world. It was a likely region for a young merchant, a rapidly developing place where he might heed his father's dictum, gleaned from a proverb, to "first creep and then go." This is a cautious piece of business advice, expressing a father's concern about the money he was investing and perhaps about his son's judgment.[33]

"Billy is now gone to Carolina," John told Collinson, "but whether he is arrived or when he will come back I know not." Yes, John was concerned for his investment, but mostly about the boy who was now a man. He didn't know whether Billy was dead or alive, or whether he'd ever see him again. Imagine the guilt John would bear if something happened to William—especially down there—after he had insisted on this career for his son. "Dear Father," the letter finally came, the first one that survives in William's hand,

> I am just arrived at this place after a most severe attack from that most dangerous disorder of sea sickness. We had a tedious passage of about seven days from the capes. We rode out two dangerous gales of wind. The first was last Thursday night, a little to the east of Cape Hatteras and was miraculously delivered from the dangerous shoals.

It's a miracle, he tells his father, that I'm still alive. Billy is sharing good news and bad, while adding a small burden of guilt to his father's relief.[34]

Two weeks later, William wrote to his father again to let him know that things weren't going well. "I am unfortunate in arriving to a bad market," he was sorry to say, "a wrong season of the year and the excessive rain has almost destroyed the country." He waited for a boat, while his goods languished on a dock with nobody to buy them and no way to get out. He'd have to pay as much to transport his goods locally as it cost to get them all the way from Philadelphia to North Carolina. With rivers flooded and crops destroyed in the fields, finding customers who could pay was going to be tough. For all the danger around him, William was happy to report that, "I have my health, with thank[s to] Heaven, hope I may enjoy it in this country, God willing." He had already shipped John a beautiful plant that he thought John would like, sent love to his siblings "and all those that'll accept it," and expressed hope that his parents would write to him.[35]

John wrote back right away: the plant was swept overboard because Billy didn't pack it right, but even if it had gotten to Philadelphia it wouldn't have lived because this is the wrong time of year to send plants. Some tension is there, some disappointment, too, but mostly the letter is filled with paternal love. "My dear child," John writes,

> I have no new advice to give thee but to remind thee of my former general instructions; fear God and walk humble before him; practice all virtues and eschew all vice; take care of being beguiled by vain recreations. They are like the hornets [that] hath a sting in their tail. But keep close to industry, temperance and frugality. Thee hath left a good character behind in town. Pray don't forget it. Now is the time to gain it there and establish it in both provinces by making good remittances to thy creditors here. Be complaisant and obliging to all so far as consistent with thy credit and no honest man will desire more.

It's your character that will make a difference, John is telling his son. The converse, he implies, is that failure will just as surely be a consequence of your behavior; it is under your control. "I have thy welfare much at heart," he tells William. Listen to your uncle; he knows the people there. Ingratiate yourself with the better sort; pay your respects to the governor whenever possible. And, John continues, there are a few curious plants that you can send me when you get a chance. "I must close with much love," the letter concludes; the ship that will carry this letter is about to leave port. I'm powerless to help you; I've taught you everything that I know; platitudes are all I have left. You're on your own now. Remember what I taught you and keep your priorities straight. Work hard, act wisely and politely, and things will work out.[36]

It's as if William's letter, with its list of problems external to him, has been read by a blind man who lays a heavy responsibility on his son. There is no answer from William as the summer slips by. Was he angry, frustrated, embarrassed to tell his father the same things again? John writes in September, as he's about to leave for Pittsburgh, driving himself forward after his bad fall from the tree and injuring his hip. "Dear Billy keep to virtue, piety, moderation and frugality," John reminds William again; "be obliging to all, but don't join with the vicious. Beware of the deluding snares of excess. Keep in the narrow paths of strict temperance in all things, which leads to the bowers of tranquility." John really believes that for good men things eventually work out.

Poor William; does he think this, too? Does he carry the burden of failure so heavily that he can't recover from his own fall? "Dear Billy, I heartily wish thee well in all thy undertakings and remain thy loving father," the letter concludes after another request for just a few plants. A postscript from his mother endorses John's counsel, wishes "Bill" health and prosperity, and shares her desire "to hear from thee at all opportunities."[37]

A month later, upon John's return, there is no letter from Billy, so he writes again. I had a good trip, but didn't find any plants that we don't already have growing here in the garden. Please send a few that I need from down there. I hope you will never forfeit our good name. Please give my love to my brother and his family. "I remain thy affectionate father," this short letter ends. The artist George Edwards is also a little annoyed by William's lack of response. "It being upwards of two years since I've had the pleasure of a letter from you," Edwards chides his young friend. I sent you my books, with their generous acknowledgment of your help, and you haven't sent me a word of thanks, never mind some praise for my art. Yet another friend writes at about the same time, with the same request for a word to let him know that William still lives, still cares, still grows.[38]

No letters come in response. John grows more worried; he doesn't know how to interpret the silence, but fears the worst. "I and most of my son Billy's relations [are] concerned," John writes to his brother, "that he never writes how his trade affairs succeed. We are afraid he doth not make out so well as he expected." On the same date in late December 1761, John also writes to Billy again. Kindly, he doesn't ask about business, but complains about seeds. "I want seed of everything we have not and thee is a good judge of that. . . . Thee disappointed my expectation[s] much in not sending to me any seeds. . . . I have not received one single seed from my son who glories so much in the knowledge of plants and whom I have been at so much charge to instruct therein." John lays it on pretty thick: "I don't want thee to hinder thy own affairs to oblige me, but thee might easily gather a few seeds when thee need not hinder half an hour's time to gather them or turn 20 yards out of thy way to pluck them." He sure sounds mad, seems hurt by his son. Perhaps William intended to wound John; all he had wanted in the first place was to gather seeds, but his father insisted that nature wasn't enough. Now I've got my career, William might have thought, such as it is, and I'm out on my own; I never wanted to do this and it's not going well. Just leave me alone. William couldn't bring himself to say, perhaps even consciously to feel, such hostility as this toward the man whom he loved, admired, cared for so much. He was silent, keeping his pain to himself, as well as his ambitions and harsh judgments of the mess he had made of his life and couldn't clean up.[39]

John continued to build. In the winter of 1761 it was a greenhouse, constructed of stone and glass, with two flues for the stoves that would keep the plants warm. Again, as he finished, he chiseled a quotation from Alexander Pope into the stone lintel over the door: "Slave to no sect, who takes no private road, But looks through Nature up to Nature's God." Disowned by Darby Meeting three years earlier, and perhaps still smarting from the affront, John proclaims his independence and testifies, in Pope's words, to his view of nature as a telescope through which to view God. His business was growing at the same time, with up to twenty-nine boxes of seeds and plants sent to England in any one year, and £590 in receipts during the period from 1760 through 1762.[40]

There were no letters from Billy in 1762 and, almost as bad, no plants or seeds either. "I can't get one plant from Billy," John complained to Collinson. Not a word, not a seed—then, one day, Billy appears. In June, William returned to Philadelphia, "to settle his affairs there," according to his uncle. That's all anyone says.[41]

How did it feel to come home? Not a word from John or William about the arrival or how the summer passed with Billy again in the house. What was his welcome home like? He surely was missed and worried over; but why didn't he write, send plants, let them know that he was alive? There must have been some anger, resentment at least, about how Billy had acted toward his family. Perhaps his parents said nothing, kept their hurt inside, but that doesn't sound like John.

What about William's attempt to settle his business affairs? The lack of comment doesn't sound good. Did he need to borrow money? Was he deeply in debt? He did collect for one shipment of turpentine that he had sent north: "Recd. Sept 1, 1762 of William Fisher eighteen pounds seventeen shillings and sixpence for 35 Bb turpentine in full. £10.17.6 Wm. Bartram." That's good news; perhaps there was more. How did John respond to Billy's stories about bad debts, unpredictable markets, or ships lost at sea? If John offered more platitudes about the relationships among good character, hard work, and success, it couldn't have felt good to William, might even have angered him. Perhaps the silence in surviving correspondence is a good reflection of what passed between father and son. Maybe they tried to say nothing, lest they make the strain worse.[42]

John and his sons Billy and Moses departed Philadelphia together in September 1762. Moses was headed to North Carolina to make contacts for the apothecary business that he ran with his older brother Isaac. John wanted to botanize the Carolinas again. William was going back to his uncle's, his business, his adult life. The boys traveled with their father as far as the Yadkin River, where they struck out east to the coast and John stayed inland, heading south toward more plants before he went home.

John wrote to his sons when he got back. "I had the most prosperous journey that ever I was favoured with," he reported enthusiastically about the specimens he found, having lost none of his childlike ardor for discovering plants in his old age. "I was pleased with Billy's temperance and patience in his journey, and shall soon be daily expecting a packet of seeds and a box of plants from you which with hearing of your welfare will make glad the heart of your loving father." This linkage of a shipment of plants and his affection is typical of John, who was neither subtle nor reluctant to make his love sound contingent on his children's behavior. Dutifully, if not soon enough for their father's satisfaction, William and Moses sent their father a box of plants the next spring.[43]

The most curious line in John's letter refers to Billy's behavior during their trip. The father was "pleased" with his son's "temperance and patience." Does that mean that John was pleasantly surprised; is it a comparison to past experience or what he had witnessed that summer in his home? Did William now drink, however little being too much in his father's eyes; did he often lose patience, perhaps with his father? Or maybe he had a temper that John found intemperate, too. Maybe this tells us something about how the summer had gone—badly, both cold and hot.

Whatever was there in the silences, whatever meanings these few words about William carry, by the first week in March 1764 both John Bartram and Peter Collinson had lost faith in the "boy." "My [son]

John is a worthy, sober, industrious son," John senior writes, "and delights in plants. But I doubt Will[iam]. He will be ruined in Carolina. Everything goes wrong with him there." Collinson writes three days later, long before his friend's letter crosses the Atlantic, to say the same things. "William was a very ingenious lad," he recalls, "but I am afraid made some mistakes that I hear nothing of him. Johnny seems now to be our sheet anchor. I hope he will inherit his father's virtues and at leisure and suitable opportunities make nature his studies."44

John Jr. is a "worthy, sober, industrious son" in his father's eyes, a compliment apparently intended as a specific comparison to William, whom John doubts and sees as "ruined" in ways that matter to him. William is unworthy of his father's confidence and trust—frivolous, if not inebriate and indolent—the opposite of what John respects, of the way that he has instructed his sons. Is it failure in business alone that reveals these traits to John's eyes or is he reflecting on specific characteristics that he sees in his boy? Has he got cause and effect right or has William slipped into a lethargic fog, a depression, that is caused by his failure to make his way in the profession that his father has chosen for him?

Collinson is saddened to hear that "Billy, so ingenious a lad, is as it were lost in indolence and obscurity." John was not a man to give up so easily on anything or anyone, let alone the "dear child" in whom he had placed so much hope. Already in the fall of 1764, he had a plan in mind to find the boy and some curious specimens at the same time. "If I should be appointed by authority [or] private subscription to travail thro[ugh] Florida or the Illinois," he writes to Collinson, "I am too old to go alone and I think my son William will be a fit person to accompany me as by this time I believe can draw well."45

When the King's appointment came through that's exactly what John wanted to do: reclaim his son's nature through art, begin over again by demolishing the walls that had come between them, rebuild the foundation of affection and trust upon which their relationship once rested, and enlist Billy's help in the business of nature that they both loved. John wrote to Billy on June 7, 1765, informing him of the King's appointment and his imminent trip south. "I am daily waiting for orders and recommendations from Court," John explained, but our friend Peter ordered me to take my son or a servant with me and as thee wrote to me last winter and seemed so very desirous to go there, now thee hath a fair opportunity, so pray let me know as soon as possible. Our vessel is to sail in about two or three weeks. Therefore, I advise thee to sell of[f] all thy goods at a public vendue and give thy account into the hands of an attorney there properly proved, who will recover thy debts better and with a quicker dispatch than thee can thyself and write directly to thy creditors to let them know how the affairs stand.

John was giving his blessing for Billy to quit, to make a new start with his father and with his life. He didn't have to ask twice. William was ready to give the mess up and was waiting for an excuse, perhaps for permission, to start over again. He shared in John's dream, writing to his brother Isaac that he would put his business aside and join their father on this, probably the old man's last, expedition, to "help and comfort" him—at least that is what Isaac says—"in whatever afflictions or trouble thee should meet with in thy long and tedious journey." William and John wanted to save each other, to redeem themselves from the recent past, to find each other in nature and discover themselves.[46]

It's hard to say which of them most needed redemption and whether either could be saved by anyone but himself. And it is equally difficult to know their greatest fears as they anticipated the trip that lay ahead. Nature was scary, but they had been there before. Each also had the sting of the other's judgment to fear. Then, of course, there were the venomous snakes—and not just the ones on the ground; for those inside ourselves, the ones that inhabit our hearts, are perhaps the most frightening of all and the most difficult to kill.

CHAPTER SIX

Snakes

 OHN BARTRAM WAS BORN into a world at war against snakes. The warfare was total; no prisoners were taken and ranks were assigned. "I killed a snake," wrote Dr. Alexander Hamilton in his diary at midcentury; "had it been a rattlesnake I should have been entitled to a colonel's commission, for it is a common saying here that a man has no right to that dignity until he has killed a rattlesnake." Whacking a rattler was something of a male rite of passage in colonial America—a moral obligation, a public service, and dangerous fun all in one.[1]

John killed his share. By my count he whacked three rattlesnakes on his 1743 trip to Canada. On his 1765–1766 Florida trek with William he clubbed a water moccasin, "a monstrous rattler," and one other, unnamed. He killed "a few" black snakes over six feet in length, but doesn't even bother to mention how many smaller ones he thumped. Then there is the rattlesnake he "found" near his home and dissected, which probably belongs in this imperfect tally, the event of stomping a snake, even a rattler, being so commonplace as not to constitute news.[2]

What makes John unusual for his time and place is that he didn't try to kill *every* snake that came into his view. "We commonly let them go unhurt," John wrote of himself and his sons, "as we are not murderers." Quaker influences are evident here, but not enough to explain the behavior entirely. The problem is that John wasn't the most pacific of Quakers when it came to war among men; and, in the reverse, other Quakers who were more peaceful than he had fewer qualms about squashing snakes.[3]

There was a practical quality to John's mercy, which we see in his approach to nonvenomous reptiles. Since the bite of a black snake causes no harm, "they are permitted to harbour about the house to destroy rats, mice, frogs, &c." These snakes he describes as "domestick" inhabitants of the barnyard, living in harmony with the other animals and the human household. Their proximity to John's family bred familiarity and a decline in fear on both sides. It seems likely that John's tolerance for poisonous snakes in the wild was also a consequence of the frequency of his contact with rattlers, as well as the philosophical influences that led him to see nature as a system of interlocking relationships created by God.

We may justly admire the goodness of Providence in giving this noxious animal a rattle in his tail to give notice where he is when in motion, for it happens that most that are bit are by accident, by treading on them at unawares as they lie coiled up or asleep. And we may further admire that not withstanding they are great increasers, breeding of sixty at a time . . . yet the wisdom of Providence is great in preserving a balance by preventing their increase by providing animals to destroy them.[4]

John's approach to vipers was also an extension of his views on violence toward humans, which were inspired by the traditional Quaker peace testimony but not entirely in accordance with its pacifist principles. He was willing, in theory, to kill men for reasons of self-defense, vengeance, or in a principled war. He held himself to the same standards in his dealings with snakes. What's exceptional about John is his application of such principles across species lines. Not that he didn't see differences between snakes and people, but he focused on connections in ways that others did not.

In a draft letter, John wrote about one of his sons teasing a snake with a stick. John was right there, observing it all. For the man this was the work of a naturalist and a father. For the boy we can guess it was play. For the snake this was a life-and-death struggle against monstrous foes armed with a weapon against which it lacked a defense. Again, John wants his correspondent to know that he and his sons often "tease" snakes and "then let them go unhurt for we are not murderers."

The snake hisses, attracting one of the family's cats. A new hunter thus enters the scene, an added enemy for the snake, which must now fend off three. "The cat directly walked before the snake," John reports, "and with one claw of her foot struck him quite through the middle of his skull into his mouth at which the snake turned upon his back and died instantly." Although, John tells us, neither he nor his son would have murdered the snake, he permits the cat to pursue its instinct without interference and has no remorse for the dead. Instead, what strikes him is the "natural prudent conduct of this young cat, [who] had no example nor a material being to direct her" to strike the snake in precisely the way safest to her and most deadly to her prey. John's approach to nature was tolerant, humane, curious, observant, experimental, and not a bit sentimental.

What gave her that knowledge that she could not hurt him with her mouth and paws on his body? What directed her to strike him on the head, the only part where she could annoy him and with one claw in the middle of his skull the only spot that she could strike him dead? What instructed her that she could better enter farther with one than if she had struck with all the nails of her paw? What shall we say to the actions of many of the kinds of what is called the brute animals which seem to be acted with more cunning forethought and caution, indeed reason, than many actions and indeed opinions of the human species? They have love, hatred, fear, and revenge if not foreknowledge, thought, will, and desire, faculties of the soul, mem[ory], and reason in a great degree and some in a greater than some of our species. Indeed, I have a much higher opinion of the spirit and soul of brutes than our mystery mongers have. Call it all instinct, but what is instinct but a stream from the universal fountain or an emanation from the deity.[5]

That's how John thought, in terms of connections and patterns throughout nature. He admired the "brutes" that are in some ways superior to us. He had less respect for the "mystery mongers" of organized religion than he did for the cat and the snake. The contrast that preachers made between animal "spirits" and human "souls" seemed nonsense to him. He saw the distinction as unnatural, as an artificial elevation of man above nature. His Quaker disdain for paid, professional clergy was showing itself again, his sense that preachers obscure what any person with eyesight and common sense can see for himself. They were blind leaders, ignorant men with college degrees, unfit for their calling because they lacked the sensibility to read the great book of nature, where God reveals his divine plan. "I have a very different opinion," John wrote, "of what the priests have told us in all ages and nations, of the world relating to their imported and imaginary notions, of their superstitious worship and attributes of their gods." Itinerant preachers associated with the so-called New Light movement were even worse—charlatans who duped common folks with appeals to their emotions rather than to their brains.[6]

As a man of science, John sought truth in observable facts. He had no patience with either mysteries or mongers, who gave supernatural explanations for the natural and real. He liked the Germantown physician Christopher Witt and respected the old man, enjoying walks in Witt's garden and conversations on all manner of philosophy and plants. Witt's library, though, was filled with books for which John had no use, "philosophy, natural magic, divinity, nay even mystic divinity." Those weren't the sources upon which John drew for knowledge about snakes or remedies against bites. "I could have wished thee the enjoyment of so much diversion," he wrote to Peter Collinson about one of his visits to Witt, "as to have heard our discourse, provided thee had been well swathed from hips to armpits." The swathing is prescribed in a jocular tone, as protection from the nonsense that Witt slung around.

> A little of our spiritual discourse was interrupted by a material object within doors, for the Doctor had lately purchased of a great traveller in Spain and Italy a sample of what was imposed upon him for snake stones, which took me up a little time beside laughing at him to convince the Doctor that they were nothing but calcined [calcified] old horse bones.

How silly, John thought, that a curious man, a man of learning who knew nature firsthand, could believe that rubbing old bones over the wound cured a snakebite. John's science broke with the medieval past from which such stories came. He had no use for the amalgam of astrology, folklore, and mystical medicine endorsed by his friend Dr. Witt. "When we are upon the topic of astrology, magic, and mystic divinity," John wrote of his conversations with the older man,

> I am apt to be a little troublesome, by inquiring into the foundation and reasonableness of these notions which thee knows will not bear to be searched and examined into, though I handle these fancies with more tenderness with him than I should with many others that are so superstitiously inclined because I respect the man.[7]

He respects Witt, but doesn't share his view of the world. John's curiosity ran to experiment rather than to theory, in any event, but the theories that made sense to him weren't products of "superstition" or "fancy." They were "science" that viewed nature on its own terms and God's. There was no conflict, no tension, no stress between John Bartram's spiritual and scientific beliefs. The breach was between his moral science and the mystical past.

Asked for his opinion on snake fascination by Peter Collinson, John replied in 1737 that "what I have heard and remarked of the Rattle-Snake's power of charming is surprising to me, for I have received many particular relations from very judicious persons, who have told me the whole process," which they saw with their own eyes. "I have had accounts from several persons of undoubted credit," John repeated himself, "who have affirmed to me that there is a surprising fascination in the looks of this snake."

What he heard was "surprising" to him. In other words, it was hard to believe. And yet, the people who reported seeing a snake charm its victim were so credible and so sure that the prey had not been previously bitten. He found experiments in which a rodent was released and scampered quickly away a sort of proof that infection by venom couldn't account for the scene. John remained suspicious of his sources, but unwilling to dismiss out of hand what others saw. Such testimony "confirms to me," he wrote to his friend, "that there proceeds such subtle emanations from the eyes of this creature beyond what we can comprehend." Something we cannot see must be going on, so he fell back on the century's catch-all "scientific" response, not the spells and charms of the past or the hypnotic trances to come, but effusion theory with all of its emissions, aromas, and rot.

He wasn't even locked into the "emanations" that other curious men discussed as the explanation for what others witnessed and what they could not. "It may be possible," John reasoned, that

> many creatures may come within their reach, as she lies coiled up and motionless in rage or anger against their common enemy or else in surprise or admiration at the shape and different colors of this subtle serpent, who by the power of muscular motion can appear or change to various shades of colours, to allure squirrels or bird[s] to come within its reach. The Snake lying so still, they apprehend no danger.[8]

Again, John lacks the words to discuss this theory of his, but is aiming for a physical explanation, finding spirits not worthy of comment and lacking the language of psychology in his quill. Perhaps the animals are lured into a mistake by color that attracts victims and hides what really is there. John's is an ingenious speculation about nature's use of disguise, which has more credit in our world than his and shows a creative mind at work in the field. For John was no theorist, as he explained any number of times. He was not an educated man, although he dearly loved books. He was a hands-on observer of nature in the raw, risking bites, water, and sun, smelling, tasting, and listening to nature alive, and watching it die.

John's curiosity catapulted him out of his chair, through the door, and away from his farm. Surfaces weren't all that he saw; his inquisitiveness penetrated to what lay under, beneath, and inside. He dissected the head of a dead rattler, carefully examining the teeth that others held in such awe, finding them intriguing and complex, clustered together with the two largest ones sheathed, raising for him more questions about the relationship between their design and their use. He saw nothing magical about a snake's mouth and had no fear that a scratch might end his life, as others still had.

One year after he responded to Collinson's question about a snake's power to charm, John shared a personal experience with a live snake in a letter to his friend.

One day as I was searching the woods over the [Susquehanna] River my guide had like to run over a large rattle snake. I being just behind went round the snake. He drew up in a quoil and rattled. Then I stood staring at him to observe whether he would have any way affected me by his looks, but found no alteration. Then I got a green stick and put it towards his mouth for him to bite it, that I might have seen the venom run up the pores thereof as some relate, but he would not offer to bite although provoked by gently striking and turning him over.[9]

For all his trying, John never could work himself into a snake's spell or even get a rattler to take a good shot. He attempted to replicate stories about snakes biting trees that immediately fell over dead, but there, too, he found these creatures more fragile, more fearful, more passive than mystically fierce. Experience must have led John to doubt, but he still reported what other credible people witnessed as if he believed it himself.

John would "tease" nature to see how it worked, but he resisted killing any creature unless for a good cause. Defense and hunger were high on his list of reasons to slay. John sometimes also succumbed to fear or revenge, emotions he wished to subdue with the higher spirit he sought in himself. Murdering a snake that meant no one harm was an example of conduct that, to John, reveals humans as the real brutes. In a Christian culture just emerging from its medieval past, on a continent still so wild and scary as the one where he lived, such an attitude marked John as eccentric.

Recall John's experience, discussed in the last chapter, while he was plant hunting in the Catskill Mountains with Billy along. The boy "spied" a large rattlesnake, but couldn't paint it because he'd left his artist's tools at home.

We dismounted and cut a stick to try to anger him, drawing him out at length but he offered to run away from us. I stopped him and put him back and he drew in his quoil again, rattled and flattened his body by which his colors brightened much. . . . we could not make him offer to bite so we mercifully let him go without harm.[10]

John appreciated the danger. He relished the opportunity for scientific enquiry. The rattler didn't try to fascinate him or even attack. As usual with the snakes that John met, it was just scared and wanted to go its own way. He saw the beauty of the living serpent as superior to that of the dead.

John was a philosopher of nature whose real passion was plants. Indeed, his friend Peter Collinson complained upon reading a journal from one of John's trips about "how few or none of your wild animals came under thy notice except snakes." John's replies were pretty lame—animals come out only at night; nature is not so abundant as it once was. Yet we have William's drawings and observations over much the same terrain and see through his eyes a wilderness teeming with life at all times of the day. John's gaze was fixed close to the ground, not sweeping the horizon or looking up through the trees. He had no interest in bugs, which were only annoyances that kept him from sleep; to him, animals were mainly something to eat. Snakes, though, were close by, where he could see them even with his myopic eyes.[11]

John saw the snakes and their threat, saving Billy from stepping on rattlers at least twice. "Being youthful and vigorous in the pursuit of botanical and novel objects," William writes,

> I had gained the summit of a steep rocky precipice, ahead of our guide; when just entering a shady vale, I saw, at the root of a small shrub, a singular and beautiful appearance, which I remember to have instantly apprehended to be a large kind of fungus which we call Jews ears, and was just drawing back my foot to kick it over; when at the instant, my father being near, cried out, 'A rattle snake, my son!' and jerked me back, which probably saved my life. I had never before seen one. This was of the kind which our guide called a yellow one, it was very beautiful, speckled and clouded. My father pleaded for his life, but our guide was inexorable, saying he never spared the life of a rattle snake, and killed him; my father took his skin and fangs.[12]

William's eyes, even in pursuit of a plant on the ground, didn't focus on the danger right there; swept away by nature's beauty, the plant is all that he saw. William's ken was so very broad, even when searching the ground, taking in the larger sweep of the horizon, the bigger picture that he, as an artist and writer, wanted to draw.

The energy and incautiousness of a fourteen-year-old youth led William to run on ahead; yet John, at age fifty-four, was right at his son's heels just the same. John, with his eyes looking down, was always the cautious botanist and father, less prone to mistakes. The son spotted more snakes as experience grew and energy waned, but John would continue to view Billy, with reasonable cause, as the same foolhardy youth bounding right into a man's middle age.

John pleads with the guide for the snake's life, the snake that was to the son's eyes "very beautiful" and to the father's a threat. No quarter is granted in this natural war, so John the scientist saves the most curious parts of an enemy killed and then scalped. Off the small party marches into the wilderness—this time, perhaps, with the guide in the lead and Billy walking between the two men.

Thirteen years later, in 1765, with the son now a man failed in business and without a career, and the father old and near blind, they are again traveling together in the swamps of East Florida, still looking for plants. "I being ahead a few paces," writes William, "my father bid me observe the rattlesnake before and just at my feet." Some things never change.

I stopped and saw the monster formed in a high spiral coil, not half his length from my feet: another step forward would have put my life in his power, as I must have touched if not stumbled over him.

What was Billy watching this time? This was a dangerous place and he knew better, but his mind wandered. No doubt he was too old, in his opinion, for another fatherly lecture. Perhaps John showed some restraint.

The fright and perturbation of my spirits at once excited resentment; at that time I was entirely insensible to gratitude or mercy. I instantly cut off a little sapling, and soon dispatched him: this serpent was about six feet in length, and as thick as an ordinary man's leg.

William reacted in anger, he tells us, but at whom? He says at the snake, but more likely at himself for messing up once again. Also at his father, for William lacked both gratitude and mercy. Mercy he denied to the snake. Thanks, if reserved, he withheld from John. They had reached stages in life where William, twenty-seven, should have walked first, scouting for danger, protecting the older man now entering his sixty-eighth year, but he still was just Billy, once again rescued from his own nature by his father. How William ached to tell a story about saving John; but it simply was not to be: not now and not later, either in the wilderness or at home. He let go all his anger and frustration on the "monster" by murdering the snake.

The rencounter deterred us from proceeding on our researches for that day. So I cut off a long tough withe or vine, which fastening round the neck of the slain serpent, I dragged him after me, his scaly body sounding over the ground, and entering the camp with him in triumph, was soon surrounded by the amazed multitude, both Indians and my countrymen.

William reverted to boyhood, lacking in his own mind the requisite qualities for being a man. He doesn't say why they cannot go on, whether he or his father is too upset. Both are shaken. It's his fault they cannot continue men's work, so he turns the snake into a toy and returns to camp with his conquest in tow. The men ask for the snake's body to cook for a meal, and William, the rattlesnake colonel, complies.

I tasted of it, but could not swallow it. I, however, was sorry after killing the serpent, when coolly recollecting every circumstance. He certainly had it in his power to kill me almost instantly, and I make no doubt but that he was conscious of it. I promised myself that I would never again be accessory to the death of a rattle snake, which promise I have invariably kept to.

The killing was for William a transforming event, resulting in guilt and a pledge for reform. Having vented his anger at his own nature, William reverted to Billy and came out a new William again.

Really, the story concludes, "this dreaded animal is easily killed; a stick no thicker than a man's thumb is sufficient to kill the largest at one stroke, if well directed, either on the head or across the back; nor can they make their escape by running off, nor indeed do they attempt it when attacked."[13]

In other words, killing snakes is a boy's job. The more manly task is letting them live. In William's telling, the credit for this insight is his, not his father's, not the consequence of youthful instruction, but of adult experience. The gratitude, it seems, is reserved still, a quarter century after the event he recounts and a decade after his father's death. In his eyes, he deserved to be William, not Billy, from this point in time, but his father continued to see him as an incompetent son. That is not fair to John, and William is being too hard on himself, but that's how he saw it, lived it, suffered it still. William is angry that it took him this long to grow up, resentful that even then he couldn't break free from the father he loved, his mentor, his savior from death and from life. Snakes were the least of it; but the symbol is stronger than the serpent itself, and the identities of the snake and the man are insolubly linked in the stories he tells.

Others saw William differently, though, or at least such was his hope and his claim. "Within my circle of acquaintance," he writes, "I am known to be an advocate or vindicator of the benevolent and peaceable disposition of animal creation in general," including snakes. The benevolence of snakes extends to the humans they encounter, "whom they seem to venerate." Just like his father, then, William portrays nature as kind, snakes as compassionate, and humans as brutes. Together they argued the snake's case to a jury armed with long sticks and a longer tradition of hacking serpents to bits.[14]

Unlike his father, William was prone to meddle in the workings of nature, being more sentimental than John, who let the cat and the guide kill their snakes. "I observed a large hawk on the ground in the middle of the road," William tells us;

> he seemed to be in distress endeavouring to rise; when, coming up near him, I found him closely bound up by a very long coach-whip snake, that had wreathed himself several times round the hawk's body, who had but one of his wings at liberty: beholding their struggles a while, I alighted off my horse with an intention of part-

ing them; when, on coming up, they mutually agreed to separate themselves, each one seeking his own safety, probably considering me as their common enemy. The bird rose aloft and fled away as soon as he recovered his liberty, and the snake as eagerly made off.

William's interference in this life-and-death struggle is a significant departure from the philosophy of John. The father's goal was a rational, hardheaded, hands-off squint at nature, followed by a report of the "facts." The son dove right in, breaching the physical and emotional distance that John tried to keep from the subjects he studied.

It is at such points of philosophical divergence between the two men that I wonder about the influence of others, particularly the elusive relationship between mother and son. John once told the story of a barnyard battle between two reptiles witnessed by his wife.

The black snake lay still with his eyes fixed on the striped one, which crept directly into the black snake's mouth. My wife seeing this fetched the tongs and pulled very hard to get him out of the black snake's mouth for he was near half-swallowed down. But the black snake, far from being scared at such usage, crept about as in search of his prey that he had been robbed of and would not go of[f] the premises till a stick made him run away.[15]

What interested John here was his wife's claim to having witnessed one snake charm another, the survival of the victim after her intervention, and the predator's lack of fear of Ann Bartram. Her aggressive intervention is fascinating as well; what inspired her to run for the tongs and struggle to save one snake from another of its kind? Whether Ann's inspiration was a sentimental humanity or the science of a curious woman can't be discerned from John's brief account. Since her son William was a sentimental intervener, though, and her husband was not, I am tantalized by the probability that William's nature was a product of Ann's influence as much as it was of John's.

To be sure, the differences between John and William are less obvious than those between them and their curious friends. Their shared tolerance for living snakes represents a dramatic break between the Bartrams and the cultural imperative to kill. Nonetheless, John would have left the snake and the hawk to themselves and observed the combat with a philosopher's eye. He would have used the story to instruct us on the snake's constricting powers, its awesome capacity to consume much larger prey, and the flaws in the larger predator's defense. He would have seen nature's justice in the snake's defeat of the enemy who attacked. John was bound by his nature, his science, and God to let nature's battle follow its course.

William's approach is an extension of John's, but one that moves from curiosity, dispassion, and tolerance to compassion. The son took the father's belief in the linkage between nature and man one great leap forward to a place that his father never saw. William became part of nature in a way that John never did. He surrendered his spirit, rather than just his body and mind. Whether that made William less of a scientist and more of a poet is a question that others asked at the time, but it was a possibility he vehemently denied.

"I shall strictly confine myself to facts," he tells us. The protestation to "fact" is one I take seriously, even when it's hard to believe. As a claim to honesty it is true. It is also defensive and expressive of self-doubt. He has little confidence that we'll believe him, being unsure himself about the interplay of imagination and perception, about the reliability of the senses in which his father's generation placed greater trust. Like the novelist Charles Brockden Brown, whom William knew, and the later writers Hawthorne and Poe, who mined the same gothic shaft, William could never be sure, at least as sure as his father, that he saw what he saw or knew what he believed to be true.[16]

The question of knowing is significant here, at least partly because William's snake stories are so self-referential. He uses snakes to tell us about himself and his father, his transformation late in life into a man, his courage, humanity, foolishness, and his perception of beauty even in vipers that slink through the mud. He wants us to know that he is brave, merciful, and has mastered himself; but he's not sure that he's right, so he gives us a jumble of contradictory images of himself and of snakes. Sometimes he is unsure who's the brute, who's the viper, and whether he is a man.

Having heard about his transformation from a childish murderer of serpents to a merciful man, we may wonder at the meaning of another story that William narrates about a rattler he murdered at the request of Seminole Indians. The juxtaposition of these two stories within William's *Travels* reveals unresolved tensions in his narrative and his life. Although the Seminole story takes place about a decade later than the transformation, their telling is reversed in the book. This creates a chronological challenge for readers attentive to such things, but a smoother narrative flow, which defies time and ignores contradictions in character and plot.

The first story—in time, though second in the *Travels*—was about the metamorphosis from Billy to William, while this one reveals another change that took place during the second Florida trip, when he traveled alone. Now he is "Puc-Puggy" or Flower Hunter, having been so named by his Indian hosts. "I was in the forenoon busy in my apartment in the council-house, drawing some curious flowers; when, on a sudden, my attention was taken off by a tumult without, at the Indian camp." He was inside, doing a man's work, William wants us to know. The interruption came from outside his head. "I stepped to the door opening to the piazza, where I met my friend the old interpreter, who informed me that there was a very large rattle snake in the Indian camp, which had taken possession of it, having driven the men, women and children out."

Possession and fear inspire the Indians, the men who aren't manly as well as the rest. Puc-Puggy isn't afraid and he has better things to do. The reference to a "piazza" on a Seminole dwelling suggests inspiration from European travelers' accounts, which pit the courageous man of culture against the cowardice of ignorant folk. This is an unusual identity for William, who values Indian culture with a romantic eye. It reflects an insecurity about who he is that William reveals by sharing his new name at this point in the book. As narrator of the *Travels*, he has myriad identities available to him—Billy, William, Puc-Puggy, the representative of a superior culture, the brave man among cowards, the scientist, the artist, the Romantic, the Quaker, a man scared and alone who is unsure of his nature and of nature itself—but none of them calms the squall in his soul, so he drifts from one to another as if lost at sea.

William wasn't conscious of how autobiographical his writings were—especially when he altered the record or attempted to disguise his true self. Since he wasn't in control of the self-images that he presents, what readers get is more revealing than it might otherwise be. William's intentions were overwhelmed by his nature, his failings, his self-doubts, and the margins where his self-knowledge ends. Whether the stories are about snakes, alligators, or tropical storms, whether tales of triumph, defeat, turmoil, serenity, hope, despair, sadness, or joy, they are about William and nature and the nature of William at the same time.

As the story unfolds, the interpreter tells William that the Indians are calling for Puc-Puggy to kill the snake or, at least, remove it from camp.

> I answered, that I desired to have nothing to do with him, apprehending some disagreeable consequences; and desired that the Indians might be acquainted that I was engaged in business that required application and quiet.

The "disagreeable consequences" he fears are not just from the snake, but from the "superstitious" beliefs of his Seminole hosts and from himself. The pose he takes of the man who needs quiet to do real and mysterious work is a typical European ploy that is uncharacteristic of William, as narrator at least. Puc-Puggy is more arrogant, less courteous, less brave, and less kind than William transformed. He's more childish, more Indian, more free than "William" could be. Both Puc-Puggy the actor and William the narrator are torn by contradictions unresolved in the story and inside the man. The vow William took against killing snakes, "a promise I have invariably kept to" he will tell us a few pages later, is about to be broken with "disagreeable consequences" for the narrative flow of the book.

> My old friend turned about to carry my answer to the Indians. I presently heard them approaching and calling for Puc-Puggy. Starting up to escape from their sight by a back door, a party consisting of three young fellows, richly dressed and ornamented, stepped in, and with a countenance and action of noble simplicity, amity and complaisance, requested me to accompany them to their encampment. I desired them to excuse me at this time; they pleaded and entreated me to go with them, in order to free them from a great rattle snake which had entered their camp; that none of them had freedom or courage to expel him; and understanding that it was my pleasure to collect all their animals and other nat-

ural productions of their land, desired that I would come with them and take him away, that I was welcome to him.

The Indians wouldn't hear no; they presented themselves well; William couldn't escape; they begged; they were his friends. The hunter was hunted; predator was prey. The Indians lacked "freedom" and he couldn't get free. They were braves without courage. They thought he was intrepid, but he was afraid. What a jumble of excuses inspire the breach of his vow. Perhaps even a threat was implied in the braves' observation that it was Puc-Puggy's "pleasure" to take their plants and other animal specimens away. William, he tells us, just had no choice.

At last, Puc-Puggy gave in and followed the young men back to their camp, where he found chaos inspired by fear of the "dreaded and revered serpent" that slithered around helping himself to provisions and licking the Seminoles' platters with his forked tongue. Puc-Puggy walked up to the snake and threw a stick at his head, which instantly killed the monster before everyone's eyes. He threw the stick rather than whacking the snake, a curious variation on other contemporary reports. Make no mistake about it, he was afraid. What William wants us to know is that the act was necessary and called for courage and skill.

I took out my knife, severed his head from his body, then turning about, the Indians complimented me with every demonstration of satisfaction and approbation for my heroism, and friendship for them. I carried off the head of the serpent bleeding in my hand as a trophy of victory; and taking out the mortal fangs, deposited them carefully amongst my collections.

Puc-Puggy is a man without the Seminoles' reverence and dread of the snake when alive or its spirit when dead. William, the scientist, saved the rattler's most "curious" parts. Again, though, there's a kind of primal reversion, a reveling in blood that comes from the boy/hunter that William denies he still is. Puc-Puggy would triumph in his "victory," taking a "trophy" as Indians do in a war, but William would feel guilty and ashamed. Part of William's fear, which led him initially to deny the Indians' request, was a terror of himself, for his soul, for the Quaker-in-nature whom he wanted to be and whom he wants us to see.

The other fear, the one that William consciously shares with us, is a dread of the Indians' celebration of him as a slayer of serpents who had no fear of snakes' ghosts. He had sufficient knowledge of the Seminoles to suspect that their "superstitions" about snakes and spirits would not allow the story to end here, with him walking back to his dwelling to continue his work. He was right.

I had not been long retired to my apartment, before I was again roused from it by a tumult in the yard. . . . Before I could . . . effect my escape, three young fellows singing, arm in arm, came up to me. I observed one of the three was a young prince who had, on my first interview with him, declared himself my friend and protector, when he told me that if ever occasion should offer in his presence, he would risk his life to defend mine or my property. This young champion stood by his two associates, one on each side of him: the two affecting a countenance and air of displeasure and importance, instantly presenting their scratching instruments, and flourishing them, spoke boldly, and said that I was too heroic and violent, that it would be good for me to lose some of my blood to make me more mild and tame, and for that purpose they were come to scratch me. They gave me no time to expostulate or reply, but attempted to lay hold on me, which I resisted; and my friend, the young prince, interposed and pushed them off, saying that I was a brave warrior and his friend.

The braves slapped him on the shoulder, with good humor, and let him go. Of what was William afraid—of the loss of some blood or of what it meant? Why not go along with a ceremonial bloodletting, in the name of politeness if nothing else? He terms it a "ludicrous farce to satisfy their people and appease the manes of the dead rattle snake." Why such harsh words for another culture that the narrator generally respects and portrays as, in some ways, superior to his own? William knows, as he tells us, that "these people never kill the rattle snake or any other serpent, saying if they do so, the spirit of the killed snake will excite or influence his living kindred or relatives to revenge the injury or violence done to him when alive."[17]

Fear is still the operative emotion here, on all sides. The whole episode was an emotional drain, one that challenged a fragile sense of who William was. The ceremony was "ludicrous," unlike any other that he ever described in his published writings, commonplace books, or correspondence on Indian ways. If he didn't believe in such superstitions, what would be the harm? The Seminoles' assessment of his character caused him more pain than their knives ever could. The man who murdered and beheaded that rattlesnake is not the man whom William wanted to be or whom he wants us to see. Indeed, although the story messes up the whole book, he couldn't leave it out because he's giving us "facts" and because he (partly) is proud of it. It's a good story because it shows he is courageous, something he's not sure about; it presents him as unafraid of rattlesnakes, ghosts, and Indian braves. He understands its complications clearly enough to shuffle the tale out of chronological time in the telling, lest we think Puc-Puggy to be the man that William still is.

This isn't the only snake William killed in his travels nor the only time he breached Indian conventions about the spirits of serpents. On another occasion, William went off hunting with some Indian boys.

> We returned to camp with a load of very fine fish and in my way took a very large and beautiful glass snake, which however was not generally so acceptable as the fish, as none chose to have him in the mess.[18]

They had plenty of fish, William says, and he knew that Indians didn't eat snakes. Was he trying to impress the boys with his courage; did he not want to return empty-handed, the boys having speared all the fish; had he a need to display his disdain for the "superstitions" associated with serpents? Perhaps he simply needed the specimen for drawing or sending his patron some parts. The viper posed him no threat that he mentions and there was, of course, the promise that he had made to himself. This story doesn't make it into the *Travels*, as it has nothing positive to tell us about William, contradicts the narrator's persona, and isn't even a good tale.

No more than his father was William an indiscriminate murderer of snakes. He was no more superstitious and even more prone to see beauty where others could not. "The coach-whip snake is a beautiful creature," he tells us. The rattlesnake is "a wonderful creature," he writes, "when we consider his form, nature, and disposition." It's a

William Bartram, rattlesnake (Private collection)

"generous," "magnanimous" animal with "beautiful" skin. The rattler is also a "dreadful reptile," quite capable of killing by a scratch or a bite, that moves "like a vapour," so swiftly as to beguile our eyes.[19]

And yet, look at the rattler that William eventually caught when he had his paper and paints along on a trip. It was in New Jersey, not that far from home, on the banks of the Great Egg Harbor River that he spotted the snake or the snake hissed at him. What William captured was a serpent trying to slither away, not one that wanted to bite or fascinate him. It's not the biggest, scariest, or most colorful rattler that he has ever seen. He's painting what is there as dispassionately as he can, true to the snake's nature in browns, blacks, and whites glimmering and shaded to represent depth. The snake blends into his surroundings, which William omits, but not well enough to escape its principal enemy, man.

On close observation, it seems the snake is dead, which may be why it has lost its terror for William (and also for us). It is posed rather than poised to slink off the page and into the underbrush where it once lived. There is no life in those eyes, no threat in the rattles, no hiss in the tongue. This isn't the snake that his father wanted him to paint or the way that John thought it should be drawn. It looks dead on the page; perhaps this is the only way that William could get one to hold still without poking, prodding, and putting his brush down, without touching the serpent and risking his hand. It's one more snake to haunt William.

Once, William and the party with which he traveled made camp near a cool spring after dark. During the night they all had occasion to walk down to the spring, William says, himself several times. Shortly after dawn, he was making yet another trip, to quench an "unconquerable thirst," when

> thoughtless of harm or danger, my hasty steps were suddenly stopped by the sight of a hideous serpent, the formidable rattle snake, in a high spiral coil, forming a circular mound half the height of my knees, within six inches of the narrow path. . . . My imagination and spirits were in a tumult, almost equally divided betwixt thanksgiving to the supreme Creator and Preserver, and the dignified nature of the generous though terrible creature, who had suffered us all to pass many times by him during the night, without injuring us in the least, although we must have touched him, or our steps guided therefrom by a supreme guardian spirit.

William may still have been thoughtless, but this time he was thankful and merciful, too. Saved by the good nature of the snake and the providence of God, William was grateful that he hadn't been struck.

I hastened back to acquaint my associates, but with a determination to protect the life of the generous serpent. I presently brought my companions to the place, who were, beyond expression, surprised and terrified at the sight of the animal, and in a moment acknowledged their escape from destruction to be miraculous; and I am proud to assert, that all of us, except one person, agreed to let him lie undisturbed, and that person was at length prevailed upon to suffer him to escape.[20]

This time William won his plea for the snake's life, as his father never had. Perhaps he was a better orator, a more impassioned advocate than his father had been. This, at any rate, was the William he wanted to be, a man of peace and compassion, a savior and friend of flowers and brutes.

When William's friend, the physician and scientist Benjamin Smith Barton, took swipes at those who believed in snake fascination, he wrote at his desk, in his house, in the city, where snakes no longer lived. He wrote about nature with the assurance of a man surrounded by books. Dispassion was easy. He knew superstition when he saw it and, like William and John, felt a compulsion to challenge the spirits that he didn't fear. He would not have handled Christopher Witt as gently as John or the huge rattler at the spring as compassionately as William. He would see Witt as an old fool, not worthy of a scientist's time, and the rattlesnake as a biological organism that would be more useful dead on the dissecting table than living loose in a swamp. That's the perspective an academic scientist such as Barton represents, what he sees as progress.

It was the Bartrams who walked the snake's path and stared into its eyes. So Barton used William as his principal source for the memoir he wrote attacking "superstitious" beliefs about rattlesnakes. Barton had a theory that offensive odors, "fetid emanations," from a snake's body, could be the cause that led small animals to freeze in their tracks and then wander into a predator's mouth. Not that he had ever witnessed such scenes himself or smelled a live snake, but "some creditable persons of my acquaintance" told Barton that this was the case.

Mr. William Bartram assures me that he has observed "horses to be sensible of, and greatly agitated by, it at the distance of forty or fifty yards from the snake. They showed," he says "their abhorrence, by snorting, winnowing, and starting from the road, endeavouring to throw their riders, in order to make their escape."

What gave William's testimony such value as evidence was his standing in Barton's eyes as "a man of rigid veracity." Barton's method was much less "scientific" than John Bartram's, who relied on a combination of reliable testimony and his own experiments poking and staring at snakes. Barton was dependent entirely on others, since the "duties" and "responsibilities" of his medical practice kept him closer to home than the rattlers now lived.[21]

Despite the fact that Barton could not have written his book on snake fascination without the information provided by William, his gratitude was limited by his ego, his science, and his friend William's humility. For all his dependence on the "rigid veracity" of his source, Barton wrote with absolute assurance about differences between animal and man, science and superstition, truth and lies, which is what led him to take a gentle poke at William for sharing his father's modesty and respect for what others had seen. "Several American writers have adopted the notion that snakes are endued with a fascinating faculty. Fearful that their authority may extend the empire of this error, I have been the more anxious to offer my sentiments on the subject to the society," Barton writes. The note to this passage mentions only one name and one book that make such an egregious mistake: "William Bartram says: 'They are supposed to have the power of fascination.' "[22]

In one sense, Barton got William all wrong. "They are supposed to have the power of fascination," William does write, which doesn't associate him with what others suppose. "It is generally believed that they charm birds, rabbits, squirrels and other animals," which Barton would have to admit, having offered this explanation for why he felt compelled to challenge these lies. "Be the cause what it may," William continues with the same cautious words that put some distance between himself and those who believe in such things,

> the miserable creatures undoubtedly strive by every possible means to escape, but alas! their endeavours are in vain, they at last lose the power of resistance, and flutter or move slowly, but reluctantly, towards the yawning jaws of their devourers, and creep into

their mouths, or lie down and suffer themselves to be taken and swallowed.[23]

William is not telling us what he believes, but rather what he's been told. Having several times stumbled upon a rattlesnake at his feet, he knew what it was like to be "so shocked with surprise and horror as to be in a manner rivetted to the spot, for a short time not having strength to go away." He thought that horror, not effusions from a snake's eyes or the smell of its skin, froze brutes smaller and weaker of mind than he was. And yet, there were the reports from credible people, his mother for one, who saw something that neither he nor his father ever could find.[24]

Barton was not alone, though, in reading William's *Travels* the way he did. Others also saw William as a credulous man. How someone with such knowledge, so usually wise, could credit such "fables, heightened and embellished by the charms of poetry," how he could allow superstition to cloud his vision, was more than a "philosopher" such as Barton could see. Barton was a man of science, a man who aimed at a "correct" view of things, "uninfluenced by the bold assertions of ignorance," "plausible conjectures," or poetry, he might have said. "I have sought for facts," Barton said; "these have been my guide."[25]

Had he still lived, John Bartram would not quite have agreed with this man of science. His goals were the same as Barton's, gathering facts unvarnished by prejudice and superstition, but he wasn't so quick to dismiss the spirit of nature from the science of man. For John, God is not only visible in nature; he's still present there. What's more, imbedded in John's science is a doubt that Barton didn't share, a tension that Barton suppressed. Both men's studies of nature were predicated upon the assumption that we can observe through reliable senses. And yet John Bartram suspected, even if Barton did not, that our imaginations sometimes take control of our eyes.

William not only knew what led his father to doubt his own sight; he reveled in his imagination even while searching for "facts." His nightmares were "real" and just as "true" as what he saw when awake; his art was also science, so was his writing, and so was his life. How could he possibly "know" in the way that Barton could, when he was not even sure whether he was a man, not sure where the snake ended and where he began?

CHAPTER SEVEN

Journeys

ILLIAM HAD A NUMBER OF REASONS for traveling with his father in 1765. The trip through Florida provided an escape from his failing business, an opportunity to rekindle the closeness that previous journeys had stoked, a chance to make amends, to show himself better, to help and care for the old man, to revel in nature, and to find himself if he could. These were his dreams. In reality, he was still son to his father, not quite a man; his business still beckoned with unresolved debts at the trip's end. He needed his father more than John needed him. He couldn't see the snakes at his feet, but he felt the ones between him and John and continued to suffer the ones in his heart. Still, William enjoyed the movement across space in the forest that seemed to freeze time. He could lose himself, find novel plants that would please John, sketch specimens, and watch birds about whose habits he was curious.

William also had another agenda: he wanted his father's ear. Finally, he had a plan for his life, something besides drawing that he wanted to do. He would be a rice planter, like the wealthy men around Charleston who led leisured lives. Once established, he would be free to collect plants his father desired and to sketch nature as suited him. The great plantation owners had overseers who supervised slaves. Slaves did the work; planters reaped the profits. It would take diligence on his part to begin—to get the swampy lowland that suited the crop cleared, diked, and the rice sown. He'd have to be his own overseer for a while, working shoulder to shoulder with slaves; building shelter; planting food crops to feed his plantation "family"; disciplining his workforce, serving as physician, patriarch, and priest to the slaves—caring for their bodies and souls and making them work.

In the end, John wasn't really convinced, but he acquiesced. William begged for his help. The venture needed capital that only John could supply. Since John saw this ambition as a "frolic" that was doomed from the start, why did he provide the funds to help his son fail again? Perhaps it was a case of love overwhelming good judgment, guilt that he'd pushed William into a merchant's profession that clearly wasn't right for the boy. Maybe he hoped that Billy's enthusiasm for the project—a passion that no career had before sparked in his son—forecast success. Possibly he just couldn't bear to say no. "I have left my son Billy in Florida," John wrote to Peter Collinson upon his arrival home; "nothing will do with him now, but he will be a planter upon St. John's River about 24 mile[s] from Augustine. . . . This frolic of his hath, and our maintenance, drove me to great straits."[1]

What had gotten into William; what pulled him out of his lethargy and inspired this plea? He loved the region, the savannas, forests, and swamps; it's not surprising that he wanted to stay and, short of becoming a hunter, a guide, or a merchant, planting was the most likely way to support himself in the wilderness that he adored. Hunting rubbed against his nature; he wasn't a reliable observer of practical things like distances, directions, and snakes; and he'd already determined that commerce wasn't for him. That may be enough, or at least all there is, to explain William's new need; possessed by the beauty of nature, he contrived the only plausible plan to enlist John's support.

John, ever the practical one, handled details. From Charleston, he told William to grow yams from the cuttings of good vines, how to plant rice in his twenty-acre marsh so the young shoots wouldn't rot, and where on his land corn would do well. He sent rice for seed, an iron pot, a heavy Pennsylvania axe, broad axe, adze, shovel, saw, whetstone for sharpening tools, and a bass line and hook. A lady friend helped John select household supplies: three stone cups, a bed cloth to fill with turkey and duck feathers, a kettle, a couple bushels of peas, a pot of sugar, ground nuts, and seeds for a kitchen garden. John sent coarser materials to be filled with moss for slaves' beds, two barrels of corn for eating, one of rice, one of pork, and a cask of salt from Henry Laurens, who wouldn't accept payment, but just wanted to help.[2]

Friends in Charleston, John reported to his son, thought William was making a bad, perhaps fatal, decision.

All thy friends here lament thy resolute choice to live at St. Johns and leave off drawing or writing. They say the negroes will run away or murder thee. They all seem to have a miserable opinion of negroes and reckon the new the best as not yet having learnt the mischievous practices of the negroes born in the country and town, which the people generally represent as if they [were] all either murderers, runaways, or robbers or thieves, especially the plantation negroes.[3]

How did William react to this delivery of necessities, generosity, advice, and bad news? His friends thought he'd be better off writing and drawing; William did, too, but was John now endorsing this view, which he had so thoroughly resisted in the past, or just reporting, sharing his own fears for his son and self-doubt about whether he should have agreed to finance this "frolic," which would be anything but fun?

John also selected, purchased, and shipped the slaves that William would "need." Four friends, including Dr. Garden and Colonel Laurens, helped John choose the right ones. Garden checked the slaves' health; the others gave their expert advice on other qualities that a slaveowner would want. John had six slaves put on board the *East Florida* for transport to St. Augustine, along with a pair of millstones, a grindstone, a pair of smoothing irons (for ironing clothes), six sickles, a plane, and a bar of lead for making shot. He threw in advice about how to catch mullet at night and keep the slaves from contracting pleurisy and flux. He also enquired whether William wanted a lancet for letting blood when the slaves were taken ill.[4]

John continued to worry—to think and to plan for his son. He arranged for the slaves' delivery right to William's miry new home, sent more advice about catching fish and about how to land barrels without getting them wet in the swamp. Draw a butterfly to thank Mrs. Lamboll for all her help; plant limes; I'm enclosing two guineas. A ship just arrived from St. Augustine, "but no letter from my son." John remained Billy's "loving father," and was afraid to let go. John's friends had scared him about the slaves; had he chosen the right piece of land; could Billy handle the responsibility, the heat, the malaria?[5]

Back home in Philadelphia, John finally received a letter from Billy, which hasn't survived. Whatever William said, it wasn't enough and came too late. John was angry, fell back into his retributive fatherly tone—the one that was missing from his two previous letters to Billy, the one he took when Billy declined to choose a career and when he was failing as a merchant, for which John blamed him entirely. "I received thy letter of June 6th," John replied in July; "I wish it had come a little sooner." Clearly, the letter asked for more than John had already sent, than he had already laid out for William's benefit. "Thee write that thee received my letter, but I sent two," John complains; you don't even thank me for the two guineas, the grindstone, or the millstones and other tools, "which I suppose thy usual ingratitude would not suffer thee to mention. They cost me dear and so much that I am still in debt for them. I am very sorry thee was so hindered by the bad weather as to lose a crop," John extends a fatherly hand before slapping his son, "but I hope thee may plant some corn, if not rice, if it be but two or three acres it will help some and thee hath been and [are] very indolent if thee hath not planted much garden [vegetables]."

In other words, you've had some misfortune, but if you're as bad off as you claim it's your irresponsibility, your laziness, your lack of practical planning that have done you in again. William could blame the weather, just as he did for his failures as a merchant, but John wasn't buying that excuse. There came a time, long since past in John's opinion for Billy, when a man had to take responsibility for his own fate. "I will not answer any extravagant draught," John adds with real venom. Don't feel that you can draw on my credit as long or as deep as you please. "I am not against finding thee real necessaries this year," which John believed that he'd already done generously and with little gratitude from his son, "but thee must expect to suffer the first year as all do in new settlements." Suffer, John says; "in the meantime I remain thy loving father."[6]

William suffered, almost to death. His father had done all he could, all he would; Billy had nowhere to turn. By the time Henry Laurens paid him a visit during the summer of 1766, only a handful of months since John returned home, there wasn't much of William left. Laurens didn't want to offend, to intrude between father and son, "but I hope you will not think me quite impertinent," he wrote John, "if I detain you to say a word or two touching the particular situation and circumstances of that poor young man; and the less so, when you know that it is done partly at his request." William hadn't the nerve to write on his own to his father again, to play the prodigal's role one more time. He asked Laurens to intercede for him, to help him get out. A letter from William accompanied Laurens's. John saved the one from his friend, but the one from his son is now lost.

First of all, William's plight was not entirely his own fault, according to Laurens; John had to share some of the blame. "His situation on the river is the least agreeable of all the places that I have seen," Laurens explained forthrightly; you chose badly for him. It's a particularly unhealthy place; the swamp and marsh are too narrow and "will require more strength to put them in tolerable order than Mr. Bartram is at present possessed of to make any progress above daily bread." The pine land, Laurens continued, "(I am sorry to differ in opinion with you) is very ordinary; indeed, I saw none good in the whole country; but that piece of his may justly be ranked in an inferior class, even there."

William did plant peas, beans, corn, and yams for his own use, but the excessive rain destroyed them. Only two of the six slaves that you bought him could handle an axe, and one of those was "exceedingly insolent."

The house, or rather hovel, that he lives in, is extremely confined, and not proof against the weather. He had not proper assistance to make a better, and from its situation it is very hot, the only disagreeably hot place that I found in East Florida. . . . His provision of grain, flesh, and spirits is scanty, even to penury, the latter article very much so. His own health very imperfect. He had the fever, when I was first with him, and looked very poorly the second visit.

Laurens ordered some supplies for William, which he would gladly have provided gratis, but for fear of offending John had them charged to his account.

The entire blame for the fiasco shouldn't fall on John's shoulders, Laurens continued; he wasn't letting William off that easily or merely taking the son's side against his father. He was, at William's request, interceding to relieve Billy of the entire responsibility for his failure.

Possibly, sir, your son, though a worthy, ingenious man, may not have resolution, or not that sort of resolution, that is necessary to encounter the difficulties incident to, and unavoidable in his present state of life. You and I, probably, could surmount all those hardships without much chagrin. I verily believe that I could. But, at the same time, I protest that I should think it less grievous to disinherit my own son, and turn him into the wide world, if he was of a tender and delicate frame of body and intellects, as yours seems to be, than to restrict him, in my favour, just in the state that your son is reduced to. This is no doubt more than ever you apprehended.

This must have been very difficult for John to read. Not only was Billy in dire straits; John was, in Laurens's opinion, largely to blame both for advising Billy poorly and for misreading his own son's capacity to cope with the situation that John left him in. John might have responded that it was Billy's idea, that his son would hear no reason against such a "frolic" as this. That wouldn't relieve John's responsibility, though, or ease his conscience a bit. He would be embarrassed by his own mistakes, some of them about nature, in addition to misjudging the nature of his boy. He would be upset with his friends; after all, hadn't Laurens and others advised him on the choice of these particular slaves? He would be angry at Billy, at the loss of his funds, at the trouble and expense he'd have saving this son from danger again. Yes, it was more than John apprehended; he certainly didn't mean to kill Billy or banish him from the world. "No colouring can do justice to the forlorn state of poor Billy Bartram," the letter continues, laying on the guilt pretty thickly, painting a picture that was painful for John to view.

A gentle, mild young man, no human inhabitant within nine miles of him, the nearest by water, no boat to come at them, and those only common soldiers seated upon a beggarly spot of land, scant of the bare necessaries, and totally void of all the comforts of life, except an inimitable degree of patience, for which he deserves a thousand times better fate; an unpleasant, unhealthy situation; six negroes, rather plagues than aids to him, of whom one is so insolent as to threaten his life, one a useless expense, one a helpless child in arms.

All right, John might have felt, I've read enough. But there was more about Billy to see.

> These, I say, are discouragements enough to break the spirit of any modest young man; and more than any man should be exposed to, without his own free acceptance, unless his crimes had been so great as to merit a state of exile.
>
> I had been informed, indeed, before my visit to Mr. W. B., that he had felt the pressure of his solitary and hopeless condition so heavily, as almost to drive him to despondency.[7]

Laurens and his source are on to something here; they have provided a glimpse of one battle in William's lifelong war against what was then called melancholia—what we term depression, a despondency that drove him to the greatest depths of mental anguish that a person can know. Laurens suggests suicidal tendencies. I suspect this wasn't the only time that William balanced unsteadily on the brink of self-destruction. Whether melancholia was the cause or the consequence of his failures is difficult to say; quite possibly it was both, but at most his problems were triggers rather than explanations for what he went through.

Depression, a mysterious disease in our day, was even less comprehensible in the Bartrams'. A sense of self-hatred is common to those enduring the illness; a failure of self-esteem is sometimes precipitated by difficulties, but depression often lays sufferers low at what, for others, would be the most joyous of occasions. William suffered, at times, from an inability to make active decisions and from disrupted sleep patterns; he appeared lethargic when energy was called for, and was unable to connect with others or even to communicate for months on end. Symptoms show themselves early, in his inability to make choices about a career as part of the teenage crisis that so thoroughly depressed him. Others found William's behavior frustrating and blamed him for lethargy, unresponsiveness, irresponsibility, and rudeness; he blamed himself, too. As William Styron writes eloquently about his own case,

> I was feeling in my mind a sensation close to, but indescribably different from, actual pain. This leads me to touch again on the elusive nature of such distress. That the word "indescribable"

should present itself is not fortuitous, since it has to be emphasized that if the pain were readily describable most of the countless sufferers from this ancient affliction would have been able to confidently depict for their friends and loved ones (even their physicians) some of the actual dimensions of their torment, and perhaps elicit a comprehension that has been generally lacking; such incomprehension has usually been due not to a failure of sympathy but to the basic inability of healthy people to imagine a form of torment so alien to everyday experience. For myself, the pain is most closely connected to drowning or suffocation—but even these images are off the mark.[8]

William couldn't explain; others couldn't comprehend, weren't sympathetic. For some reason, people of an artistic bent, such as William, suffer disproportionately from melancholia, from what Styron describes as a helpless stupor in which cognition is replaced by "positive and active anguish."[9] William simply wasn't fit for the world in which other men lived. Now he knew that for sure, if he hadn't known it before.

"Whimsical and unhappy" is the way John described Billy shortly before he received Laurens's long, painful letter.[10] Styron depicts some of his own symptoms in much the same way, but rather than "whimsical" would use one of its synonyms—capricious, erratic, fickle, inconsistent, unreliable, unpredictable, or quixotic—to capture the essence of this particular kind of whimsy, words that describe William's condition equally well. "Detached," "remote," and "isolated" also address aspects of behavior that others observed in Styron and Bartram. Sometimes, people would say, they didn't seem all there; these "normally" eloquent writers became inarticulate or garbled communications pathetically. Sometimes they weren't fit company for anyone, especially themselves.

Entries in William's commonplace book from this period reveal his own view of the problem, which, not surprisingly, is less clear than his father's. From the swamp, through the mist of melancholia, he couldn't always see himself well but had lucid moments when self-knowledge made the pain all the greater, when seeing was worse than not knowing what was going on. William knew that he couldn't endure his miry habitat long and that, should he survive, he needed to contemplate a great change. "If I seem to neglect any friend I have," William explained in his commonplace book, "I do more than seem to neglect myself as I find daily by the increasing ill constitution of my body and mind." The muddiness of this passage reflects a state of mind rather than incomprehension. He drops a negative and otherwise garbles the sentence, but what he's trying to say is that in neglecting friends he's doing *no* more than what he does by neglecting himself.[11]

Even from the depths of his despair, William recognized that his body and mind were desperately ill. He suffered from bitterness, anger, and self-doubt. He lashed out at himself, at others, at his lack of control. He blamed himself for his failures, for not knowing what he really wanted, and for trying to live in a way that pleased his father rather than seeking and satisfying his true self.

> I still resolve this course shall not, nay I see it cannot, be long: and I determine to retreat within myself to the only business I was born for, and which I am only good for (if I am entitled to use that phrase for anything). It is great folly to sacrifice one's self, one's time, one's quiet (the very life of life itself) to forms, complaisances, and amusements, which do not inwardly please me, and only please a set of people who regard me no farther than a musical instrument of their present idleness or vanity.[12]

He proposes inward retreat as a solution, as a recognition of his true nature, of what God meant for him. He postures the folly of conformity to others' rules for right living and the moral necessity of living a less tempestuous life. He blames others, whom he believes regard him lightly, for using him as an instrument on which to play their own songs, a powerful image that reveals the return of lucidity in an anger that he pivots outside himself. William would write his own lyrics, play his own music, march to the beat of his own drum, to borrow an image from Thoreau, whom Bartram influenced greatly by what he would write after this transforming moment in his life. "Is it not much more wise [to] live to ourselves and of ourselves," William asks rhetorically, a question that Thoreau would answer in the same affirmative way.[13]

Out of the mire, the gloom, from his own slough of despond, William emerged a new man. It was time to put dreams behind him— nightmares as well, if he could. It's important that John released him from the swamp, but more meaningful that William is trying to free himself from dependence, conformity, ambition—in a certain sense even from hope. It was time to say goodbye to any pretense that he was like other men, even to fancy that he, someday, would have a wife.

Collinson had thought that John acted "prudently" in settling his son on a remote plantation, but predicted success only if a wife were also found for the young man. "One thing is not to be omitted," Collinson wrote,

> and that is to get him a virtuous industrious wife such as knows how to share the toils as well as the comforts of a marriage state. He will not settle rightly to business until this is done for then home will be always agreeable to him; if this is not done he'll fall into the snares of a loose unlawful way of life from whence no good can come but much evil and inconvenience.[14]

Later, when Collinson heard of William's failure, he tendered the same cure again: "If my advice may have any weight with him, it is to get him a notable wife, a farmer's daughter and return to his estate and set his shoulders heartily to work to improve it, a moderate industry goes a great way."[15]

However uncomprehending the diagnoses and prescriptions were, William may once have thought, too, that what his life really needed to turn it around was the sort of lover, helpmate, and anchor that his mother was for John. There are tantalizing clues that a love in William's life may have spurred his lobbying for funds to become a planter in the first place. Family tradition says there was a romance during William's sojourn in North Carolina as a merchant and that a cousin, Mary, was the object of his desire.

Perhaps William's burning need to establish himself as a planter was lit, or at least the flame fanned, by his wish to build a hearth for a wife. When it became clear that the plantation wasn't going to work out, William drafted a letter to someone, but to whom is unclear. "My dear companion farewell," the epistle begins. "All other temporal enjoyments have I banished from my heart, but friendship lingers long and tis with tears I say farewell." This wasn't necessarily addressed to a woman, although it has an air of finality, which suggests either a suicide note or the ending of a romance. The "dear companion" could have been a man, but the permanence of the condition implies that this was a relationship tragically broken, contrary to the wishes of both parties, and that the end was a consequence of William's failure to establish a plantation. "Whatever situation of live [*sic*] you can wish or propose for yourself," William continues somewhat bitterly, "acquire a lucid and clear idea of all the inconveniences attending it."

As he emerges from the soul-wrenching darkness of melancholia, William values lucidity and clearness, doesn't take them for granted, basks in their light. I now see that I wasn't cut out for plantation work, he admits; I had a romantic image of what such a life would be like. "I utterly condemned and rejected after a month's experience the very condition I had all my lifetime been solicitous to procure." His hopes were misguided, unrealistic, not right for him; attaining his heart's desire was more painful than not getting it could ever have been. Now William knew that he must take another course, far different from the one that he had once planned with his friend. That sounds like a love lost.[16]

"Fresh blown flowers are and ever have been the symbol of joy." What a mysterious closing line. Perhaps the meaning was clear to the intimate friend; possibly they shared memories of nature's beauty to which this refers. Whatever he meant, it was to the study, nurturing, and appreciation of "fresh blown flowers" that William devoted the rest of his life; it was such blossoms that gave him joy. Maybe this was his testament of intent. Was this letter to Mary, the Mary whose name he wrote over and over again once he got home, his "Dear Cozen," to whom he scribbled eight salutations for a letter that he couldn't write, never mind send? The passion was still there in his heart; the memories still burned; his sense of loss and of being alone, but

Dear D D

Dear Cozen
    Dear Cozin D Dear I write a few lines
    Dear Cozen I write a few

BC Lines Dear cozen
    Cozin I write a few
    D Deare Cozen

I wright a few lines
8   8 8 8 8 8 8 8 8 8 8 8

D Dear Cozen
I write

Mary

was all he could say when he got home.[17]

Why couldn't he write? This man with a poet's heart, an artist's paintbrush, a novelist's quill, couldn't express himself. The pen sputtered, the words stuttered, the hand stopped. What tortures us so besides love and the pain of love lost? What drove him away? Was it her, was it him? Why didn't he succumb, pursue? Why didn't he jump into the snake's mouth, consume the moth with his flame? Was he really better than Adam, a less natural man? Something held him back. He needed to face his father, to come to terms with who he was and never would be, and since he didn't fully comprehend all those needs he couldn't explain. He couldn't love a woman without becoming somebody else. He lacked a career, a steady source of income that would support a family. He wasn't fit for public life, for commerce, engraving, medicine, science, or plantation farming. But if that were the whole story, he might have lived with an Indian woman in the woods.

William couldn't live in either place, though. He was neither "them" nor "us." He wasn't an Indian; he wasn't in his own eyes, in his father's, a man. He couldn't commit to a woman. Why? There's the rub. Perhaps he feared being trapped, being responsible, being an adult, and feared losing what he wanted to be. And what was that—an artist, a poet, a writer, a gardener, a man who charted the migratory habits of birds? Where? Another problem. Ultimately, William would learn that he was a civilized man with no place in the world save a garden, a spot in between city and wilderness, where there was no room for a woman, because it wasn't home for a man. How? There were financial considerations, a perennial barrier to young love, but it was more than that, too. The patriarchal presence was too powerful, too intimidating in his life. He couldn't be the father, the husband, the lover, the provider that his father was.

Not fully comprehending either his plight or a way out, William went the only way that he could imagine at this point. He returned to a house full of others whom he loved and who loved him, but with unfinished business that would draw him back to his cousin's house and to the forest again. The garbled salutation was all he could write because there was no way to explain better how his heart had betrayed her, betrayed him, how he knew that it was his nature, for good and for ill, to walk life's path alone.

Like Thoreau, William would reach his midlife with just this one, unconsummated, love affair and would look ahead, when he looked, to an inward retreat. That's how William became the first native-born American to devote his life, his entire life, to the study of nature. Out of an unresolved teenage crisis, failure, depression, a lost love, and a sense that he didn't fit and had to follow his own light rather than that of his father or anyone else, William transformed himself from a failed man of commerce and commercial agriculture into the saintly eccentric that he would become. That's where he turned from the broad avenues of civilization, from the clear lane of his father's long journey, down a path of his own: that of the nature artist, botanist, explorer, gardener, and "philosophical pilgrim," as he called himself. There just wasn't anything else he could be. That's the way he went even though there was no career pattern for such things or any good way to make his way in the world as a pilgrim to nature. Those "fresh blown flowers" symbolized his joy, his freedom in nature's breeze. They were William's epiphany, just as the daisy was for Crèvecoeur's John Bertram.

Eventually, William would make a virtue of his failures, congratulate himself for being different, develop a stinging critique of those who pursued the main chance that eluded him. But his theory of nature and human nature was more than a rationalization for what he couldn't be; it was a way of life that he achieved with struggle over time, a better self that he labored hard to become. Although the corner was turned when William abandoned his swampy plantation, the destination was still miles and years away. First there was a shipwreck off the coast of Florida, in which he was for a time presumed killed. Surely his father couldn't blame him for that; he really did have bad luck. Certainly they both were scared. John didn't know whether his son was alive; William knew just how close he came to death at least twice, once from the storm inside his head and again from a tempest at sea.[18]

When he returned to Philadelphia in 1767, William still had three painful, unsettling years before him in his father's house. He had to face the old lion in his den, hear his recriminations or, worse still, imagine them in the tense silences that substituted for growls from the great man. Perhaps worst of all, he had to accept John's forgiveness when he didn't think that he had done any more wrong than have some meteorological misfortunes and misjudge himself, no more badly than his father still misjudged him. John's life, both as he lived it in ways visible to all and in the myth that he created about himself and that his son accepted as fact, was an indictment of William every day that he lived under the roof that John built. He worked as a common agricultural laborer, which was an embarrassment to the father who had financed a college education and an apprenticeship for his son. It was a mortifying penance for William, but it proved to them both that he knew how to work hard. He tried to clear up his debts, collect on accounts, extract himself from previous failures so that he could be free of the past and begin over again.

William also drew, more and better than he'd drawn before, to even greater acclaim from old and new English friends. Collinson encouraged him again, no longer fearful that he'd be distracting William from the work of a man. At first, the Englishman feared that Billy would be too melancholic, "under such a dejection from his late disappointments that he has not spirits to undertake such a business" as drawing, which, in fact, proved therapeutic instead. Collinson hoped that this "ingenious young man" could "be got into some business above the servile drudgery of a day labourer, but that should operate in his favour as an instance of his industry and humility, which I hope will be rewarded at last with something more suitable to his abilities." In other words, the penance should work, John should forgive, and Billy's friends should try to find him a better place in the world. Collinson was doing his best, but nothing yet had turned up. Unfortunately, the king wasn't interested in flowers or drawings, so that avenue of potential patronage was closed off, but Collinson would keep trying to find patrons for William's art.[19]

Once William started sending new sketches, those who had been so enthusiastic in the past were utterly amazed by how much better he had gotten over the years. "I and my son opened my ingenious fr[iend] William's inimitable picture of the colocasia," Collinson wrote.

So great was the deception it being a candle light that we disputed for some time whether it was an engraving or a drawing. It is really a noble piece of pencil work and the skill of the artist is shown in following nature in her progressive operations. I will not say more in its commendation because I shall say too little where so much [is] due.[20]

This was a high compliment. To be sure, it's a merchant speaking, not an art critic—a man of John's generation, who couldn't detect that William was aiming for greater truths than those discernible in the precision of lines, for greater accomplishments than came from careers, for the kind of success that brought peace rather than pounds sterling. Collinson sent money, for an artist must live; he showed the pictures around. Dr. Solander admired them; the Duchess of Portland commissioned drawings of sea shells. Then, in August 1768, Collinson died of a kidney ailment at age seventy-four.[21]

As great as was the loss of the Bartrams' patron and friend, they were fortunate that another such figure stepped immediately into the breach for William—a man with deep pockets, a generous spirit, and an appreciation of nature and art. This is exactly what William needed, yet another new start. Dr. John Fothergill was a distinguished London physician, a Quaker, a graduate of the University of Edinburgh, a fellow of the Royal Society, and a man with wide-ranging scientific interests. Shortly before Collinson's death the previous summer, Fothergill visited him and saw William's "exquisite drawings." Collinson proposed, as Fothergill explained in a letter that fall to John, "that I should engage thy son to make drawings of all your land tortoises," which he now proposed to do. Fothergill wanted the drawings at whatever price William thought fair and at William's own pace. "I would not limit him, either in respect to time or expense," this generous patron explained.[22]

It looked, finally, as if things were about to go William's way. He had a wealthy patron who didn't care about time. What could better suit William's artistic temperament, which was guided by neither compass nor clock? Again, though, William managed to pluck failure from the jaws of success. "Poor Billy," John explained to Fothergill in the fall of 1770,

> hath had the greatest misfortunes in trade that could be and [has] gone through the most grievous disappointments and is now absconded I know not whither. He would not take his friends advice, yet kept very temperate.[23]

John is more sympathetic to Billy's plight this time than he was when the plantation failed. The passive voice portrays William as a victim of misfortune and disappointment; and yet, ultimately, John lays blame on his son for not taking advice. Now William has run away from his creditors, to where John doesn't know, and the father is worried about his thirty-one-year-old boy.

A letter from William arrived in December, another letter that's lost, informing his father that he was again with the Bartram family in North Carolina, where he'd been for several months. The bad news was that John's brother had died several weeks after Billy's arrival; his uncle's son, also named William, died not long after that. And so John got news of the deaths of two Williams and learned that one, his son, survived. It took John five months to respond, in a note that William had not yet received in June. Why the long silence after John got the bad and good news isn't clear; whether the mix of emotions held him back, it's difficult to say.

When he didn't hear from his father, William wrote to him again. That this letter is missing, as are the previous three, can't be a coincidence; somebody must have gone through John's voluminous correspondence and destroyed them. At first I suspected that John passed them on to other family members, perhaps Moses and Isaac, whose papers weren't saved. This might be true, but now I surmise that William sifted through his father's papers in the years after John's death, when he lived in the house and used his father's den as his own. As he went about re-creating himself, becoming a new man, the letters pained him. These weren't the work of the new William; they were letters from the Billy whom he wished to deny, to forget, to relegate to the past. He had determined to change in 1767 when he left the swamp, but here it was 1771 and he was still struggling with his old self.

When he wrote in April, and then again in July, John wanted Billy to know that he need no longer fear for his life. William's cousin George, his sister Ann's husband, had convinced the creditors to settle accounts for £100 ready cash. John agreed to pay that amount, bailing Billy out once again. As for "that troublesome man who threatened thee on his own account," George paid him off himself.[24]

"My eyes are so dim," John continued, "that I can't know my own children a foot distance and I write with trouble and must hold my face within two or three inches of the paper." I'm growing old and won't be long on earth, John wanted his son to know; writing this letter causes me pain, is an act of love. John's brother James was sick unto death and John Jr. had married Eliza, taken over the nursery business, and moved into the northern half of the house. William's twin sister, Elizabeth, would marry the next month, and Benjamin and Mary were courting. William would miss all the weddings, but he must have shared his siblings' happiness and perhaps envied them, too. "We shall be glad to hear of thy welfare. Thy mother, brothers, and sisters join with [me] in love to thee and I remain thy affectionate father." No recriminations, no advice this time; perhaps John had given up.[25]

The reason that William apparently gave his father for absconding to North Carolina was to collect old debts from his period there as a merchant. John didn't have much hope that Billy would be successful in "that poor country"; and apparently he was right. William was undoubtedly also drawn back to his uncle's by the family attachments and perhaps by the severed romance with his cousin Mary, but his motives and actions over the course of the following year have not left a trace.

In July 1772, after at least one more letter from William, also lost, John wrote to his son again. This time he is angry. "We are surprised at thy wild notion of going to Augustine," John says; "indeed, I don't intend to have any more of my estate spent there or to the southward upon any pretense whatever." He was amazed by this "wild" notion, by the expectation that he would finance such a venture again, and, he might have said but didn't this time, by the ingratitude of his son.

What had gotten into William? How and why did he lose his resolve? Depression and/or his infatuation with Mary seem to be at work again. John thought that he should return home, "dwell amongst thy relatives and friends, who I doubt not will endeavour to put thee in a way of profitable business if thee will take their advice and be industrious and careful." Come back in failure again, reform yourself, draw energy from somewhere and put your shoulder to the wheel. These were the old prescriptions for what John, at least, perceived as the same problems again. Billy returned home.[26]

William had been away for two years with nothing to show for his efforts, but perhaps he wasn't as lost as he seemed to John. He continued to draw or started drawing again, sending the sketches to Fothergill, but not filling the commission to draft all the turtles in North America and nothing else. He drew phenomenal things, although in what order and when he did each isn't clear. He drew what he wanted, when and how he wanted to draw, and sent what he felt like sending when he got the chance, perhaps when he needed the cash. He wasn't an easy protégé; but artists are renowned for biting the hands that feed them and he was turning out interesting, by this time unique, work.

Fothergill was impressed. "It is a pity that such genius should sink under distress," he wrote to John, still dealing with the father as middleman to the thirty-three-year-old son. "Is he sober and diligent?" Fothergill wanted to know.

This may be an uncommon question to ask a father of his son and yet I know thy integrity will not suffer thee to mislead me. I would not have it understood that I mean to support him. I would lend, however, some little assistance if he is worthy.

No answer survives. John's eyes had deteriorated to the point that he didn't draft letters himself, perhaps dictating responses of which copies weren't saved. What a spot to be in; John had his doubts, but would have seen this as Billy's best chance for success. He did respond and responded positively, since Fothergill later thanks him for his letter and decides to proceed.

He proposes to go to Florida. It is a country abounding with great variety of plants and many of them unknown. . . . I shall endeavour to assist his inclination for a tour of Florida, and if he succeeds shall perhaps wish him to see the back parts of Canada.[27]

What William's patron had in mind was a journey of two to three years' duration in which he would collect rare plants, much as John had done for Peter Collinson and his clients. William, as it turned out to Fothergill's great frustration, had other plans and a poor sense of time; he traveled for four years, believing that he'd been gone only three. His father's talent was scanning the ground for venomous snakes, rare plants, and new seeds. William saw differently; he wanted to draw, to write, to seek clarity and inspiration in the tree tops, to lose himself in the woods. Two years later, in the summer of 1774, Fothergill had received from his protégé about a hundred dried plants, a "very few" drawings, but "neither a seed nor a [live] plant." Granted, William's patron had suggested that he "keep a little journal" of his trip and expressed admiration for his drawings; but it was, Fothergill clearly said, "plants remarkable for their beauty, fragrance, singularity of appearance or known usefulness, I should be glad to possess."[28]

The journal or report of the journey, the drawings, and the *Travels* were what Fothergill's money bought. From a literary, natural history, and artistic perspective, it was money very well spent. For William, within a shorter temporal context, the money bought freedom to explore who he was; to collect himself rather than seeds; to continue the transformation that he'd begun half a dozen years past; to be brave, competent, and successful; to traffic in feelings rather than a merchant's goods; to become in midlife his own man; to master himself rather than slaves; and to find God in the swamps.

William left Charleston in May 1773 on a trip that would take almost four years. He still held resentments against his father, still voiced complaints about the way others had treated him like an old violin. "Indeed it surprises me," Lionel Chalmers chastised John after dining with his embittered, ungrateful son, "that you should not have encouraged this genius of his as a naturalist sooner; for, though you endeavoured to cure it by [apprenticing] him to a merchant &c, yet nature prevailed so far as to disqualify him from pursuits of this sort." This postscript to a letter written before the dinner in an entirely different tone might have been dictated by William, for the thoughts surely were his. Again, as he had with Henry Laurens, perhaps William asked the older man to make his case to John, who thought so poorly of his son. "On the whole," Chalmers continued, "John Bartram has a son, who I hope will perpetuate both his father's and his own name, for the advancement of natural philosophy, as well as of science in general."[29]

William dreamed of even more. He had not yet conquered ambition as he had hoped; he competed with his father, Chalmers's passage suggests, and sought his father's love. He still wasn't the man who he, who his father, wanted him to be. He didn't write often to anyone, spent very little of anyone's money (drawing on Fothergill for only £12 in over a year), and was often feared dead.[30] The journey was a passage out of the past, through his own heart of darkness, that had to be made alone.

By March 1775, when he returned to Charleston for a spell, William was much closer to becoming the man he wants us to know. After two years in the wilderness, he could write a letter to his father that he wouldn't later regret. "Honored and Benevolent Father," the letter begins, gratefully, respectfully, with no trace of past resentments and emotional chills. "I am happy by the blessing of the Almighty God by whose care I have been protected and led safe through a Pilgrimage these three and twenty months till my return to Charleston two days since." He is happy, something never said in his letters before; he has returned from the desert, a pilgrim who survived the biblical trial reflected in the language he uses to write about time—"three and twenty months." I was threatened by hostile Indians, was struck down with a malarial fever for two months, met important people, and saw amazing things. The Alachua Savanna, for one, "is vast and beautiful beyond description," which didn't stop William from drawing it twice and writing about it at least three more times. "The face and constitution of the country is Indian wild now and pleasing," he continues, revealing his excitement about the wilderness just as it was.

"Dear Father," he sustains the effusive affection without so much as a hint of hurt, anger, or fear, "it is the greatest pleasure that I hear . . . that you are alive and well with my Dear Mother, which I pray may continue." For all he knew until his arrival in Charleston two days ago, they might have been dead, which wouldn't have, couldn't have changed his plans in the least. They both were old, might not live long, but "I am resolved . . . to continue my travels another year." He wasn't yet quite done. William had come up for air, which he inhaled breathlessly, but he had to plunge back into the wilderness, where he would remain for closer to two years than one. "I am ever your faithful son." Well, at least now he is. "I have not had the favour of a line from my Father or Mother whom God ever preserve." Even this complaint, which turns the tables on the one often made of him, ends with affection, the expression of eternal love.[31]

One peculiar thing about William's journey is how he lost track of time—not *that* he lost track, but *how*. He gained a year in the woods. At some point, apparently in 1774, he began to think it was later than it really was. When he wrote to Lachlan McIntosh, a good Georgia friend, he believed it was July 1775, which it wouldn't be for twelve months.[32] This was not a mistake that he made only once; it's one he stuck to tenaciously for the rest of his life in recalling the five years preceding 1778. For over a century and a half after that, those who wrote about William's travels believed that he returned to Philadelphia shortly after John's death, which, if true, would be evidence that William's resentments and self-doubts hadn't dimmed. It is the date William gives in the *Travels* for his return that threw everyone off, but since he mistakes John's death date in his eulogy by the same increment of twelve months, it's not the psychologically significant error bearing on their relationship that it appears to be. William would meet with his father, live with him once again in the house that he built, make his peace, show John who he had become, and witness John's end.

William would find his way out of the past's labyrinth in his own time and in his own way. Alone—at least, more alone than he was as a twin in a home full of children, at school, in college, or in a mercantile house—days and nights stretched before him, lagged behind. Slowly, in his late thirties, with his life almost half done, William was becoming what he wanted, who he already claimed to be. But he wasn't there yet; he still had to write his book, tell nature's story, before he could rest content that he'd had his say.

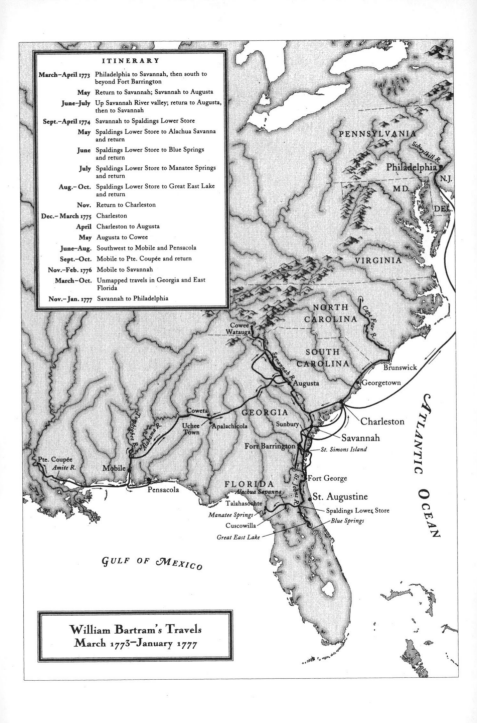

ITINERARY

March–April 1773	Philadelphia to Savannah, then south to beyond Fort Barrington
May	Return to Savannah; Savannah to Augusta
June–July	Up Savannah River valley; return to Augusta, then to Savannah
Sept.–April 1774	Savannah to Spaldings Lower Store
May	Spaldings Lower Store to Alachua Savanna and return
June	Spaldings Lower Store to Blue Springs and return
July	Spaldings Lower Store to Manatee Springs and return
Aug.– Oct.	Spaldings Lower Store to Great East Lake and return
Nov.	Return to Charleston
Dec.– March 1775	Charleston
April	Charleston to Augusta
May	Augusta to Cowee
June–Aug.	Southwest to Mobile and Pensacola
Sept.–Oct.	Mobile to Pte. Coupée and return
Nov.–Feb. 1776	Mobile to Savannah
March–Oct.	Unmapped travels in Georgia and East Florida
Nov.– Jan. 1777	Savannah to Philadelphia

PENNSYLVANIA

Schuylkill R.

Philadelphia

N.J.

MD.

DEL.

VIRGINIA

Cowee
Watauga

NORTH
CAROLINA

Cape Fear R.

SOUTH
CAROLINA

Savannah R.

Augusta

Brunswick

Georgetown

Coweta

GEORGIA

Charleston

Uchee
Town

Apalachicola

Sunbury

Savannah

Tombigbee R.

Alabama R.

Fort Barrington

St. Simons Island

Pte. Coupée
Amite R.

Mobile

Pensacola

FLORIDA

St. Johns R.

Fort George

Alachua Savanna

Talahasochte

St. Augustine

Manatee Springs

Spaldings Lower Store

Cuscowilla

Blue Springs

Great East Lake

ATLANTIC OCEAN

GULF OF MEXICO

William Bartram's Travels
March 1773–January 1777

CHAPTER EIGHT

Perspectives

S WILLIAM BARTRAM'S *TRAVELS* POETRY, readers have asked, fiction, or science? Are the author and the "philosophical pilgrim" the same person or different ones sharing the same name? Is the story true, readers have always wanted to know, or did the author alter the record and transfigure time—create, transform, embellish, recall things that never happened, and forget some that did? The answer to all these questions is yes; the book is all these things and more.

The *Travels* is a complicated story told by a person who wanted to tell the truth, but who didn't always know what it was; it was written by a man who didn't let smaller truths obscure larger ones that he wanted to share. William Bartram was a persona, a character in a book whom the author imagined back in his plantation swamp and whom he became over the course of his travels, in writing his *Travels*, in the garden after his traveling was done. The personal transformation was a self-conscious act, but the creation of the pilgrim's persona was not, so the book is richly autobiographical in ways that William never intended, didn't recognize, would never know, and would have denied.

Is the author of the *Travels* an Enlightenment figure, a Romantic, or a pre-Romantic writer? other readers have asked. Does the book bear structural resemblances to the novels, natural histories, or travel accounts of William's day? Again, the answer is that William and the book are all those things. Since the principal character in the *Travels* isn't a literal rendering of the author, since his story is an idealization of nature and self, the book should be approached cautiously as a biographical source, with attention to contextual materials and internal evidence that suggest it isn't always what it appears to be. The ancillary sources include William's life, the drawings he made on his journey, the three surviving manuscript chapters written and corrected in his hand, and the Report that he wrote for his patron, Dr. Fothergill, which parallels events in the *Travels*, but offers a strikingly different account of William's journey from April 1773 to January 1777.

In all these revelations about nature and self, William had but one message that he consciously shared, and he voiced it with a clarity and simplicity that defined who he became as he entered his forties and continued becoming for the last forty years of his life. All of nature is one, he believed, and infused with the spirit of its creator; this common soul reveals God and is an active spiritual presence in the natural world, an essence that connects all nature and makes the characteristics shared by animals and plants more significant than the differences among us. If such ideas sound familiar, it may be because they were inspired by John's strikingly similar philosophy. William's message was a distinctive combination of traditional notions, lessons learned at his father's knee, and visionary ideals of his own, a view of the natural world that had a greater kinship with both seventeenth-century spiritualism and nineteenth-century Transcendentalism than did the nature writings of such contemporaries as Crèvecoeur, Kalm, and Jefferson.[1]

William accepted nature on its own terms—on God's terms, he would say. Wilderness was just as God intended without any improvement by man, without the clearing, tilling, and fencing that others, including his father, saw as natural beauty. No American of his day waxed so romantic about wilderness settings. The *Travels* is, among other things, an ode to unspoiled natural beauty. Inhale William's reverie on the Altamaha River:

> How gently flow thy peaceful floods, O Altamaha! How sublimely rise to view, on thy elevated shores, yon magnolian groves, from whose tops the surrounding expanse is perfumed, by clouds of incense, blended with the exhaling balm of the liquidambar, and odours continually arising from circumambient aromatic groves of illicium, myrica, laurus and bignonia. . . . Thus secure and tranquil, and meditating on the marvellous scenes of primitive nature, as yet unmodified by the hand of man, I gently descended the peaceful stream, on whose polished surface were depicted the

mutable shadows from its pensile banks; whilst myriads of finny inhabitants sported in its pellucid floods.[2]

Hear William's drawing of Florida's Alachua Savanna. Everything wondrous he has to say about the shared nature of all creation echoes there, too. The picture is really a series of mirror images that display the connections among animal and plant life. The central focus of the drawing is the lowland feature that begins with the sinkhole in the top center. The swamp is shaped like the leaf of a tree, with the streams running out of the sinkhole taking on the characteristics of both the veins of the large leaf and of branches leading to interior leaf-shaped lowlands and ponds. The cranes flying through the top right of the picture are reflected in two terrestrial features below them.[3]

The drawing evokes classical imagery, with the columnlike tree framing the foreground and left side of the scene. The elevated perspective of the viewer is also traditional in European landscape art, and is often interpreted as an expression of dominance, a declaration of control over nature by artists steeped in Western cultural conventions, who see with imperial eyes. As always for William, though, dominance and control are deeply troubling prospects, implying responsibilities that he's not prepared to accept, a confidence that he doesn't really have, and a hierarchical configuration of nature to which he isn't emotionally attached. He undermines these messages within his own portrayal by representing humans as less significant in the savanna than animals and plants.

If he had simply left out mankind altogether, implying our presence as the elevated viewers of the scene, our dominance would be clear; but he muddies the story by including at least some of us on his landscape. Humans are represented by the building in the lower central part of the drawing. We know from a key to William's map of the savanna that this structure stands for the Seminole village of Cuscowilla. Typical of William, where humans are visible in his scenes, our place is modest in scale and scope, not a dominating presence, more Eastern than Western in the way he situates mankind in nature. We saw this as well in the sketch of his father's house, in which William included a man dwarfed by his trees (page 36).

His drawing of the *arethusa divaricata* also portrays a tiny figure in a canoe and a town on the opposite bank. The lone paddler may again

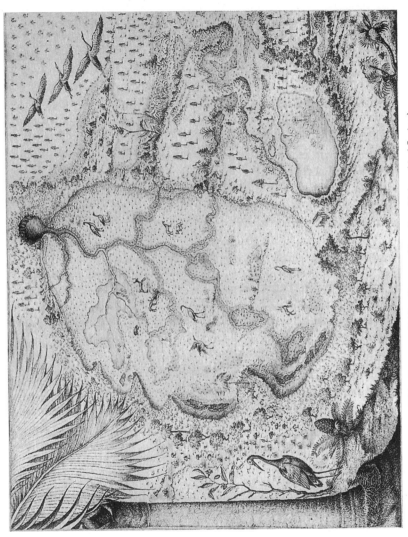

William Bartram, Alachua Savanna (American Philosophical Society)

be the artist, as the fisherman may be in the sketch of John's house. Plants dominate; birds are an interior focus, detailed enough to discern species and their graceful ease gliding across the landscape. Humans are more remote, but we are part of the natural habitat, nonetheless. The meticulously drawn frame defines the portrait as a pose that freezes the subjects in place.

By representing Indians in the Alachua Savanna, the artist has left open the interpretive possibility that a European "we," who exist above and outside the image field, rule this domain, thereby "othering" nature in ways typical of Western conventions of seeing dating back to the "discovery" of the Americas in the late fifteenth century. Since the drawing subverts such conventions, though, challenging the very perspectives it takes, this is a reading to which we shouldn't leap. Indeed, the fisherman and the paddler show that William sees the Cuscowilla Seminoles in nature just as he views the rest of us, including himself.

In William's landscape, there are flowers larger than the trees that surround them, which suggests that foreground and background don't have the relationship traditional in Western pictorial art. Animal size doesn't shrink as we move toward the top of the picture; the scene does not recede into either a distant horizon or a dim past. Our view takes in the whole savanna with the same focus and depth. Such novel perspectives imply a timelessness or, at least, that change comes slowly here.

As in William's description of the Altamaha, the wilderness present is "primitive," "as yet unmodified by the hand of man," still "peaceful." The drawing stops time, as all pictures do, and constructs an unnatural view that bounds reality in ways our eyes and the terrain never could. It freezes a view into a scene; vision becomes a bounded field with a central focus and clearly defined edges that exist only in the artist's mind, telling us his story rather than reporting visual "facts" that anyone else would behold. The picture is true to William's feelings and to the sensations that others might experience at the savanna, thereby discerning a different "Truth" than his father perceived in the same place. In another subversion of the expected, the viewer looks *backward* in time from an imagined perspective beside the classical tree. This feature, which at its base so resembles the column William may have helped John build on his house, stands for the present, civilization, and the structures of man—including the artificial frame constructed by the artist—rather than simply evoking an idealized

William Bartram, arethusa divaricata (American Philosophical Society)

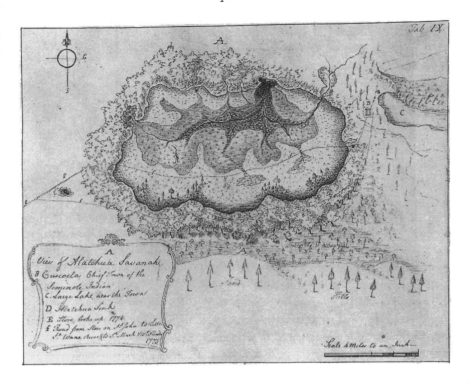

William Bartram, map of Alachua Savanna (Natural History Museum, London)

European past. The column is imposed to give shape, to define an edge of the image field, to hide from our eyes what exists beyond the lined borders that William draws.

As viewers, we are much closer to the column than we are to the savanna below. The idealized savanna is a memory, not just of the place that William saw, but of one that we must struggle inside our hearts to reach. It's an attempt to escape from the past through a back door, to a world that existed before the failures of William's life, before Europeans disturbed the savanna's tranquility, which is why he leaves out the roads that transect the "map" he sent to Fothergill.

The presence of commercial highways on this map would alter the story, dampen the emotional fires of sublimity that William is trying to stoke for the reader, and introduce change. This drawing not only stops time; it captures a moment now past. It's unclear whether this reflects an antidevelopmental prejudice, because like his father William can both admire nature on its own terms *and* imagine fences and fields as pleasant prospects. A letter that he wrote to Lachlan McIntosh about the savanna captures William's wilderness idyll and a developmental dream in the same paragraph.

> The wide and almost unlimited prospect of this verdant plain varied with glittering pieces of water and jetting points of the hammocks forms a scene inchangingly beautiful. . . . The land about it very good and extremely proper for indigo, would grow good corn &c., the whole savanna in the summer and fall a meadow of very good kind of grass. . . . In short would those Indians part with this land, it would admit of a very valuable settlement and would be a very considerable acquisition.[4]

In the *Travels* as well, there are odes to wilderness beauty juxtaposed with developmental proposals. This isn't surprising in light of John's easy blending of these two ways of seeing one place. There are reasons to believe, though, that William experienced a tension between these two visions closer in some ways to those a modern advocate for unspoiled nature would feel than to what his father ever revealed. The adverb "inchangingly" from the letter provides a clue that William may have felt conflicted about developing this particular plot of land, perhaps more than he did about others that he witnessed in his travels. The invented word conflates "unchanging" and "inchantingly," to use William's usual spelling, which implies that the savanna's beauty, its enchantment, would be shattered by change. A passage in his Report likewise contemplates

> the wonderful harmony and perfection in the lovely simplicity of Nature tho naked yet unviolated by the rude touch of the human hand. Tho admitting that human inventions, arts and sciences to be a part in the progress of Nature, yet [they] are perpetually productive of innovations, and events, that show the defects of human policy; What a beautiful scenery is Vegetable Nature![5]

What we see here are the opening eyes of a man who has a greater fear of the future, less confidence in science, commerce, and man, and a greater love of unspoiled nature than John had. Compared to his father, William was a more romantic, less constrained, celebrant of wild nature. William also had mixed feelings about civilization as a consequence of his inability to find a place where he fit. Whether he realized the complex, sometimes conflicted, nature of his thinking, he didn't edit the *Travels* for a false consistency. That's why some readers have pegged him—based on their reading of this one writing of his— as a natural, who favored the wild over civilized life, while others have seen him—again based solely on a reading of the *Travels*—as another European exploiter of virgin lands and native peoples. William was to some extent torn between the lure of the natural and the culture that was imbedded in him, but we tend to exaggerate the conflict that we feel more than he did, because we know that development will not end with farms, because of our own guilt, perhaps, our own sense of consumptive complicity in a culture that overdeveloped the land, drove the manatees out, and bulldozed Indian burial mounds for road-paving materials.[6]

What William did in his 1774 letter to Lachlan McIntosh and the Report to Fothergill was reverse the reportorial style of his father, using the more private genre of personal correspondence for his discussion of productive potential and reserving his most romantic prose for the public audience of the *Travels*. Where John presented a scientific persona in public writings, waxing romantic about nature only in letters to a close friend, William's public agenda was emotional and aesthetic, not advocacy for development and use. The Report to Fothergill is stylistically the closest of William's writings to John's published journals, adopting the tone of the philosophical reporter of size, distances, terrain, and "useful" plant life. The differences between William's Report and John's journals are also instructive, because William is a more active, visible presence even in his most philosophical pose than John ever was in his.

The Report covers the first two years of William's journey, 1773 and 1774, and was composed in two volumes, which are numbered separately and were apparently sent to Fothergill at different times. William corrected the spelling of only the second volume, suggesting that the first came wild from the field and the second was domesticated back in Charleston with a dictionary in hand. The Report's twentieth-century editor values it as "a far fresher document than the *Travels*, and . . . almost wholly free from the disturbing discrepancies that the discriminating student finds in the published work."[7] As a scientist himself, the editor sees William's reportage as "careless," his memory as "faulty," and his frequent inaccuracies as a "blind spot in his mental vision." He's disturbed that William's lunar eclipse of 1773 actually occurred three years later, that his chronology is "sadly confused," and that chapters of the *Travels* are shuffled out of the order in which events took place. The editor offers illness, damaged eyesight, and scandalous editing by the *Travels*'s publisher as excuses for William. The Report is better "science" by modern lights and by the standards of John's published journals as well.[8]

The Report gets its starting date wrong, hardly an auspicious beginning for a "scientist," revealing that William lost track of years early on. The opening is similar in structure to that of the *Travels*'s first chapter, but there is no identity of language; some passages have more information, others less. He leaves out many of the philosophical flights of fancy that so richly adorn the book. Such phrases as "the face of the angry ocean" reveal William's authorial voice. He tells us in the Report that two horses washed overboard in his ocean journey and that he heard a good sermon in Georgia, delivered to a "respectable and genteel congregation," which is the sort of detail that the reader of the *Travels* doesn't learn, but he leaves out any mention of a long visit with McIntosh upon his arrival and provides fewer particulars here than in the *Travels* about a clay urn that he found.

Like his father's journals, William's Report includes practical information about "the soil being very rich" and "very good mills." Even such "useful" details, though, are cast in a less restrained prose: "the land flat, the soil sandy, but the country everywhere clad with green grass in the forests and beautiful savannas, richly painted over with various colored flowers." There's no restraining the poet, no repressing the artist who sees color as paint—viewing landscape as "pictures from the surrounding painted hills." Also differently from John, William sees abundant animal life—wolves, vultures, eagles, cranes, alligators, snakes, panthers, buffalo, scorpions, spiders, possums, fish, weasels, vast "herds and flocks of deer and turkeys bounding and tripping over the hills and savannas"—and witnesses signs of an animal presence even when fauna hide from his sight. Nor does he often dig beneath the surface, feel and taste nature as John did, "as I attempt only to exhibit to your notice the outward furniture of Nature, or the productions of the surface of the earth."[9] William smells nature, but he is irrepressibly visual in his Report. Where he digs, it isn't to explore rocks or determine the fitness of soil for crops; it's into the human past that he tunnels, through the burial mounds of "ancient civilizations" about which he wants to know more. The scariness of wilderness travel is more visible in William's account. Whether he's "enveloped in an almost endless savage wilderness" that damps his spirits "with a kind of gloomy horror" or finds a kind of sublime "terror" in the flight of a bald eagle, his Report is more emotionally accessible than John wanted his journals to be.[10]

Why did William retrace the trip that he took with his father in 1765, write a Report about the same places they "discovered" together, and botanize the same ground that he and John had already searched? John's journal was already published in multiple editions; why didn't William seek out a spot of his own? What had he lost the last time; what did he hope to find; what was he trying to say to his father, to others, and to himself? William tells much that John didn't, records things that John couldn't see, finds plants that they had both overlooked. Was he competing, revising his father; had he a need to better his father's courage, competence, science, and art? Perhaps he imagined a book about the emotional experience of travel in this wilderness as virgin literary ground. Maybe he wanted to see the "enchanted" Alachua Savanna again.

William's personal failures as a merchant, from which he fled in both 1765 and 1773, have a bright side in the story that he tells about the Alachua Savanna, for he won't be one of those harbingers of civilization who brings his wares here or who, like his father, shows others the way. By leaving the roads out of his picture, romanticizing the savanna in his Report, and mythologizing it in the *Travels*, he indicts the dominant culture that he represents, but from which he wants to distance himself, hide himself, find himself in a newer self than the one who sold pots, bought rice, accompanied his father, and owned slaves. William's view of the savanna as a refuge from time, trouble, and want also explains why he rotates the map's eastern features by ninety degrees, subverting any effort to find this special place in the world. A traveler can't reach William's savanna by walking down the roads that he draws on the map, making the idealized portrait and "Romantic" *Travels* more reliable guides to the terrain than the "scientific" Report and "objective" map. The scientist/editor of the Report got the story wrong, mistaking facts for truth, as perhaps William thought that John did, not realizing that William was a philosopher of the emotions, an even higher calling in his eyes than the philosopher of birds and flowers he also was.

William was not the same explorer for empire that his father became; it wasn't his intent to help Europeans master this place, to write a guide for locating, clearing, plowing, and fencing the scene that he drew. The map's artifices also imply that the Alachua Savanna is more a state of mind than a feature on the face of the earth. To see what William saw the viewer and reader must change as William was changing, as he wanted to believe, wanted us to believe, that he already had. He began writing while he was still in the woods, sketching a primitive outline for a section of the *Travels* on a scrap of paper from one of Fothergill's letters, drafting the manuscript chapter about the savanna while he was still in Florida, then correcting it back in Charleston, when he had a dictionary and a copy of Linnaeus's *Systema Naturae* close at hand.[11] The bracketed deletions and insertions in the manuscript conform exactly with the published version. Both the *Travels* and the draft have a much more extensive discussion of the savanna than the Report to Fothergill, which doesn't seem drawn from the manuscript any more than the *Travels* was drawn from the Report in any obvious sense.

William wrote the manuscript before he sent the second of the Report's two parts to Fothergill, where he corrected spelling and substituted scientific names for more general descriptions. Given this relationship among the three written texts, it makes sense to call the manuscript a field journal, even though it doesn't conform to botanists' expectations for what the genre looks like, even though scientists still lament that William's field notes are "lost." Again, as in his drawings and published writings, William challenged form and convention in the way that he worked. His "notes" were more reveries, explications of states of mind, evocations of God in nature, and explorations of themes developed through the *Travels*, than they were dates, distances, and lists of flora and fauna that he saw as he crossed the landscape.

William added the lists of Latin names to his book for credibility's sake, to recover authority from a dead Roman past. They are now the passages that seem most antique, giving the *Travels* a clear border in time, just as the columnlike tree bounds his drawing of the Alachua Savanna in culture and place. The lists also add beauty, to some readers' eyes, even as they provide "facts" that the scientist craves. The poet James Dickey experiences the lists as

> a kind of shade, and because the names themselves are strange, special and beautiful, and taken together with Bartram's descriptions of the creatures and plants they designate, call up an entire flora and fauna that hover with Edenic colors in the reader's uninformed—that is, still virgin—mind. A state of innocence not unlike Bartram's is possible for him, too.[12]

Although that is not an effect the author anticipated—a way that he calculated his writing—it is a cogent insight into why the book still lives long after science, literature, and art have adopted other fashions, when the authority of Latin has died yet again, when our innocence is a product of ignorance, as Dickey remarks. The reader is still with William under the trees, struggling with the same torments of alienation and self, and trying to find the redemption in nature that the sylvan pilgrim sought, that he found, that he promises us.

As the text written the nearest in time to William's visit and the one least recalculated for an audience of others, the manuscript chapter on the Alachua Savanna is a place to continue exploring nature's meaning for him. All other versions were revisions of this original story. Since the published section is the one he chose to represent the whole book when his editor produced a sample for recruiting subscribers in 1791, there is good reason to believe that it's the one that pleased him most and that he anticipated would appeal best to an audience of like-minded readers.[13]

Because William calculated the descriptions in the Report and the map so differently from the other depictions, the contrasting accounts provide access to the ways that William told his stories with different audiences in mind. With two drawings and three written accounts, William's literary encounters with the Alachua Savanna reveal the process of his personal transformation and desire to recast his tale for an audience of others in whose eyes he hoped to redeem himself as he refashioned who he really was. The revisions to this and the other two surviving manuscript chapters provide clues to the ways in which the transformation was incomplete, where he struggled to delete his "old" self from the text, and where he couldn't see that "Billy" was still part of him.

The principal variations from the manuscript chapters to the book are an editing for style, grammar, spelling, syntax, and tone, a shortening of the most rhapsodic commentaries about landscape, and deletion of some prayerful references to God. The revisions are toward a more secular, less romantic text that he hoped would be a more authoritative one. The changes consistently aim for scientific credibility, greater precision in naming, measuring, and counting than his methods of observation actually supplied. Since the "facts" are consistently erroneous, the changes are a ploy, but a psychologically complicated one, because at a conscious level William wanted to get the story right and was deeply hurt when people challenged his objectivity as a scientist. He doubles the acreage of the Alachua Savanna, overstates the magnitude of plains, rivers, and trees, writes "yards" when "feet" would be the accurate measure, and reports such phenomena as a 200-egg average for alligator nests when 40 is the real norm and a twenty-foot alligator, which is unlikely at best.[14]

These errors consistently exaggerate size, number, and distance, which suggests that William's "science" was calculated for literary effect. His numbers reported the true feelings of the sylvan pilgrim and are thus better considered guides to emotionality than lies, bad science, or failed efforts at literal counts. As such they reflect an eighteenth-century rhetorical revolution that also affected art. As Jay Fliegelman describes the philosophy behind this search for "natural" expression, it was a "new model of representation that defines truth as truthfulness to feelings rather than to facts," in which "the misrepresentation of . . . [an] event serves to make possible the accurate representation of an emotion or emotions that otherwise could not be represented."[15] That is what William wanted—to share how he felt and elicit the same feelings in those who read his book or witnessed his art.

The emotion that William sought in these exaggerated counts was the sublime, which could be a product of size, number, variety, height, sound, beauty, or fear. Willing, indeed eager, to sacrifice mere numbers for emotional truth, he drew on the aesthetic theory that he'd been exposed to in school, of Joseph Addison, Lord Kames, William Hogarth, and Edmund Burke. He saw the same emotionality in the poetry of Mark Akenside, and he would have found it also in Jefferson's Declaration and Paine's *Common Sense* had he not been off in the woods when they first appeared. He would have plenty of time later, though, in the serenity of his family's garden, to read about the sublime in the writings of Immanuel Kant, Archibald Alison, William Smellie, and Gilbert White.[16]

Addison's *Spectator* essays on "The Pleasures of the Imagination" articulated a vision of nature as God's creation for improving men's souls. Since imagination is the vehicle for receiving God's lessons inscribed in nature, the imaginative faculty is elevated to new heights that are seized by artists, poets, novelists, and natural historians as the focal point of their work. In the latter part of the century, theories of the sublime, Deism, and Romanticism merge with classical traditions furthering this process of emotionalizing nature. So, for example, John's generation venerated Virgil's *Georgics* as both a poem and a didactic work on scientific agriculture, one that proclaimed a gospel of work and idealized rural life. William's contemporaries would find greater appeal in Virgil's *Eclogues*, which portrayed an Arcadian myth about an imaginary existence far removed from real life. The two pastoral visions aren't so much conflicting ones as celebrations of "natural" life in different forms. Emphasizing, as they do, alternative visions of nature, the poems appealed to the different tastes, different sensibilities, and different values of William and John. It was the concept of the sublime that fomented this process of change.[17]

Cultural transformations illustrated by the natural sublime redefined "imagination" even as it was becoming more highly esteemed. The more traditional role of the imaginative faculty, as defined by Samuel Johnson, saw poetry as the "art of uniting pleasure with truth by calling the imagination to the help of reason." Others, more affected by the new sensibilities than Johnson, proclaimed that only by divorcing the poetic imagination from reason can poetry achieve the highest accomplishment.[18] This, to be sure, was contested terrain, and William was not an exemplar of the most extreme advocacy of imagination over and apart from reason. However, he was affected by this revolution in artistic consciousness in ways that John, and many of William's readers, never appreciated.

Just as Thomas Burnet's *The Sacred Theory of the Earth* gave John a theoretical focus and *The Morals of Confucius* supported what he already believed, so there were books that either influenced William or reinforced his existing views. Mark Akenside's *Pleasures of Imagination*, for example, illustrates one of the fissures between the writings of William and John. The poem and its didactic introduction endorse the powers and pleasures of the imagination, elevating subjective over objective perception. Theoretically indebted to Addison's essays on the sublime, Akenside seeks the emotional effects of nature on humanity.

> With what attractive charms this goodly frame
>   of nature touches the consenting hearts
> of mortal men

Having set the frame thus in the first line, Akenside celebrates "indulgent fancy," and proclaims "Let FICTION come," which, he predicts, will result in a liberating "Majestic TRUTH" superior to other claims to mere lower-case truths derived from nature.[19]

The key biological metaphor is the heart, not the mind, but Akenside's endorsement of an imaginative approach to nature isn't a call for aesthetic or emotional chaos. Indeed, the expectation is that universal comprehension and feeling will be achieved, uniting the senses of mankind with the revelations of the natural world. As Edmund Burke explains in his *Philosophical Enquiry*, "we do and must suppose, that as the conformation of their organs are nearly, or altogether the same in all men, so the manner of perceiving external objects is in all men the same, or with little difference."[20]

The goal was quite similar in some respects to that of John's generation, but the locus of exploration had changed. From a sensory search for physically discernible phenomena, the quest was now for emotional truths discovered by a man of universal feeling. The confidence of eighteenth-century aestheticians that they could identify and classify emotions was of a piece with the botanical enterprise and no more humble than scientists' faith in objective sight. If William was a reliable witness, his sensations upon experiencing nature would be substantiated by those of other writers and artists. He would convey those emotions in a fashion that elicited the same response in his readers, thereby replicating the discoveries of other nature poets and artists in the same manner that the Royal Society directed its philosophical travelers to achieve a high degree of "probabilism" by the use of identical scientific methods. The limits on the artist's discernment of Truth were those of talent, integrity, and imagination; any doubt or disbelief by readers was a very personal assault on the man of feeling.

Sublimity can be a pleasant and/or an awful experience, but must evoke a passion comparable to horror. As Burke explained,

> whatever is fitted in any sort to excite the ideas of pain, and danger, that is to say, whatever is in any sort terrible, or is conversant about terrible objects, or operates in a manner analogous to terror, is a source of the *sublime;* that is, it is productive of the strongest emotion which the mind is capable of feeling. I say the strongest emotion, because I am satisfied the ideas of pain are much more powerful than those which enter on the part of pleasure.[21]

Such theories of the sublime led William to find terror even in the way that a bird flaps its wings.

> . . . the eagle closes the points of his wings towards his body, and with collected power cleaves the elastic air and seems to rend the skies which indeed can be only equalled by the Terror of sudden and unexpected thunder.[22]

The sublime helps explain the degree of emotionality William aims for in describing great beauty, such as that of the Altamaha River, and why he takes what Burke would call "delight" from frights that he survives. What William tries to capture is the degree of sublime astonishment that, according to Burke, is a state of the soul "in which all its motions are suspended, with some degree of horror."[23]

William wants to appear credible in the same ways that John did, but some part of him with which he is not entirely in touch challenges the scientific method, thereby undermining his self-confidence and the reliability of his reporting in ways that trouble him. This leads him to edit his draft of the *Travels* by adding the sort of details, largely manufactured, that his father scrupulously noted when he traveled this same wilderness a decade before, melding the approaches of aesthetics and science, which weren't necessarily in conflict in any event. That's not to say that William got everything wrong, distorted the facts purposely, or that the book isn't "science" at all. It is the seminal source for much botanical and anthropological data, and the author intended the *Travels* to report what was true. It's simply that truth is elusive and William lacked the discipline and desire to tell what seemed to him sterile tales, to take careful notes, and to see specimens, locations, and relations in nature as John had. Even more importantly, William lacked John's confidence that Truth lay in those details rather than in the emotions with which he was more closely in touch, especially the darkness of the sublime. With the rest of his culture, but ahead of the crowd, William contemplated inner truth; state of mind assumed a greater significance for him than external "facts."[24]

In both its unedited and edited versions, William's chapter on the Alachua Savanna is the most moving passage that he ever wrote. It shows him at his greatest emotional height, inspired by the beauty of this most wondrous site and the poetry and aesthetic theories of the sublime that he read. He feared that his writing was too religious and waxed too romantical (an opinion with which reviewers agreed even about the edited, published version), but that's what the place meant to him. The first draft was emotionally honest; in the second he tried to refine the effect that it would have on his readers. He deleted descriptions of "inchanted ground," "bewitching" birds, and fireflies as the moon's "ministering agents of Light"; substituted "elevated mind" for "inraptured soul"; changed "sacred" to "grand"; and removed the prayerful phrase that ended a paragraph: "O most bountifull & benificent Creator!" He dropped references to a flight of birds at sunset as a "solemn religious rite" and to their song as an "evening hymn." And he eliminated the bracketed phrases from the passage below.

> I am sensible that my countrymen, the refined civilised nations of white people, will conclude & say [to one another] these paradisial scenes are surely [are] nothing more than [the] mere visionary dreams [of the Sylvan Pilgrim] or [mere] phantoms of a sickly mind [or deranged imagination] [but such] Yet I speak but the truth.[25]

William's audience is precisely the "refined, civilised nations of white people" to whom he refers, a readership about which we can detect in his tone a mix of fear and disdain. He dreads rejection, having felt it before, and thinks he can anticipate civilized men's reaction to him. Perhaps the "sylvan pilgrim" apprehends some truth in the rejection that he predicts. Is he merely a dreamer, who experiences "phantoms" in his "sickly mind," a man cursed with a "deranged imagination"? No, he insists, answering himself rather than them, "I speak but the truth." He toned down the passage's indictment of himself and made it a little less personal, a little less offensive and defensive at the same time, but essentially left his resentment, fear, and response. He also dropped another self-reference describing his "apprehensions" as "bewildered," again perhaps because, although true, the depiction was too revealing, leaving him more vulnerable to a charge that he wished to deny.

William also deleted long passages that were even harder on his audience than those he left in. Having depicted nature's "rational system of social fraternal intercourse," which rejects avarice and diminishes the impact of war, he compares humans unfavorably to our animal kin.

> How unseemly it looks! How debasing to humanity to see every day and everywhere amongst what are called civilised nations such a disparity, such an inequality in the conditions and situations of men.
>
> It appears to me to be within the reach or ability of a man to live in this world, and even in this depraved age and Nation to a good old age without greatly injuring himself or his neighbor and if one man can continue in a state of innocence as long as he lives why not all men? If they would unite seriously in the cause of righteousness we should gain upon the common enemy every day and in time it would be as easy and natural to do right as to do wrong. Is it not in the power of every one of us to do justly, love mercy, and walk humbly before God?

William apparently drafted this passage, along with the rest of the chapter on the Alachua Savanna, during or shortly after his visit in 1774. Although the Boston Tea Party had already occurred, it was by no means certain that an actual war would ensue. Even here, though, in this natural retreat from the failings of mankind and of a man, news reached William's ears of the "depraved age and nation" in which he lived. What a strong indictment of his country and countrymen, which it makes good sense to edit out after the war, during an era that celebrated independence and resented what was seen as Quakers' closet Toryism, when he was looking for a sympathetic audience to read his book.

William also deleted another passage that casts his peace testimony in a more positive tone: "I profess myself of the Christian sect of the people called Quakers and consequently am against War and violence in any form or manner whatever." This line, too, might have narrowed his potential readership, offended others with different views and harsh feelings toward the Quakers, who were still denounced as traitors or cowards unwilling to risk themselves and their fortunes for liberty's cause. It was consistent with his pilgrim's persona, a biographical link between himself and his text, which might have seemed too personal, too preachy, and that wasn't even literally true.

William served, at least briefly, as a spy for Patriot forces in 1776 during his travels. He often said that Charles Thomson, his beloved college tutor and future secretary of the Continental Congress, had instilled "republican principles" in his mind. He also had family members who joined the "Free Quakers"—those who broke with the peace testimony to actively support the war in 1781; publicly praised some of the Revolution's leaders—dedicating his book to one (Thomas Mifflin) after another (George Washington) turned him down; rejoiced in American independence; and supported a nephew-in-law's application for an army commission later in life. No, this wasn't the real William he deleted to enhance his standing with readers. It was the Quaker pilgrim persona that he brought closer in line with the man he was and remained. Like his father, William's pacifism was contingent; there were, he believed, good reasons to fight, good causes to fight for, and bad people whom we have an obligation to kill. Such beliefs are not those of the Society of Friends, which makes no such exceptions, but a product of the Bartrams' shared view that violence was natural, however regrettable; one of nature's ways of balancing life.[26]

CHAPTER NINE

Travels

F OR ALL HIS CELEBRATION OF NATURE, William's wilderness was much less romanticized than that of Rousseau or Crèvecoeur's Farmer James. His was a clear-eyed knowledge of the harshness of nature, an acceptance of the violence and pain that were as natural as the serenity of a summer's blue sky. All consumed all in William's wilderness, in a relentless warfare among animals and plants. The message is there in William's denunciations of sport hunting, in his stories about larger fish stalking smaller ones in a state of continual war replete with citadels, brilliant tacticians, and "a warrior in a gilded coat of mail," of alligator battles, of the ferocity of hurricanes, and of a spider stalking a bee.

> . . . at length, in about a quarter of an hour, the bee quite exhausted by his struggles, and the repeated wounds of the butcher, became motionless, and quickly expired in the arms of the devouring spider, who, ascending the rope with his game, retired to feast on it under cover of the leaves; and perhaps before night, became himself the delicious evening repast of a bird or lizard.[1]

The message is also there in his drawing *The Sarasena*. This is William's most striking image of all nature as somebody's meal. The picture is most effective if you start by looking at the lower left-hand corner and then scan it counterclockwise. He need not put us in the scene to make our place clear. Mankind, the great hunter of all, becomes in our turn the prey of insects and worms. The circle is full.

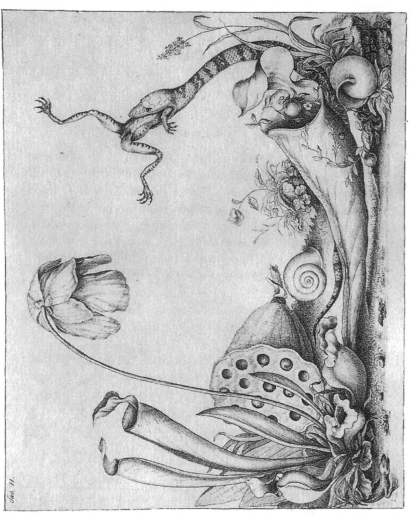

William Bartram, The Sarasena (Natural History Museum, London)

There is often in William's stories on this theme a sense both of regret, even sometimes of moral outrage, and of acceptance of things as they are. Sometimes, as in the drawing of the sarasena, he even displays a sense of humor, or at least takes an ironic tone, about the whole thing. There are tensions, by no means unique to him, in knowing the ways of the world, accepting the reality, yet still wishing for a place of asylum. He found such havens of sanctuary in Indian lore about "a most blissful spot of the earth," which was inaccessible to mortals, in a Seminole "elysium," and in an "inchanting little Isle of Palms." William even saw in his travels a tranquil fishy paradise, which seemingly conquered the violent nature shared by all creatures. "There are no signs of enmity," he wrote, "no attempt to devour each other; the different bands seem peaceably and complaisantly to move a little aside, as it were to make room for others to pass by."[2]

In each of these cases, in each of these places, William knew that the laws of nature rule everywhere on earth, except perhaps in our imagination. The best we can hope for, the most that we can achieve, is a truce in the unending warfare of creature against creature. Even the aquatic Eden that he described was ruled more by a balance of terror than a pacific exception to nature's laws.

> And although this paradise of fish may seem to exhibit a just representation of the peaceable and happy state of nature which existed before the fall, yet in reality it is a mere representation; for the nature of the fish is the same as if they were in lake George or the river; but here the water or element in which they live and move, is so perfectly clear and transparent, it places them all on an equality with regard to their ability to injure or escape from one another.[3]

The seeming exceptions we find to the relentless horrors of life are islands of the imagination, oases of time, mere temporary shelters in space from nature's storms.

There are also, in William's view, natural "representations" or approximations of hell. These, too, can be creatures, geographical locales, or states of mind. William gives us all three in his eyewitness descriptions of the alligator's haunts, undeniably the most famous passages in all of his writings, the ones that were least believed in his lifetime and that have been anthologized time and again as representative of the nature he saw.

I have seen an alligator take up out of the water several great fish at a time, and just squeeze them betwixt his jaws, while the tails of the great trout flapped about his eyes and lips, ere he had swallowed them. The horrid noise of their closing jaws, their plunging amidst the broken banks of fish, and rising with their prey some feet upright above the water, the floods of water and blood rushing out of their mouths, and the clouds of vapour issuing from their wide nostrils, were truly frightful.[4]

Make no mistake about it, William's alligators are monsters on a heroic scale. His drawing *The Alegator of St. Johns* resembles medieval representations of the dragons battled by St. George more than the photos of modern naturalists. The alligators are huge in their setting. William's account of his own encounters with the roaring, steam-blowing, not quite fire-breathing creatures is one of the most psychologically tense in the *Travels*. The triumph of the lone pilgrim against such great odds, which could be right out of John Bunyan's *Pilgrim's Progress*, was orchestrated for just such dramatic effect.

I was attacked on all sides, several endeavouring to overset the canoe. My situation now became precarious to the last degree: two very large ones attacked me closely, at the same instant, rushing up with their heads and part of their bodies above the water, roaring terribly and belching floods of water over me. They struck their jaws together so close to my ears, as almost to stun me, and I expected every moment to be dragged out of the boat and instantly devoured.[5]

Indeed, William wasn't actually alone, as he claims, during these battles, but neither was Bunyan's Christian for most of his trip. In the *Travels*, William says he's by himself after a young Indian guide abandons him; in the Report, his companion is a man, presumably a white one since he always tells us when the case is otherwise, and his departure is described *after* the alligator attack and the hurricane William

William Bartram, The Alegator of St. Johns (Natural History Museum, London)

survived on Lake George. What's more, alligators are cold-blooded animals, so they don't emit steam.[6]

We should read these stories for their psychological truths, in addition to searching them for literal facts about William's journey. We can value them for their romantic qualities, for their emotional depth, for their insights into the state of mind of the author as he engaged his own worst fears in a sublime natural hell. To say that they were calculated and recast for effect isn't to criticize them; indeed, they orchestrate facts and fancies into an emotional symphony that is William's Truth, his art, his gift to us.

Perhaps this is a place to recall the possibility that William suffered from bouts of melancholia, and to ask whether the stories about spiders and alligators, as well as the drawings of monsters and predatory insects, were as much representations of what William felt inside his head as they were of what no other eyes ever saw, have ever seen, in a Florida swamp. If depression wasn't as influential on his nature as the new science and aesthetics, the classics, pastoral poetry, Quakerism, novels, the literatures of travel and natural history, and John's philosophy, then something is missing, unaccounted for, in our comprehension of William's view of the world. What he shared in his *Travels* was more than a literary convention, something closer to a dream. "For a time I would feel I belonged still to a world of straight-forward facts," Marlow explains in Joseph Conrad's *Heart of Darkness;* "but the feeling would not last long. Something would turn up to scare it away." Ferocious beasts, terrible hurricanes, a blistering, baking sun, insects by the thousands, the millions, sometimes William believed, an unremitting fever, and solitude of the worst kind, one from which he couldn't imagine escape—these were his fate. "It was like a weary pilgrimage amongst hints for nightmares," Marlow recalled.[7] William knew how that felt. His could be as dark a vision of nature as American art and literature have ever produced, and none of the literary influences, alone or combined, tell the whole story of what went on in William's head.

It is humans, in William's telling, not roaring, dragonlike alligators, who have made earth a more violent place than it needs to be, and William developed over the course of his life a withering critique of civilized man. "Man is cruel," he wrote in an unpublished essay on morality, "hypocritical, a dissembler, his dissimulation exceeds that of any being we are acquainted with for he dissembles dissimulation itself . . . in order more completely to dissemble and deceive." He lectured himself frequently in his commonplace books on the evils of ambition, the connections between avarice and war, the superiority of instinct over book learning, and the destructively busy pace of civilized life.

Again, in a long passage of his manuscript chapter on the Alachua Savanna, William indicts us all for our unnatural violence, then removes the insult to his readers from the published book.

> And if it be so that we are their Lords and have dominion over them in this world, yet they are our fellow creatures and perhaps it would demonstrate more wisdom and propriety in us if we would at seasonable times demean ourselves and associate more peaceably with them; I mean the animal creation at large. . . . This would be humanity and we should be considered as their superiors by such a peaceable familiar and merciful conduct towards them:

But alas! How contrary is our behavior, our conduct in this life won't bear a retrospect, not even a slight examination. We act inconsistently and contrary to the consent of our own reason and judgement amongst ourselves and perhaps like tyrants and demons in the opinion of the animal creation. . . . O Men! The highly distinguished and favoured creature of God! Let us stop a little in our mad career, let us look back and examine our actions, our conduct; Are we not bewildered and lost in error?

Yes, we are lost, William believed; what he hoped was that he had found the Truth that would save us, deliver him, from the jaws of avarice, ambition, and greed. What he prayed was that the violence of mankind and the horrors inside his own head could be diminished, thereby bringing us into greater harmony with nature, not in unnatural passivity, but with a truce such as that in the pellucid pond.

The lecture that he leaves in the published account at this point was as much aimed at himself as it is at the rest of us.

Our life here is spent in continual warfare and strife; we act contrary to the immediate convictions and dictates of our own consciences and the divine dictates of Truth and Reason.

We toil and thirst continually for superiority and like children pursue headlong and wrangle for the power and riches of this world, which we know by [sad] experience are transitory [perishable and prey to each other] and soon perish [forever] with the possessor.

Again, William is rationalizing his failure as a man of the world and justifying his decision not to return to his "sad" experience as a merchant.

We labour continually [for] to enslave our own species, [those] whilst visionary alluring scenes lead us wandering in a labyrinth of errors and [we are lost] and are led astray from the glorious eternal abodes of future tranquility.

It is William, as much as any of his readers, who has committed these sins, who has been lost in a "labyrinth of errors" by buying and selling slaves, which he does as late as 1773, accepting a slave woman named Jenny as payment on a debt and then selling her through his cousin and brother to pay some of his own bills.[8]

In his youth and into his middle age, William accepted without exception the rule, which he saw as a natural law, that everybody eats someone else, a world of predator and prey, dominion and deference, of brute force in which slavery was a "natural" exploitation by the strong of the weak. Perhaps his father saw slavery and slaves in the same way. Still, particularly in the case of William, it is perplexing to a late-twentieth-century reader that a man who could feel so poignantly the heartbreak of an orphaned bear, who made such an impassioned plea for the life of a rattlesnake, could buy and sell people.

Throughout the *Travels*, there are references to slaves without any comments about slavery. Just like his father, William gratefully accepted the loan of slaves from planter acquaintances during his travels. "We sat [*sic*] sail in a handsome pleasure-boat," he reports at one point, "manned with four stout negro slaves, to row in case of necessity." At another, a planter sends slaves to fetch and repair his small boat. Later in the book, William recounts his amazement that no slaves died on the plantation he was visiting, despite the severity of the hurricane he describes. He even discusses enslaved Indians, whom he met in his travels, with an anthropologist's detachment and no moral commentary at all. He portrays in admiring words a frontier family of slave owners and quotes the patriarch's self-praise for how well he took care of his slaves. William tells us on other occasions about a gentleman, who "very obligingly sent a young Negro slave to assist and pilot me," and another, who furnished him "with horses to ride, and a Negro to pilot and take care of me." If William had any qualms about the institution of slavery or about benefiting personally from the labor of slaves, we hear nothing about it in the *Travels*.[9]

What we do see, though, are several references to his horse as "my faithful slave," and "my old trusty slave." Towards the end of the journey, William narrates his need for a new horse, the old one being worn out, and his concern for the fate of his "slave."

> About the middle of the afternoon, we were joyfully surprised at the distant prospect of the trading company coming up . . . and before night I struck up a bargain with them for a handsome

strong young horse, which cost me about ten pounds sterling. I was now constrained to leave my old slave behind, to feed in rich cane pastures, where he was to remain and recruit until the return of his new master from Mobile; from whom I extorted a promise to use him gently, and if possible not to make a pack-horse of him.

Like the frontier farmer who fed his slaves well, William considered himself a good master, and seems to have equated the institution across species lines.[10]

In other words, a pure naturalism, which accepts the law of the jungle as the fate of mankind, cuts two ways, contrary to modern tendencies to romanticize the natural as superior to our ways of life. In William's eyes, and perhaps in his father's as well, naturalistic moralism rationalized complicity in the exploitation of fellow humans for profitable ends. It helped them not see what they didn't want to; it provided dark glasses for the darkest of their moral nights just as surely as it enlightened them on the shared qualities of all life and the senselessness of killing without cause or for sport. There were limits to John's and William's vision just as surely as there are to ours, which isn't a good cause for dismissing their wisdom, judging harshly their whole lives, or declaring "us" superior to "them." Simply put, they were no more morally consistent than any of the rest of us are.

I might leave my consideration of William's attitudes toward slavery right there, with a sense that he—like his father—was somewhat behind the more enlightened Quaker morality of his times (which he was) and that he found a comfortable rationale in his fatalistic naturalism (which he apparently did). It seems, though, that William saw the light on this social issue after he returned from his travels, some time during his years of retirement in the Kingsessing garden. The essay on his father, in which he praised John for manumitting a slave at great financial cost, was probably written in 1804, and no doubt reflected his own current views better than those of his father, to whom William attributes an antislavery zealotry that was now his own. There's also an unpublished essay on slavery that William drafted sometime after his father's death, but exactly when we can't know.

At some point in the second half of his life, William came to see slavery as unnatural, as inconsistent with "the dignity of human nature" and contrary to God's plan for the earth. "The present plan of civilisation must be changed," William wrote, "in time for a better one more consonant to reason and general happiness, according to the first determined intentions and will of the Supreme creator and only Lord." He believed that "God is no respecter of persons and that the Black, White, Red and Yellow People are equally dear to him and under his protection and favour."[11]

William is using the language of "nature" to support his moral system, as he did all along. Now, though, it is a distinctive human nature that he writes about. Civilization needs reform, but it's not a return to the wilderness that William advocates here. The natural laws that rule the forest seem not to apply. He's looking for humans to transcend in civilization the relationships he discusses most fully in his *Travels*, those between predator and prey; and the similarities that he and his father found among all species appear irrelevant to this line of thought. William's theory that humans are no better, no worse, than snakes no longer works for him, because he now knows in ways that his conscious mind can't ignore that all people are equal in God's eyes and slavery is wrong.

There is nothing extraordinary about an eighteenth-century Quaker expressing such views. This was, after all, long after the antislavery testimony of Benjamin Lay, and during the era when such men as Anthony Benezet and John Woolman worked against slavery and in behalf of African-Americans. It was after the Philadelphia Yearly Meeting had moved against the slave trade and decided to rid its membership of slave-owning's taint, after Pennsylvania—among other Northern states—had moved to gradually abolish the institution within its boundaries. William's thoughts now were consistent with traditional Quaker ideas about the brotherhood of mankind, which included women, and the equality of humans before God.[12]

William isn't inventing doctrine here; he's only catching up. In this he was no slower than many other Quakers, and a lot quicker than most of the rest of his race. There is nothing odd about William's views on slavery either before or after he wrote his antislavery tract. His self-interest and sense of the natural may have slowed him down, providing him a rationalization for action that he would otherwise have lacked, but eventually his compassion for enslaved humans conforms with his appreciation for wild Seminole horses, "who never yet felt the weight of the collar or the galling chains of servitude."[13]

William's belief in the connectedness of all life, including plants, led him to see Indians, if not African-Americans, as people rather than simply "others" better or worse than himself. Again, if this seems inconsistent, that's because it is, which only reveals William's humanity, his capacity, shared with the rest of us, for allowing self-interest and prejudice to obscure his moral vision. It was the Indians' comparative closeness to nature, which William could observe in the field, that led him to see their natures in ways that he couldn't with Blacks. It doesn't dilute William's uniqueness, in his own day, for having Indian ideals who were neither the noble savages of Rousseau nor the ignoble savages about whom his father wrote. His Indians were people with strengths and weaknesses, in some ways different, but ultimately much like whites.

There's no evidence directly addressing why William's approach to Native Americans wasn't more affected by the nature of his grandfather's death. A number of circumstances, though, point the same way. One generation removed from the horror, growing up as he did with Indians around, they weren't an abstraction for him and he saw too much variety among individuals and across tribal groups to generalize in either a romantic or bigoted way. Possibly, too, William mirrored his father in this regard, reflecting the reverse of John's image, engaging in some humanitarian rebellion against the patriarch's rage. This was an ideal arena for William to compete with his father, to be a better, more tolerant, more Christian Quaker, thereby defining himself positively in contrast to John.

Finally, provocatively in this regard, William was named for his grandfather, though he would misremember his grandfather's name. Denying, at least in a subconscious sense, the potent legacy of namesake relationships, William wrote in the 1804 eulogy to John that his father and grandfather shared the same name. To him the identities of his father and grandfather were much more closely linked than was his to the namesake whose name he forgot. This mistake is a telling error of identity—a breaking, even if unconscious—with his grandfatherly past. By forgetting William's name was he possibly even forgiving the Indians for killing "John"? This supplies one surviving clue to the formation of William's identity in relationship to two significant male figures, only one of whom he ever met, and to the significance of Indians in all three men's lives.

Just like his father, William had an encounter with a fearsome Indian "other" deep in the woods. The story he tells is so different, though, from John's that it encapsulates the gulf between father and son as much as it describes William's sense of the distance between "them" and "us." The scene is set in the *Travels*; he has passed the "utmost frontier of the white settlements" and would have the reader believe that he was as alone as a man can ever be.

As we know, William isn't above claiming to be alone when he really was not. Were he to tell us that there was another young, virile, white man along, which meant that the Indian was outnumbered and out-armed, the story would not be the same one at all. Whether or not William was literally by himself, he faced "his" Indian in a way that defined his identity unsullied by that of anyone else. This was essential to him. The story is about two representative men, about two cultures, two civilizations, two ways of life come together in nature to reveal their true selves. The story ultimately tells us that their natures were one.

The scene is set with particular care, with William's poetic sense of beauty, his novelist's flair for description, and his dramatic capture of tension in peace.

> It was drawing on towards the close of day, the skies serene and calm, the air temperately cool, and gentle zephyrs breathing through the fragrant pines; the prospect around enchantingly varied and beautiful; endless green savannas, chequered with coppices of fragrant shrubs, filled the air with the richest perfume.

"Nature seemed silent," but nature is never just what it seems and sometimes it's cruelly deceptive.

> Nothing appeared to ruffle the happy moments of evening contemplation; when, on a sudden, an Indian appeared crossing the path, at a considerable distance before me. On perceiving that he was armed with a rifle, the first sight of him startled me, and I endeavoured to elude his sight, by stopping my pace, and keeping large trees between us; but he espied me, and turning short about, sat spurs to his horse, and came up on full gallop.

The contrast implied here is deceptive, too, but essential for the story it tells. Just as we know that he may not have been alone, we also know, as William tells us elsewhere, that he carried a rifle and rode a horse. But the emotions are more important to William than facts, and we need to keep his moral in mind.

> I never before this was afraid at the sight of an Indian, but at this time, I must own that my spirits were very much agitated: I saw at once, that, being unarmed, I was in his power; and having now but a few moments to prepare, I resigned myself entirely to the will of the Almighty, trusting to his mercies for my preservation: my mind then became tranquil, and I resolved to meet the dreaded foe with resolution and cheerful confidence.

God gave William strength—very important here; the facts could obscure the reader's view of the real scene, so we must forgive the license, poetic or not, that the author takes in the name of a larger truth.

> The intrepid Siminole stopped suddenly, three or four yards before me, and silently viewed me, his countenance angry and fierce, shifting his rifle from shoulder to shoulder, and looking about instantly on all sides.

The Indian was looking to see if the two of them were alone, for the purpose of knowing if he was free to do as he would with this white fellow, to see if he was safe from attack. The look betrays his purpose, the story implies, and the intentions aren't good. You can see how the Indian's subsequent actions might be misinterpreted, from William's perspective, if we are told that another armed, mounted, white man rode at his side.

> I advanced towards him, and with an air of confidence offered him my hand, hailing him, brother; at this he hastily jerked back his arm, with a look of malice, rage, and disdain, seeming every way discontented; when again looking at me more attentively, he instantly spurred up to me, and with dignity in his look and action, gave me his hand.

Nature is scary in its own right, but the principal predator of man, besides the unknown, is surely a man such as this.

> Possibly the silent language of his soul, during the moment of suspense (for I believe his design was to kill me when he first came up) was after this manner: "White man, thou art my enemy, and thou and thy brethren may have killed mine; yet it may not be so, and even were that the case, thou art now alone, and in my power. Live; the Great Spirit forbids me to touch thy life; go to thy brethren, tell them thou sawest an Indian in the forests, who knew how to be humane and compassionate."

Tell your brethren, perhaps tell your father, as well, that we aren't all savages any more than you are, that we can distinguish one white man from others who have done us harm. Tell them we're men, not cannibals, that we have souls, too, that we can be moved to compassion by Christian comportment, that it was God, not your weapon, horse, and companion who saved you. Tell them that I respect bravery, that your Quaker passivity is remarkable to me, that I have an integrity of my own kind, that I love and am loved, too.

> In fine, we shook hands, and parted in a friendly manner, in the midst of a dreary wilderness; and he informed me of the course and the distance to the trading-house, where I found he had been extremely ill-treated the day before.

Now the wilderness is "dreary," which it wasn't before the Indian arrived on the scene. Two people, one interhuman encounter that ended well, altered the serenity of the woods. These are powerful humans, whose spirit both transforms and is transformed by nature.

William was not in the forest to meet others; he was there to lose and to find himself. This Indian was "one of the greatest villains on earth," the traders tell him, "a noted murderer, and outlawed by his countrymen." William's nature triumphs against the worst human just as he is saved by the nature of the worst of all snakes. This is how William wants us to see him in nature, how he portrays the natural world in which he lives so much more successfully than he had in a civilized state.[14]

Indians are, to William, direct descendants of "the ancients," bearers of wisdom that civilized people had lost. The ancients were no better than nature, but they were closer to being their "natural" God-intended selves. Whether from the forests of North America, the Spanish Pyrenees, ancient China, or other remote places in the world, and whether they were truly "ancient" in a temporal sense or contemporaries who still lived naturally, William elevated their teachings above those of books. In his eyes, the Bible and organized religion may have "improved" civilization, but not enough to compensate for what our estrangement from nature has cost us.

According to William and the sources from which he drew for entries in his commonplace book, "ancients" lack ambition, which is the "real evil" plaguing the civilized world; they eschew hierarchy—being natural democrats; are free from avarice—"that destructive passion"; kill only for just cause; and covet no women besides their own. The last, of course, tells us that William's "ancients," like John's "Indians," are men. They draw no arbitrary property lines, for they believe that private ownership of the earth "is a usurpation contrary to Nature." They possess all they desire because they "desire only what is necessary" to sustain life.

> The sun warms us, the rains and dew cool and refresh, the rivers quench our thirst, herbs and roots nourish us[?]. The earth affords us a bed; anxious cares [interrupt? inhibit?] not our repose. Independence deliver[s] us from the fears[?] of subjection; we look upon one another as brothers whom nature has rendered equal and as the children of one supreme God our common father.[15]

In a natural state, which Indians approximate more closely than Europeans, William believed that humans are more innocent, less prone to adultery and war, more ingenious, more industrious, and in possession of more highly developed senses of justice and honor. Deviations are a function of corruptions of nature by civilized men.

Which is not to say that William's Indians were ideal ancients or always ideals at all. He knew them too well to ignore the corruptions and the varieties of individual behavior to which Indians were as prone as Europeans. As a generalization, though, William observed the connections across racial and cultural lines, the similarities, the shared features, just as his father taught him to recognize the connections among all forms of life. He simply carried John's natural system a logical step further by seeing Indians as not so different—wiser in some ways, if more ignorant in others—more "like" than "other" to "us."

The art of the Creek Indians, as William saw it, was closer to nature and to the art of the ancients than the "artificial" accomplishments of modern European artists. Outlines were "bold, natural, and turned or designed to convey some meaning, passion, or admonition, and thus may be said to speak to those who can read them." The drawings spoke the language of nature that was lost to civilized men, who were unable to extract meaning from the walls of Indian houses, buffalo hides, and the tattooed bodies of "ancient chiefs." The method and intent of these pictures resembled Egyptian hieroglyphics, William thought, which revealed a linkage in nature between Indians and ancients from across the sea. Both were "mystical writings" that held wisdom we no longer share. Embodied in the drawings were stories that William only dimly grasped about natural connections among animals and humans.

> Men are often depicted as having the head and other members of different kinds of animals, as a wolf, buck, hare, horse, buffalo, snake, duck, turkey, tiger, cat, crocodile, etc., etc. All these animals are, on the other hand, depicted having the human head, members, etc.

We are them; they are us. Indians, ancients, Europeans, and animals share natures, just as his father had taught him about humans and plants. If we could just see what's there, comprehend what we see, hear the language of nature in the streams and the trees, we could recover the ancient wisdom that Indians know.[16]

William asks rhetorically whether "adopting or imitating the manners and customs of white people is to be termed civilization" or whether the better measure of Indian accomplishments is the ideals set by moralists, philosophers, and divines "either of the ancients or moderns," ideals from which he believed that Europeans fell shorter than some Indian tribes. "Their religion is, perhaps, as pure as that which was in the beginning revealed to the first families of mankind," William says of the Creeks, which made them superior in his eyes to the Cherokee, who were the best imitators of European culture. His measure was a "natural" morality and "natural" religion rather than a yardstick of European customs, styles, and habits.[17]

The Creek government, of all the nations of which William was aware, was "the most simple, natural, and rational that can be imagined or desired. The same spirit that dictated to Montesquieu the idea of a rational government, seems to superintend and guide the Indians." Simple, natural, and rational, an achievement only now theorized in European culture was the ancient and ongoing accomplishment of this Indian tribe. Simplicity was natural and rational; the cumbersome systems of government were the opposite—artificial and irrational—in William's eyes. Should Europeans reach back to their ancient roots for governing forms or model their politics and law on the natural models set before them on this continent, they, too, could attune their civilization to nature, to God, and to good.[18]

Those who rejected Indian wisdom seemed to William "prejudiced, ignorant, obstinate people." Pretty harsh words for describing his father, among others, but this was written more than a decade after John's death. William didn't favor "levelling things down to the simplicity of Indians"; he wasn't advocating, as Crèvecoeur did in the twelfth of his *American Farmer* letters, a return to the woods. "We" can, though, William wrote,

> better our condition in civil society by paying some more respect to and impartially examining the system of legislation, religion, morality, and economy of these despised, persecuted *wild people*, or as they are learnedly called, *bipeds*—I suppose meaning a creature differing from quadrupeds.[19]

"We" have much to learn from "them," which can only be achieved, William believes, if we can see that "they" aren't so very much different from "us." If only we could acknowledge our place in nature, rather than asserting superiority over other animals, vegetables, and men; if only we could see that the laws binding us together are God's.

There was the occasion, which William reports in the *Travels* to illustrate this theme, when Indians' sense of the forest, their feeling for contours of land, displayed a striking superiority to the measuring tools of civilized man. He was traveling with a surveying party, whose design was to map out the bounds of an Indian treaty. One of the Indians accompanying them, who had a stake in the outcome, pointed out that the surveyor's measurements were wrong.

The surveyor replied, that he himself was certainly right, adding, that little instrument (pointing to the compass) told him so, which, he said, could not err. The Indian answered, he knew better, and that the little wicked instrument was a liar; and he would not acquiesce in its decisions, since it would wrong the Indians out of their land. This mistake (the surveyor proving to be in the wrong) displeased the Indians; the dispute arose to that height, that the chief and his party had determined to break up the business, and return the shortest way home, and forbad the surveyors to proceed any farther.[20]

Fortunately, the dispute was amicably resolved, but not before the Europeans' misplaced faith in their technology had brought them to the brink of another Indian war. A little humility, a little respect, something less than a culturally superior sneer—a willingness to appreciate knowledge that came from the Indian's lifetime of walking the woods, his ancestors' millennia of living as part of this land— would have served these Europeans well. That's William's point—not an idealization of Indian culture or a dismissal of European knowledge obtained from books and scientific instruments, but a sense that nature was the best teacher and that Europeans still had something to learn that they may have once known but had long since forgot.

Indians had their cultural defects, in William's eyes, such as a reluctance to work, which was unchallenged by logic or commitments previously made. There was no disagreement here with his father, although William's language is kinder, more tolerant, in saying about the same thing. Indians in William's acquaintance could be "savage," but that didn't lead him to generalize like his father did about the whole race. In William's experience, Indians differed "as widely from each other as the bull from the ox." Seminole warriors could be "savage" by any common understanding of the term, but Seminoles in slavery were "the tamest, the most abject creatures that we can possibly imagine: mild, peaceable, and tractable, they seem to have no will or power to act but as directed by their masters; whilst the free Indians, on the contrary, are bold, active, and clamorous." It's the difference between freedom and slavery rather than their nature that accounts for such extreme varieties as he found. Unlike the ox, the manhood of Indian slaves wasn't literally slashed. We might read an indictment of slavery in these words, but the reader must extract it, because William doesn't add a commentary about the institution's effect on the nature of man.[21]

In other words, Indians have their faults, which include waging war against their fellow creatures, "but I cannot find, upon the strictest inquiry, that their bloody contests at this day are marked with deeper stains of inhumanity or savage cruelty, than what may be observed amongst the most civilized nations." They scalp their enemies, but only after they're dead; and, contrary to his father's experience, William can't find examples of their killing women or children or even of them burning or torturing male captives, "though it is said they used to do it formerly." They are sometimes perpetrators of adultery and fornication, he notes, "but, I suppose, in no greater excess than other nations of men." They are overly fond of games and gambling, tell preposterous tales, and now hunt to "criminal excess, since the white people have dazzled their senses with foreign superfluities."[22]

Indians have the same morality as we do, William says, but find it easier to practice.

> For, however strange it may appear to us, the same moral duties which with us form the amiable, virtuous character, so difficult to maintain there, without compulsion or visible restraint, operates like instinct, with a surprising harmony and natural ease, insomuch that it seems impossible for them to act out of the common high road to virtue.

This praise specifically applies to the Upper Creeks or Muscogulges; and William is careful to distinguish among the various Indian cultures, which differ as much as the Spanish from the English or Dutch. The Seminoles seem to him admirable for their freedom from "want or desires," as yet less affected by the corrupting influence of civilized men. "Thus contented and undisturbed, they appear as blithe and free as the birds of the air, and like them as volatile and active, tuneful and vociferous." In other words, they are more natural than acculturated Indians and in that sense superior to them and to us.[23]

Again, William isn't above altering his tale to fit the story that he has to tell. In his *Report*, for example, he explains that Seminoles destroyed a Spanish settlement, the ruins of which he describes again in the *Travels* without the information about Indian "savagery." That's because such information wouldn't fit here, wouldn't carry his story of Indian nobility forward in the way that he wants. The larger truth is that these Indians are peaceful, living in harmony with nature around them—including man. Contrary facts would subvert his description of the present, play to existing prejudices against these people, detract from his portrait of men living in nature, who are much like us but more peaceful, content, in better tune with the bees and the birds.[24]

One defect that William observed in the otherwise admirable art of the Creeks was their representation of men's "private" parts. They drew "figures of mankind in various attitudes, some very ludicrous and even obscene; even the *privates* of men are sometimes represented, but never an instance of indelicacy in a female figure."[25] Drawing men's penises was too "natural" for William; the "ludicrous" quality of the drawings is likely a reference to size. He's relieved, for the sake of his argument in behalf of Indian culture, that the pornography doesn't extend to depicting women without their clothes. He's embarrassed, but not obviously titillated by the graphic portrayal of man's nature within the context of animals and plants, whose sexuality gave him less pause.

What William's critique of Indian art does introduce, though, is his "delicacy" about gender, women, and sex. No less than John, William was attracted to Indian women, but without the complications of racial repulsion that his father felt. That's not to say that William's attitudes toward women were less complex than John's, for the opposite seems true. William lacked his father's playful attitude toward sex; he never married; and there is no evidence that he consummated a love affair. And yet he liked women, was clearly sexually attracted to them. Whether there was a problem that stemmed from the developmental crisis of his teenage years, we can't really know, but something kept William from letting himself enjoy women in the ways that his father clearly did.

Whatever William's concerns about pornographic art, he had a sensual take on the sex lives of insects. Mayflies, he tells us in the

Travels, those tiny insects that rise up in clouds upon evening's approach, gladly risk being consumed by predators to procreate.

But as if insensible of their danger, gay and tranquil each meets his beloved mate in the still air, inimitably bedecked in their new nuptial robes. What eye can trace them, in their varied wanton amorous chaces, bounding and fluttering on the odoriferous air! With what peace, love, and joy, do they end the last moments of their existence![26]

The section is part of a longer philosophical aside in which he compares the lives of these insects to those of humans, and urges upon us a little humility, a bit of gratitude, that our opportunity for such rapture is so much longer than theirs. Perhaps this suggests that William still had hope for himself, writing in his mid-forties, that he might yet experience the same bliss as bugs. Possibly the passage implies that William suffered his lack of a mate as an unnatural state, as a defect in himself that there was still time to fix.

Such an interpretation implies, though, that William hadn't shared passion, had yet to know love, was still waiting for an ideal partner, or was on the verge of giving up. What I hope for him is that none of that's true, because such ecstasy never came into William's life after he finished writing his book. The second half of his life brought him some joy, but not of the kind the insects knew. Perhaps William's best chance, and my best case that he might have known what he was writing about, is revealed in another passage of the *Travels*, where he engages in his own reverie about Indian "nymphs." Again, William sets the scene splendidly for the picture he wants us to see.

Proceeding on our return to town, continued through part of this high forest skirting on the meadows: began to ascend the hills of a ridge which we were under the necessity of crossing; and having gained its summit, enjoyed a most enchanting view; a vast expanse of green meadows and strawberry fields; a meandering river gliding through, saluting in its various turnings the swelling, green, turfy knolls, embellished with parterres of flowers and fruitful strawberry beds; flocks of turkies strolling about them; herds of deer prancing in the meads or bounding over the hills; companies of young, innocent Cherokee virgins, some busy gathering the rich fragrant fruit, others having already filled their baskets, lay reclined under the shade of floriferous and fragrant native bowers . . . disclosing their beauties to the fluttering breeze, and bathing their limbs in the cool fleeting streams; whilst other parties, more gay and libertine, were yet collecting strawberries, or wantonly chasing their companions, tantalising them, staining their lips and cheeks with the rich fruit.

The sexual imagery of this "enchanting view" shows William's imagination at work. From the "swelling" knolls to the "fruitful" strawberry beds, from the prancing deer bounding over hills to the "young, innocent Cherokee virgins" with overflowing baskets of ripe, red fruit and red-stained lips and cheeks, we see his conscious and subconscious mind revealing more than he knows, more than he wants to share, much that would embarrass him had he not written for a pre-Freudian culture that was still innocent about colors, textures, language, and shapes.

The sylvan scene of primitive innocence was enchanting, and perhaps too enticing for hearty young men long to continue idle spectators.

In fine, nature prevailing over reason, we wished at least to have a more active part in their delicious sports. . . . Now, although we meant no other than an innocent frolic with this gay assembly of hamadryades, we shall leave it to the person of feeling and sensibility to form an idea to what lengths our passions might have hurried us, thus warmed and excited, had it not been for the vigilance and care of some envious matrons who lay in ambush, and espying us, gave the alarm, time enough for the nymphs to rally and assemble together.

William, he tells us, was capable of lust and there was nothing about the complexion, clothing, or culture of these young women to restrain him. If his mind or his morals got in the way, he admits that they didn't put up much of a fight. Whether the eighteenth-century "person of feeling and sensibility" would grant the young men the innocence of intention that William claims for himself, the modern reader easily imagines the lengths to which their passions might have "hurried" them. Through the diligence of the matrons, his story continues, their passions were sated only on fruit.

We accepted a basket, sat down and regaled ourselves on the delicious fruit, encircled by the whole assembly of the innocent jocose sylvan nymphs.

In the end, William writes, the young men "mounted" only the hills, arriving back in civilization "in the cool of the evening," the heat of the day having passed.[27]

At the level of symbol and tone, the passage harbors less sexual frustration than the story suggests. Either William is content with fantasy rather than flesh or he tasted more on this day than the strawberries that he tells us about. The remark at the story's end about his companion's arrangement with the young women to "bring their collections to his house at a stipulated price" might be read as a bargain for future sex. Such an interpretation introduces tensions to the tale, though, that aren't easily resolved.[28]

The objects of William's desire aren't simply women, but rather "innocent virgins," a redundancy in his language that speaks to an ideal. The juxtaposed qualities of innocence and wantonness are precisely the allure of Indians. The characterization of the young women as "nymphs" should be taken more seriously than John's parallel tale. William's specific appellation of "hamadryades" connects this story to the reverie about mayflies in an enticing way. Hamadryads are the wood nymphs of Greek and Roman mythology, whose lives are inextricably entwined with the tree whose spirit each is. They live as long as and no longer than the forest survives; their loss is one price paid for civilized life. A man can know them only in the woods, so they couldn't possibly keep a bargain to visit the man's house for any price. Making the choice that William does at the story's end, to return to the civilization from which he has come, means giving up nymphs. Whether or not anyone lost innocence on this day, William liked to imagine that it would happen this way.

If not then, in the woods with a nymph, perhaps William lost, or found, his innocence at a trading house. He certainly witnessed, if he didn't take part in, bacchanalian "festivals" of liquor, women, and song. "White and red men and women without distinction," he writes,

> passed the day merrily with these jovial, amorous topers, and the nights in convivial songs, dances, and sacrifices to Venus, as long as they could stand or move; for in these frolicks both sexes take such liberties with each other, and act, without constraint or shame, such scenes as they would abhor when sober or in their senses; and would endanger their ears and even their lives.[29]

There's danger in such behavior, even as there's absolution from responsibility for all the fun. The risk of ears and lives comes from cuckolded spouses; the Indian punishment for adultery being the cropping of both parties' ears. The common retaliation from white husbands was passionate murder that any jury of twelve husbands would excuse. William claims no innocence here—of intention or act—as he does in his frolic with nymphs. These aren't innocent women or virgins, in his accounting, but whores. When the men were sickened by drink and in search of some hair-of-the-dog,

> this was the time for the wenches to make their market, as they had the fortitude and subtlety by dissimulation and artifice to save their share of the liquor during the frolic . . . and when the comic farce is over, the wench retails this precious cordial to them at her own price.[30]

The men are trapped by women, who use dissimulation to entice their prey. It's a dangerous game in which the hunters are hunted and skinned; whether they lose the contents of their stomachs and wallets, their ears, or even worse, they're defenseless against their own natures and female predators with unnatural skills.

Whatever William's joy, bliss, or loss, whether frustrated, fantasized, or realized in sexual encounters with wanton innocents in the woods or prostitutes in camp, he chose to return from the forest; he retained an ambivalence about women, about Indian women even more, that kept him from sustaining the ecstasy that he may have known, possibly because he feared losing his ears or other parts. Another story he tells, about an Indian "charmer," a woman with qualities ascribed to a venomous snake, again shows the darker side of William's approach to women and his "othering" of Indian women in a way that he didn't generally "other" Indian men. Perhaps this comparative passion comes because he was more attracted *and* more repulsed by Indian women than he was by white, but for whatever reasons his most engaged commentary on the evil nature of women is about an Indian, and is as much about gender as it is about race.

> On our arrival at the upper store, we found it occupied by a white trader, who had for a companion a very handsome Siminole young woman.... He is at this time unhappy in his connexions with his beautiful savage. It is but a few years since he came here, I think from North Carolina ... when unfortunately meeting with this little charmer, they were married in the Indian manner. He loves her sincerely, as she possesses every perfection in her person to render a man happy. Her features are beautiful, and manners engaging. Innocence, modesty, and love, appear to a stranger in every action and movement; and these powerful graces she has so artfully played upon her beguiled and vanquished lover, and unhappy slave, as to have already drained him of all his possessions, which she dishonestly distributes amongst her savage relations. He is now poor, emaciated, and half distracted, often threatening to shoot her, and afterwards put an end to his own life; yet he has not resolution even to leave her; but now endeavours to drown and forget his sorrows in deep draughts of brandy. Her father condemns her dishonesty and cruel conduct.[31]

William is careful to exonerate the white trader, his wife's father, and the rest of her tribe. The merchant was a "stout genteel well-bred man, active, and of a heroic and amiable disposition" before he was charmed by this female viper. Her father "condemns" her. She is "condemned and detested by her own people of both sexes." Her character wasn't imbedded in her Indian nature, William wants us to know. Should her husband "turn her away ... she would not get a husband again" from among the Seminoles, who would look upon her as a "harlot."[32]

Such an entrapping woman is an exception to nature's rule, to the nature of Indians, but also of women. She shares characteristics of the tipitiwichet as well as the snake, and of the harlot, who is found across the temporal and geographic breadth of human experience, but isn't typical of the way women behave. William's reason for mentioning this woman, "so foreign to my business," is "to exhibit an instance of the power of beauty in a savage, and her art and finesse in improving it to her private ends." Her crimes are gender-specific, even more than they are racial, displaying the Indians' shared nature with Europeans both in producing such a woman and in their rejection of her.

William reveals his fear of women or, at least, the dangers of which a man must beware. Like the fly before the carnivorous plant or the squirrel in the path of a rattlesnake, he was both curious and cautious, entranced and terrified. Innocence, modesty, and beauty bewitched him: he felt the allure of "powerful graces"; womanly manners seduced him. He feared being vanquished, becoming a slave, the loss of freedom that romantic entanglements meant to him. Indian women, with their more visible sensuality, the combination of innocence and wantonness that he writes about, were the most dangerous, the most attractive, to him.

It was inner peace that William sought as his travels came to an end—not adventure or even love.

> Is it not most [clearly] evident that a very considerable degree of real happiness even in this life is within our reach if we would attend and listen to the voice of truth and obey the constant dictates and admonitions of Wisdom and reason. Observe and practice humility and give place to one another. Be contented with mediocrity in the possession and use of the bountiful gifts of Providence.

That's where William was headed, what he almost found in his travels, but this goal he could reach only at his home. It's one thing to travel lightly in the wilderness; quite another to rid oneself of possessions in a civilized state. He'd found his humility, the voice of truth in his own heart; he was wiser and more reasonable than when he fled Philadelphia and abandoned his swamp. Now he could be content with "mediocrity," by which he meant a middle path, not the life of a true natural, an ascetic, but of the pilgrim returned from his quest.

The garden was such a middle place in the world; the rural life celebrated by Virgil and Jefferson was the one right for him. Having experienced the sublime, solitude, and the stars above him at night, he now needed serenity, family, and a roof over his head. William wanted to share what he learned in his travels and tell the story of what he'd become. He had to write his book, which he had planned all along, to draw as the spirit moved him and nature inspired, to work with a spade and have a change of clean clothes, to record the earth's cycles by a warm fire, and sleep soundly at night.

William wasn't the man he was when he fled Philadelphia, when he began the journey that now brought him back. He would be thirty-eight in the spring. He had been ill, almost to death; perhaps it was scarlet fever that had laid him low for over a month in 1775 or poison ivy that infected his eyes, temporarily blinded him, and forever weakened his sight. Was he thinner, bedraggled; had he cleaned himself up and bought a new suit of clothes before he returned? When did he learn that his father and mother still lived? Who saw whom first? Was his arrival a total surprise? Who cried? Did he and John hug or shake hands? What did, what could, anyone say? I'm a man; I'm fine; I made it alone, William would want John to know. I'm sorry; I'll try to do better; I didn't run up any more debts; please forgive me and take me in, John wanted to hear. I forgive; you're my son; this is your home, John would have the words to express. I love you; I hate you; I admire and fear you more than hurricanes, alligators, and Indians, William couldn't admit to himself, so there's no way he bared his soul to his father about such complex emotions and unpleasant thoughts. Whether either man expressed love openly to the other or whether they now could better accept each other's differences, it's hard to say. John still saw his son as a failure and surely they both knew that without any words passing between them. If William believed he merited John's forgiveness, that there was anything to forgive, or if John finally saw his dear Billy as a man, we can't know.

CHAPTER TEN

Gardens

THE GARDEN WAS THERE, under the snow, for John and William to share one last time, when spring came again. Summer passed; then so did John. Leaves turned color, lost color, fell; blossoms died; birds migrated through; the river froze; snow melted, crocuses bloomed without any more fatherly lectures, recriminations, advice, affection, or the patriarch's good holiday cheer. William continued his work and started over again.

The first-floor study was now William's to use, but not alone. Perhaps he shared it with his brother, the owner of the house; certainly he shared it with other sentient creatures, some of whom were his pets. Curious guests wanted to see John's collections, so the place became a museum with William as curator and guide. Memories surrounded William: piles of rocks, some representing different minerals and others containing fossils; shards of Indian pottery that John had carted home carefully over the years; seeds, books, and a mountain of correspondence loomed over him. He went through the letters, curious to know his father better, using the backs of some to write himself notes, draft his own letters, to scribble and think. At some point, but when there is no clue, he may have burned those he had written to John when he was still "Billy," letters that embarrassed him, caused pain, reminded him of the boy and young man he once was.

The coat of arms may still have hung on the wall. Was there a portrait as well? Most likely not, but the image of John was in his son's head. William did not want to forget his father; he valued each of the specimens, declining to part with a single one "at any price, cherishing in them the memory of his father's industry," as he told one prospective purchaser.[1]

William was forty-four when the visitor offered to take these memories off his hands; his father was six years in the grave. Now he cherished recollections of John's industry, which throughout William's adult life had stood as an indictment of him. What had William accomplished in the years since he returned? He worked on his book—writing, rewriting, but not finishing it. He remembered and tried to forget. He toiled in the garden with spade and hoe; he kept the nursery business's financial records for his brother, using the skills he learned as a merchant's apprentice. He recorded bird migrations; compiled a pharmacopeia; enjoyed the garden's tranquility, his family, and his growing circle of friends. He read and he drew; he didn't stray far; he kept a commonplace book. He tried to be a better man than he was.

William looked outside himself, to make peace with others who kept him from achieving the serenity of soul that he sought. It wasn't until 1785 that he addressed publicly the creditors who thought ill of him.

Whereas William Bartram, of the township of Kingsessing, and state of Pennsylvania, being duly sensible of the signal indulgence shown by his creditors in forbearing to distress him, thinks it his duty, in this public manner, to acknowledge the same, and to make them all the compensation in his power; that having lately received a legacy left him by his father, John Bartram, he is desirous of discharging the remainder of what is so justly their due; and, though he is fearful his whole property will not be sufficient to satisfy all that may be demanded of him, is yet anxious that an equal distribution should be made as far as the same will hold out.[2]

He would meet them face to face, no longer relying on his brothers and cousins to confront his failure for him; he invited even those who had previously discharged their claims upon partial payment of what he owed, wanting to include them in the final settlement, too. It was moral, as well as financial, freedom that he sought, release from debt and from the guilt jailing his heart. On May 13, at his brother Isaac's house on Third Street in Philadelphia, William would show up, not run away again. He'd look them in the eye and act like the man he now was. How many were there; how difficult was his anticipation of the event? He'd endure the harsh words of those creditors who still felt ill-used by a partial payment of his long-standing debts. "I am obliged to the person that speaks me fair to my face," he claimed in the commonplace book; "the clown in Shakespeare's *Twelfth Night* says he is the worse for his friends because they praise him and make an ass of him; but his foes tell him plainly he's an ass so thus profit him in knowledge of himself."[3] William was more sensitive than Feste; he suffered his enemies, valued his friends more than this borrowed wisdom reveals.

When it was over, he must have been relieved. "What a pleasure it is to pay one's debts," he remarked once in his commonplace book, free of "that uneasiness which a true spirit feels from dependence and obligation." Settling accounts "affords pleasure to the creditor and it gratifies our special affections. . . . It leaves a consciousness of our own virtue." He felt good about himself and in a mood to forgive those who would never forgive him. "It has been a maxim with me," he reminded himself, "to admit of an easy reconciliation with an enemy and to forego all opportunities of revenge, to recall to remembrance the more pleasing ideas of my friends," disputing Shakespeare's clown.

Eight years had passed since his return home. His book still wasn't done. He hadn't said his piece, found his peace, yet. He struggled on, editing the manuscript section of chapter four that includes the alligator attack in the same ways that he rewrote his chapter on the Alachua Savanna, deleting phrases that burden the text with his deep religiosity—"divine influence," "feathered choir," "divine," "holy," "adoration," and "as a temple or local residence of the divine spirit, and therefore a sacred and awful retreat where to withdraw to worship the divine supreme God"—not to edit God out, but to diminish his imposing presence a bit. He rewrote another assault on mankind for our failure to exercise responsible dominion over animals, as God directed in the first chapter of Genesis. This time, though, the deletions reduce the detail of our failure, but don't soften the message a bit.

That thus [we] by the excellency of our oeconomy and government, not only among ourselves but also in our demeanour toward all creatures, [put under our charge we] may be worthy of [being guides and examples to them, and impress on their understandings a just sense of] the dignity and superiority of our high and distinguished station here on Earth!"

William also removed a long, four-paragraph passage that evokes the sublime in a stately grove of trees. The vastness, extensiveness, and "exalted aspiring stature and elegance" of the oak, cypress, elm, and cedar that "flourish in the sublime regions of the clouds" excite in us "ideas of majesty and excellence" that reveal the true nature of God. Had the passage ended there, it could have been right out of a textbook on the religious and natural sublime, telling the same story told elsewhere in the *Travels*. On those grounds alone, the reverie might have been cut out, as repetitious of others that played the same notes on the same instrument.

This one is different, though, and that is why he left it out. Instead of celebrating nature, it indicts the grand trees for sharing the hubris of great men. These "exalted chiefs of the vegetable order of nature" look down with contempt on "their humbler and lower brethren," but are actually more vulnerable to the tempests that tear them up by their roots and the lightning that strikes them down, which is the basis for a "moral or edifying lecture" on natural humility. Some cypress, like human tyrants, justly "fall victim to their own weakness and folly," but others, divinely appointed to shade those below them, prosper as protectors and guardians of the smaller and weak, just as a great man wisely elected to his position in society keeps his public trust.

The allegory doesn't quite work, as William realized himself. All the grand trees are divinely appointed to their place, there's nothing parallel to democracy that he can discern in the forest, and who's to say which ones betray their trust or how that is done. The story is more sappy than true, but the political message endorsing republican government is there even if William's art failed him in his attempt to identify "vegetable chiefs" comparable to George Washington and George III. Left in, the tale would also create a conflict between the philosophical pilgrim's denunciation of war and this praise of its consequence.

For all his obvious struggle with the manuscript, William did not toil industriously on the book or on anything else. Decades earlier, he confessed in his commonplace book to napping instead of working under his father's trees: "the instant I awakened, I found the garden by my side prepared to plant a parcel of trees and that I had slumbered away the time in which I should have given him direction." He was embarrassed, chides himself gently by entering the facts, fearful perhaps of a parental reprimand, that he wasn't the same master of men as his father, whose patriarchal industry was immortalized by Crève-coeur. The humiliation diminished, but did not disappear. William treasured leisure, accepted his own nature, knew the priceless value of time, and found as much satisfaction in a good garden nap as John did in hewing rock. "The wisdom of learned men cometh by opportunity of leisure and he that hath little business shall become wise," he wrote in the commonplace book during this phase of his life.

It was the solitude of the garden that William still craved, the leisure to remember, to pursue the state "in which the soul freely resigns itself to its own reflections." The words aren't his, but the sentiment is. When he read Johann Georg von Zimmermann's *Solitude* it spoke to his life, what he'd lived and what he had left. Zimmermann anticipated that he'd shock some readers, perhaps most, by suggesting that solitude could be a source of happiness, rather than a punishment or an inspiration for melancholy; indeed, it seemed to him a cure for the melancholic mind. "In Solitude the weight of melancholy is less-ened by the feeblest effort, but the slightest resistance," Zimmermann prescribed; "to men who possess a sensibility too refined, an imagina-tion too ardent, to mix with comfort in the society of the world . . . SOLITUDE is not only desirable, but absolutely necessary." William took copious notes in his commonplace book, not so much because he had learned something new or because he feared forgetting Zimmer-mann's point of view, but because the book justified how he lived, what he needed, why he wouldn't leave the garden again.

I love to recall to my mind the cool and silent scenes of Solitude; to oppose them to the heat and bustle of the world; to meditate on those advantages which the great and good of every age have acknowledged they possess, though perhaps too seldom when grief corrodes the mind, when disease afflicts the body, when the num-ber of our years bends us to the ground; to contemplate, in short, the benign influence of Solitude upon all the troubles of the heart.

That is what William needed, how he sought to heal his troubled heart, by surrendering himself in retirement, "without restraint or limitation, to the guidance of his own ideas," by giving free rein to the "sentiments which his taste, temper, inclination, and genius, inspire."

Simplicity was what William was after. "Be moderate in all thy aims and acquisition[s] with respect to reputation, riches or gratification of the passions," he counseled his nephew Moses. "Be honest and frugal," he advised his nephew James; "be cool and temperate." The connections between William's Quaker upbringing and his advocacy of natural simplicity are obvious, but the contrasts between his lifestyle and that of other Philadelphia Quakers—including his father—are as striking as their shared rhetoric and spiritual heritage. Insolvency made it much easier to live simply, but William also quelled desires to accumulate more. He sought and advised his nephews to seek for themselves what Zimmermann called a "mind independent of human assistances," one that relied "entirely upon the strength of its own powers," real freedom of the interior kind.[4]

The family's dog sensed that William, among all the humans in the household, had gotten life right. It was a large dog, whose lineage is now lost, which found William's pace more comprehensible than that of other people he knew. "This old dog," its master recalled, "from natural fidelity, and a particular attachment, commonly lay down near me, when I was at rest, reading or writing under the shade of a pear-tree, in the garden, near the house."[5] How many hours did they spend like that together, dozing and daydreaming in the light shade while bees buzzed overhead, while William worked on his book, drafted letters to friends, answered queries about nature and Indians, wrote essays about partridges, beetles, his father, birds, vines, and plants?

Friends still wrote to William petulantly in the mid-1780s about letters unanswered for years at a time. Perhaps he was so absorbed in the *Travels* that he couldn't write anything else. By 1786 it was done, at least a draft, but perhaps essentially the text that we now have. There was an aborted attempt to find subscribers for an edition that year. It was a hard time for booksellers, so it's not surprising that the plan fell through or that it was easier five years later to risk such a venture on such a strange text.[6] There was a conflict over whether William's friend Benjamin Smith Barton attempted to wrestle the manuscript from Enoch Story, Jr., the prospective publisher, and spirit it off to Scotland with him for the purpose of publishing it there, perhaps in his own name. Barton hotly denied the elusive accusation, and William forgave and forgot, but the details and the truth are now lost.[7]

The demise of the venture and the recriminations that Story and Barton exchanged must have perplexed William, who had worked so long on the book. Whether this failure threw him into another melancholic state is unclear, since no letter or scrap written by him for almost a year after July 1786 has survived. Perhaps the absence of correspondence or visible work is evidence of a kind. Some time in the fall of 1786, though, when the failure of the publishing venture was already clear, William fell from a tree where he was gathering seeds. He suffered a compound fracture of his right leg, was feared close to death, possibly from infection, and remained physically incapacitated for almost twelve months. The condition of his body was bleak, whatever the state of his mind. "Don't be cast down," a relative wrote, perhaps upon hearing how low William was. Barton tried to get him to draw, hoping that work would lift William's spirits, if not ease the pain in his leg, but William didn't draw the stuffed black squirrel that this friend sent or acknowledge his letter for over six years.[8]

When William wrote, it was to Mary, two years after his near-fatal fall.

> Cousin, don't doubt my assertion, when I tell you that time, vicissitudes of fortune, tribulation, I may say, indeed, the decrepitude of old age, are not sufficient to erase from my mind those impressions which it received during my residence in my uncle's family in North Carolina. Dreams by night or serious reveries by day often present to my imagination striking scenes of past transactions, which occurred to me in your delightful country; and be assured that thou, my cousin, art the foremost pleasing object in these ideal paintings.

I haven't forgotten you, William wants her to know; time hasn't cooled my feelings a bit. Mary had married, though, and there are gentlemanly limits to expressions of affection for a lost love that someone else has already found. "For although our pastimes were of the most innocent and simple nature," he assures Mary and anyone else who might read dishonor into his heart, "such as amuse brothers, sisters and friends, yet they leave sufficient impressions to be often recollected." These were his memories, his reveries, "now that I am grown old," before he turned fifty, a decade earlier than his father would describe himself in this way.[9] The leg, his pain and the limp, aged William a lot; his eyes were already dim; his book was finished, his journeys over, the past was what loomed before him.

William describes his life, awake and asleep, as a dream. "Ideal paintings" are what he has left, such as that of the *Colocasia*, which he drew. It's a surrealistic image, combining William's various ways of seeing into an extraordinary vision from the South, from his past, from nowhere to represent everything that he knows, that he saw, that's still alive in his head. As always, he sketched in ink, an unforgiving medium that allows for no mistakes. The confidence, success, belies the image of a careless man with which John burdened him and that William carried always on his back. He had time and he took it; he let his imagination run, but not wild. The details are as inspiring as the vast theme and specimens that he presents. The flowering nymphaea are huge with a purpose, of displaying nature's details scientifically and within a context that's emotionally true. The crane is much smaller, all out of proportion to the gigantic plants, but plays a role in the same story that William has told us before. A dragonfly perches on a flower, which is perhaps the next meal of the Venus flytrap in the lower left corner; next in nature's consuming plan is the crane, which stalks a small fish that, in turn, is searching for plant life to eat. Plants frame the drawing and even gently challenge the artificial edge that the artist constructs, a leaf on the left side almost imperceptibly escaping the frame. How many hours, how many days, how much serenity such a scene must have consumed and digested; how much sustenance must William have gained from his art.

The letter to Mary overflows with regrets; a litany of misfortunes floods the page. Committing the dreams, "the striking scenes" in his head, to paper helped William through the "cold and frowns of our winters," the darkness that sometimes still plagued his soul. In the dank seasons when his old bones now ached, the memories of an emotional place where "reigns spring eternal" presented themselves to his

William Bartram, Colocasia (Natural History Museum, London)

view and beckoned him back "nearer the meridian," an imaginary line that runs through the earth, William's life, his mind, his *Travels,* his natures, and his art.

There was one mistake, though, which William recognized now—however belatedly—and labored—however inadequately—to address in this, his only surviving letter to Mary.

Please present my regard to all the families of the *Black People;* they were kind and very serviceable to me; I wish it were in my power to reward their fidelity and benevolence to me. I often remember them; these acknowledgement[s] at least, are due from me to them, altho they are Negroes and Slaves.

The time in the garden rehearsing his life was having an effect on William, and a light, however dim, was beginning to dawn. What about the other slaves, the ones he had owned? What would he want to say to them? Did they haunt his dreams, along with the terrors of nature and his other mistakes? Perhaps he hadn't arrived yet at the place of real guilt about slavery—a guilt he implied in later writings. He grew in the garden, in the shade of an apple tree.

William finished the series of fifty-nine drawings that he'd begun for Fothergill. He mounted the last specimens from his travels; forwarded the lot to Robert Barclay and Sir Joseph Banks in his patron's place. This was also in 1788, after he'd finished the *Travels,* the same year that he wrote to Mary, possibly for the last time. What he sought was recognition, the "bare mention of my being the discoverer" of new plants, as his "reward due for traveling several thousand miles mostly amongs't Indian nations, which is not only difficult but dangerous, besides suffering sickness cold and hunger."[10] That seemed only fair, an ambition for just recognition of the risks that he'd taken and the accomplishments that were rightly his. Absorbed as these men now were in receiving and recording the more exotic flora of the East, and as insignificant as this former colonist was in their minds, they never quite got around to cataloguing William's discoveries. William would die without ever getting his due, suffering sorely this slight, this evidence that the world still didn't take seriously anything that he had done in his life.

William continued, nonetheless, to draw and to write for others, principally for his friend Barton, who incorporated the information into publications that furthered his own career. He drew the *Franklinia altamaha*, the tree that he and his father had found in their travels, and in 1789 answered Barton's queries about the Creek and Cherokee Indians. He persisted despite what he described in the letter accompanying his essay on Indians as "my weakness of eyesight," which obliged him "to write the greater part of this with my eyes shut, and that with pain."[11] Vision actually hindered William's ability to see what was now most important to him, memories that he created, rewrote, and redrew.

The past relinquished some of its terrors in this safe haven, helping William capture his youth and tame his middle age. Drawings and writings exorcised the horrors inside, domesticated the most ferocious predators of his mind, confined them to a page, where they shared space with the dreamy scenes and huge plants that filled his head. We can see the struggle and the success in his letter to Mary, where pleasant recollections battle the bad. Now, at last, he can write to his lost love, find words that express feelings without hurting too much. He can stare the likeness of alligators in the face, challenging the nightmares he shares with readers, making them ours. In another fifteen years, more or less, he would be able to write about his father, at the request of his friend Barton. One memory at a time, he would subdue those, too.

William hadn't left nature behind; he didn't even keep it outside. Along with the dog, he had another companion who felt equally at home in the garden and the house. He had raised Tom from infancy, from a "helpless, dependent creature" into a "tractable and benevolent, docile and humble" adult, a bird whose "genius demonstrated extraordinary acuteness, and lively sensations," a crow of prodigious intellect and wit. "He had great talents," William wrote in Tom's biography, published the same year as his remembrance of John.

> When I was engaged in weeding in the garden, he would often fly to me, and, after very attentively observing me in pulling up the small weeds and grass, he would fall to work, and with his strong beak, pluck up the grass; and the more so, when I complimented him with encouraging expressions.[12]

Tom may have helped with the gardening, which he found comprehensible in his own way, but he had a less tolerant attitude toward William's writing, which must have seemed to him both antisocial and odd. The crow had the run of the room, if not of the house; perhaps William left the outside door to the study open, at least in warm weather, creating a portal through which nature's sounds, odors, and creatures could pass. The bird often landed on the desk and made a ruckus designed to draw his friend from the room. He'd try to grab the pen from William's hand; that failing, he'd tug on the spectacles that rested on the human's beak, recognizing the essential agency of these tools in distracting William from their outside play. Tom was so intrigued by the glasses, which sparkled and reflected light, that their owner had to hide them when they weren't on his head.

But, one time, in particular, having left them a moment, the crow being then out of my sight, recollecting the bird's mischievous tricks, I returned quickly, and found him upon the table, rifling my inkstand, books, and paper. When he saw me coming, he took up my spectacles, and flew off with them.

Thus ensued a chase humorous to imagine, with William's rusty gait no match for Tom's flight. From a distance tolerated by the bird, William watched Tom play with his prize for a while at the roots of an apple tree, possibly the same one under which William and his two animal friends would sit, whiling away the hot days. The bird looked around to see if he was observed and then covered the glasses with grass and twigs; when he thought they were adequately hidden, he responded to William's call.

When he had come near me, I ran towards the tree, to regain my property. But he, judging of my intentions, by my actions, flew, and arriving there before me, picked them up again, and flew off with them, into another apple-tree. I now almost despaired of ever getting them again.

The bird remained in the tree with his hard-won prize, chattering in a language that not even William understood. When he alighted this time, Tom was even more cautious than before, less trusting of his senses, which hid the human from him, more determined to bury the shiny treasure where no one could steal it again. Dry leaves, wood chips fetched from a distance, and grass were the materials that Tom used this time; then he flew to a limb where he commanded a view of the surrounding countryside and scouted for spies. William waited him out behind a tree; when Tom flew to the house in search of other prizes, the human hobbled to the grassy grave, lowered himself to all fours, searched with his hands and gently brushed the chips and clippings aside, revealing the essential adornment that aided his eyes. Another morning passed—or was it an afternoon—in which the work of the writer and artist was put aside for more pressing matters that brought him outside. When he arrived at the table for his next meal with grass in his hair, dirt on his elbows, and grass stains on his knees, no one would have thought it odd that Uncle William's hours in the study had ended this way. Had anyone seen him outside stalking a crow from behind a grand oak or chestnut, it would have amused but couldn't possibly have surprised a family that knew him so well.

There were other tensions between Tom and the human with whom he chose to live. The bird's nature led William to physically discipline him. "When he had run to great lengths in mischief," William explained, "I was under the necessity of whipping him; which I did with a little switch." If the ambition surprises, perhaps the method is more curious still. We must picture William Bartram flailing a bird, who responded with "piteous and penitent cries." At least, that's how he interpreted the agonies expressed by the bird.

This isn't the philosophical pilgrim of the *Travels;* it is the man in real life. Even in the book, though, we learn that the majestic creatures William adores were often his next or last meal, and he did sometimes whack a snake. Still and all, William wants to alter the bird's nature, rather than accepting him on his own terms, which speaks to the nature of gardens, where animals, humans, and plants must abandon their wild ways for a bounded existence both safer and more circumscribed than the natural habitats from which all of us once came.

Underlying this enterprise is the vision of other creatures motivated by the same instincts as man. Tom's senses, William writes, "seemed, as in man, to be only the organs or instruments of his intellectual powers, and of their effects, as directed towards the accomplishment of various designs, and the gratification of the passions." The bird needed to be tamed just as William had to tame himself, just as a father, his father, disciplined sons. John favored whacking Indians to secure their "love"; William spanked birds. Such language suggests that John whacked Billy, too, without always securing the desired effect.[13]

Sometimes the crow responded obsequiously; sometimes he stole from the one who whipped him,

such as a pen-knife, or a piece of paper; in this case, he would boast and brag loudly. At other times, he would soon return, and with every token of penitence and submission, approach me for forgiveness and reconciliation. On these occasions, he would sometimes return, and settle on the ground, near my feet, and diffidently advance, with soft-soothing expressions, and a sort of circumlocution; and sit silently by me, for a considerable time. At other times, he would confidently come and settle upon my shoulder, and there solicit my favour and pardon, with soothing expressions, and caressing gesticulations; not omitting to tickle me about the neck, ears, &c.

Tom responded with the same mix of emotions—anger, fear, and penitence—that John probably received from his son. Just as in William's case, rebellion was sometimes the dominant emotion, which the crow, unlike the human, did not try to suppress. Whether the bird's sullen withdrawals reminded William of himself is unclear, but it doesn't seem from William's telling that he ever subdued Tom's passions any more than John had changed his. The crow learned from past mistakes, but not necessarily the lessons that his human "father" wanted to teach. "This bird had an excellent memory," William tells us, and that's undoubtedly true, a memory of spankings that wounded his pride, hurt his feelings, and angered him. Tom became better at protecting himself, at snatching William's material resources, at hiding from him; they also loved each other and shared tender moments in the shade. It was a complicated relationship that William remembered fondly, which is how he recalled his father, too.

Unlike William, Tom "appeared to be influenced by a lively sense of domination (an attribute prevalent in the animal creation)." The crow wasn't tyrannical or cruel, as some humans are, but he aimed to be master of every animal around him, in order to secure his independence and his self-preservation, and for the acquisition and defense of his natural rights. Yet, in general, he was peaceable and social with all the animals about him.

The parallels weren't merely between species, for that sort of simplistic vision of one creature as representative of his kind wasn't the way that William—the man rather than the character in his book—thought about any of us. In writing about Tom, he wasn't "giving an account of the whole race (since I am convinced, that these birds differ as widely as men do from each other, in point of talents and acquirements), but of a particular bird of that species, which I reared from the nest." The crow, the plant, and the Indian were individuals in William's eyes, differing as widely one from the other as they were similar across species lines.

William believed that crows, like all creatures, partake of a universal soul, thereby sharing the "truth or wisdom" upon which the cosmos is built. Humans, to be sure, have a greater portion of understanding, which God can supplement as he sees fit. Like humans, Tom had sensual appetites belonging to "the body or corporeal part of our nature." These passions were subject to the soul's reason, but sometimes had to be subdued. That's what the spanking was intended to accomplish, bring the soul back into dominion over the body. The crow, just like human children and some adults, needed help in a "continual watch" to ensure that the "designs and operation of reason and rectitude" ruled his nature.[14]

The old dog wasn't so fond of Tom as William was; and the crow found him the one creature besides William whom he couldn't conquer or control. For Tom was a jealous creature, fonder of William than he was of anyone, just as the dog chose this particular human above all the others he knew. The hierarchy was natural in William's and the animals' eyes; what wasn't clear to the crow or the dog was which of them was the second in their short chain of being under the apple tree. No sooner did Tom see that the dog was asleep, than

he would be sure to pinch his lips, and pluck his beard. At length, however, these bold and hazardous achievements had nearly cost him his life: for, one time, the dog being highly provoked, he made

so sudden and fierce a snap, that the crow narrowly escaped with
his head.

The lessons that William took from observing these creatures with
whom he shared food and shade were about the similarities of intellect, passion, logic, and action across species lines. By watching them
he learned what he already knew from his years in the wilderness, in
the garden, at family meals listening to his father, reading his father's
journals, and writing his own book. The crow was another case to
illustrate the same point, perhaps to convince others who still hadn't
the humility or wisdom derived from a knowledge of nature wild and
tamed. The examples seemed "endless" that illustrate the temperamen-
tal affinities among us, to "recount instances of this bird's understanding, cunning, and operations, which, certainly, exhibited incontestible
demonstrations of a regular combination of ideas, premeditation,
reflection, and contrivance."

When he read Gilbert White's *Natural History,* William was
struck by a passage describing baby squirrels that were mothered by a
cat.[15] White's understanding of this event is that such acts of adoption
in the animal world are a function of confusion, that the cat, for some
reason, believed the squirrels to be her own offspring. No, William
argued, fitting this example into his larger philosophy about the similar natures of all animals—including crows, dogs, and men—the
behavior was a consequence of compassion and empathy.

> I have often seen with the greatest delight several kinds of small
> birds feeding the young of other kinds or species, that have been
> abandoned, even sometimes when their own young were yet under
> their care in a helpless state. From these and many other circum-
> stances and occurrences, which daily fall under the notice of an
> accurate observer, if we could entirely divest ourselves of prejudice
> and love in favour of our own species, so as to judge and decide
> impartially and freely, it evidently appears that the animal creation
> are endowed with the same passions and affections we are and that
> their affections operate after the same manners.

William had long ago "divested" himself of inordinate love of his own
species and this comparative disdain for people is acknowledged in the

one exception to his rule about universal passions. As William always suspected, found in his wilderness travels, and now confirmed in the garden, the violent nature of humans is unique, surpassing anything he ever saw, read, or heard about animals in their natural state. In the same passage of a draft letter where he ruminated about the cat and the squirrels, William concluded "it is too true, I fear, that the malicious order abound[s] and predominate[s] in man. Not only in their actions among one another, but towards the animal creation."[16] In the last line, he even "others" man by seeming to exclude himself from "their" offensive passion. The leap he didn't make, then, and that few humans ever have, is to lay some blame for our "unnatural" violence on his own fathering instincts. William didn't realize that he was teaching his crow violence, making him a more aggressive creature than the bird naturally was, by beating him.

William doesn't say whether the crow, when he stole paper, ever escaped with a sheet upon which he'd already written, a page of an essay, a letter, or of his book, a sketch in progress or a hand-colored flower painstakingly completed. Somehow, though, through all the distractions, the injuries, and William's wounded emotions and mind, the *Travels* finally appeared in the fall of 1791. He finally had a copy in his hand, which undoubtedly thrilled before it horrified him. He was humiliated by all the typos, by the errors that he or the publisher should have caught. After all his work, the book was so far from perfect, from done, from what he'd wanted; a sense of failure must have flooded over him once again. It didn't help a bit—probably made it worse—to know the mistakes are ones that a careful proofreading would have caught, ones that he could have prevented *if* he weren't his old incautious self. Whatever he dreamed for the book wouldn't be realized in his own time. He made a list of mistakes, much shorter than the errata sheet of his life that he kept inside his head. Couldn't he ever get just one thing right? The rage must have returned, whether or not the depression again swept over him.

William had hoped that the book would be a work of art, a scientific handbook, a guide to the emotions that nature evokes. He drew more pictures than the publisher would include and meticulously hand-colored six flowers, each standing alone, designed for a larger-size format than the printer used. Perhaps the flowers were for the 1786 publication, which would have been a grander book. Now, though, he had one volume specially bound with the colorful flora sewn in just for him. He treasured this book, pasted his errata sheet in the back, creating one private copy, at least, which approached what he had wanted to share with the world.[17]

Then, in 1799, two months after he turned sixty, William gave his special copy away. Why make a gift of his work at that chronological crossroad in his life, at the same age when John wrote a letter of advice to his children, when William's culture would now agree with his self-assessment as "old"? If he'd made a calculated decision to rid himself of the book, why didn't he present it to one of his nephews, his niece, or a closer friend? William Hamilton, to whom he gave the book, was even older than William, so this wasn't an act of legacy, of passing his words down to a generation that would survive him. Hamilton may have been a father figure; he was a good family friend, fellow gardener, and owner of the Woodlands, an impressive estate just upriver from the Bartrams.

Given William's casualness toward possessions, perhaps now even toward life, the act could have been a whim. Perhaps Hamilton asked for a copy, couldn't find one to purchase, or praised William's work. Maybe either or both of the men liked the London edition of 1792 even less than the first, with its redrawn frontispiece, prints shuffled around in the text, and the editor's tinkering with William's writing style, consistently shortening his sentences and substituting the past for the author's present tense. Possibly William didn't appreciate having his spelling and grammar corrected, transformed into a style more English than American, in what one twentieth-century critic has termed the taming of the book's wild prose. However casual such a decision about giving away his special copy may appear, we can be sure that in ways William may not have understood, he relinquished attachments to more than just one more worldly thing when he passed his book on. Which isn't to say that he wasn't looking forward, because he still was.[18]

Back in January 1790, William had begun a meteorological diary, listing the dates through December 1791 in the margins at the outset, and then returning each day to enter what he felt and saw. He measured the temperature and barometric pressure at sunrise and at two in the afternoon. The method shows his modeling on the science that his father, Barton, Franklin, and Jefferson also practiced. Comparative precision was still the point. John kept such records for Peter Kalm after the Swedish botanist left him the tools that a numerate scientist needs. The idea was for curious men to take readings over a number of years, in order to compare regions and change over time. There is no point to beginning such a project if you don't plan to be around for a while. William would keep his diary somewhat differently than the other men, though to the same ends.[19]

William would record in an apparently dispassionate shorthand how the weather felt to him. The vocabulary on which he drew again turns a scientific endeavor into something more, a blend of two visions filtered through a unique mind. "Cloudy. Clear blows fresh" tells us more than it seems. "Cloudy like for snow, Ice driving in the River, Snow and sleet, rain," isn't the "objective" summary of a day that it appears or that William probably thought it to be. The language of gentle rain, fresh blowing wind, calm, uncommon darkness, flying clouds, lowering, squally, blustering, broken clouds reveals William's artistry, his visual impressions of the world around him. References to the sky predominate, which may seem an obvious focus for a weather diary, but it speaks as clearly to the sweep of his eyes, which still looked myopically heavenward.

The entries become less descriptive in April 1791. The observations are now often confined to two words representing the beginning and the end of William's day—"clear . . . . clear" (the ellipses are his), "hazy . . . . . hazy," varying by one the number of dots that define the passage of time, revealing once more that he had a constitutional inability to do most anything the same way twice, "cloudy . . . . . hazy" and "foggy . . . . clear" showing that some days got better as they went on. The handwriting was becoming larger, more hurried, sloppier still in September, with some days defined by only one word—"cloudy" or "clear"—with no change noted at all. The last entry, on September 13, 1791, is "clear clear."

Then he stops. It's not a coincidence that William becomes more agitated, less focused, as the publication of his book approaches or that the event of holding his life's work in his hand doesn't calm him, permitting a return to the old routine. He's upset, perhaps angry, possibly again depressed. Upon its arrival, such a long-anticipated event as publication of the *Travels* is profoundly disappointing to him. As William Styron explains, what for most people are the celebratory occasions of life can provoke unfathomable pain for the chronically depressed. It's possible that William cannot even look at the botched job without experiencing the agony of its imperfection, which we know he shared with family and friends. So, before the decade ends, he gives Hamilton the special copy with hand-colored prints, because— whether he knows it or not—William wants the book out of his life. He values another personal copy so little that he uses its line drawings as a practice coloring book for his niece, when teaching her the art of hand-coloring prints for which she later labors for pay. Perhaps this copy becomes Nancy's rather than his.[20]

In an April 1791 letter to Barton, William describes himself "like an old saw, or auger, or ax, worn out, rusty and cast away as useless." That's the way the world sees him, treats him, how he feels, but he knows that even such "rejected instruments after being new steeled and repaired may again be preferred to some useful purpose or other," so he has great hopes for the book. He seems sad, if resigned, before the *Travels* appears, before he sees it as a mess, before others react cruelly to his words.

One reviewer of the *Travels* was favorably impressed overall, call-ing the book a "respectable" work of science. He could have done with-out the "rhapsodical effusions," which were distractions from the facts, and he lost patience with all the details about nature's commonplace inhabitants. He especially liked the lists of Latin plant names. Science should be focused on the novel and be stylistically spare; philosophers weren't men who wasted words. William failed to affect this reader emotionally, to alter his sympathies for snakes and bears, to scare and enchant, or to engage him in a new way of experiencing what we see every day. "We are sorry," the reviewer continued critically,

> to be under the necessity of finding fault with the style of an author who has afforded us so much useful information and agree-able entertainment; but we cannot with any propriety countenance a style so very incorrect and disgustingly pompous, as that in which the greater part of these travels is written.

Incorrect, disgusting, and pompous, those words would hurt a writer with thicker skin than William, one who had revealed and invested less of himself on each page, who had experienced more success and less rejection in his life. To a man with William's hard-won self-image as a plain Quaker and philosophical man of feeling, a pilgrim to nature in search of nature's God, the particular choice of words must have wounded more deeply than we can know.

And yet, the critic liked the book. William may not even have noticed that this reader was pleased by the "many useful and curious facts contained in the work, as well as with the ingenious observations of our enterprising and philosophic traveller," that he was simply disturbed by the "garb in which they appear." Again, an attack on the Quaker author's clothes is an assault on the essence of his being; the "secondary considerations" of the reviewer were primary to William. The man failed to comprehend the very nature of the enterprise and, what's more, he thought that the author "magnifies the virtues of the Indians," calling into question William's veracity, another direct challenge to the philosophical pilgrim's Quakerly pose.[21]

Other reviewers liked the book less for many of the same reasons; the style offended, the Indians were not what the readers expected, required them to be, the landscapes were too commonplace to merit such detailed accounts, the book was too passionate, too emotionally inflamed for the genre of scientific travelers' accounts. One critic was particularly incensed by the author's affection for "rude nature," denouncing what he read as William's antidevelopmental stance.

This is a similar prejudice with that of a staunch antiquary, who would at any time oppose a new improvement to preserve a favourite ruin, which stood in the way of its execution: but such fanciful superstition ought not to impede the accommodation of growing population: for, beside the motives for clearing forests, of which Mr. B. thinks so little, he must be philosopher enough to know that such extensive groves are injurious to the climate, which the arts of clearing and cultivation render drier and more salubrious. The savage alone might be expected to lament the loss of his hunting grounds; and if he be thus driven to betake himself to any kind of agriculture, he is made a more sociable and useful being by the alteration. On such a continent, there will always be groves enough for the botanist; who, if his researches tend to useful purposes . . . will exhaust them before they severally disappear. Swamps, crocodiles, other wild beasts of prey, snakes, lizards, musquitoes, rank grass, weeds, and all their putridity, are unfriendly to man, and the enumeration of them is not very inviting to adventurers.[22]

This was the future, as well as the past; this is the view of nature and man that Thoreau and Muir would later rail against. The conflicting ways that William and this anonymous reviewer saw things represent the fissure that we now know so well, between development and preservation, among perceptions of natural beauty, alternative priorities, different notions of practicality, and contrasting predictions for what will come next. The conflict that John didn't see, didn't feel, but toward which William gropes in the *Travels* is starkly revealed in reactions to the book's emotional celebration of nature just as it was. This reviewer, among other readers and those who didn't buy, borrow, or even open the book because it seemed so naive, so unreliable, so challenging to the ways that they acted in nature, didn't see the developmental tensions that are more visible now, didn't notice that William happily imagined clear-cutting some places and saw other locales, such as the Alachua Savanna, which he wished would never be disturbed by the "rude hand" of man. There was no compromise in the reviewer's mind, in the culture's collectively, no safe place in nature, no pellucid ponds where the battle over development could achieve a truce. That would take education, greater knowledge, disastrous mistakes, and other artists, naturalists, and scientists to argue William's view differently.

William was not a natural, a radical, a revolutionary, or a hermit; he had cut down his share of trees, killed his allotment of snakes, eaten his fill of bears, venison, and beef. He was a moderate man of the garden who felt misunderstood, an artist with a keen visual sense, a romantic sensibility, a love of nature, and a wild imagination imbued with emotionality. He was an old man with weak eyes, who had lived and become wiser. He just wanted to share what he knew with others, draw, write, and be left alone.

In 1793, William finally drew Barton's stuffed squirrel, a sign that he had recovered his focus after being shaken. The Darby Library was grateful for the donated copy of his book; some people liked it, came to see him because they had read and admired his work, saw him as a remarkable person, whom they wanted to touch. They arrived uninvited, unannounced, with questions that were sometimes an excuse for stopping by, for those who were affected by the *Travels* were drawn more emotionally than intellectually to its human source. Whether they knew it themselves or not, what they really wanted was a blessing rather than another dose of facts.[23] The novelist Charles Brockden Brown and his theatrical friend William Dunlap made such a pilgrimage to the pilgrim on a spring day. They woke at sunrise and decided to walk from the city and cross the river by boat.

Arrived at the Botanist's Garden, we approached an old man who, with a rake in his hand, was breaking the clods of earth in a tulip bed. His hat was old and flapped over his face, his coarse shirt was seen near his neck, as he wore no cravat or kerchief; his waistcoat and breeches were both of leather, and his shoes were tied with leather strings. We approached and accosted him. He ceased his work, and entered into conversation with the ease and politeness of nature's noblemen. His countenance was expressive of benignity and happiness. This was the botanist, traveller, and philosopher we had come to see.[24]

Others were less polite, demanding a tour, expecting to be entertained. "I confess," wrote Henry Wansey, "I was much disappointed, to find so little to look at. One of my companions joking the old gentleman about the alligators that he had formerly fought with, he became so reserved, that we could get but little conversation with him."[25] The insults would always hurt; William knew that some people still laughed at him. His response, withdrawal into himself, was consistent with the man he now was, an old man who wasn't even safe from the world's barbs in the garden to which he had withdrawn long ago.

Then he bounced back once again, regained his sense of humor about life, about himself, feeling healthy and describing his sight as "pretty good." He even felt restless, he wrote to an old friend.

Since I have recovered my health and the free use of my limbs, my inquisitive and restless inclinations for the enjoyment of new scenes in the magnificent operations and exhibitions of nature has often excited me to attempt other discoveries.

He did go so far as Philadelphia, delivering trees for his brother the following year, which must have been arduous duty if he did more than supervise workers who unloaded the wagon and buried the roots in the earth. Before nightfall, he was back again.[26]

In 1797, still feeling fit, William began a new commonplace book, which collected facts about nature, recipes for herbal cures culled from travelers' accounts and from the reports of friends, and wisdom about life that he had acquired over the years. He also used the same notebook for personal record keeping—his niece Nancy borrowed two dollars and then paid back one—recording Bible passages, cures for hydrophobia, rheumatism, and other sundry afflictions, and a fitful stab at a new garden diary, which lasted for six consecutive days in 1801, then one final entry the following month. A description of a hawk, comments on a mouse, some further ruminations about the similarities of human and animal souls, lists of plants, and copies of several parables complete the effort into 1802 with blank pages left.[27]

As the new century began, William was again at work drawing, ultimately twenty-four of twenty-seven plates, for Barton's *Elements of Botany*. An unspecified illness forced a respite in the summer of 1801, but he returned to the task in late August. Rather than sapping his energies, William believed that the labor added greatly to his "pleasure and health." Then in October his eyes gave out again. "My dear friend," the disappointed artist wrote, "the exceeding painfulness and weakness in my eyes prevents me that pleasure and indeed I am fearful I shall no more be able to make poor drawings for your amusement."[28]

By the spring of 1802, William was sufficiently recovered to search the woods near his home for some plants that Barton wanted and to write an essay on grapevines, which an editor had requested of him. He also took ninety-one pages of notes on insects, which he illustrated with a drawing of twenty-one bugs at the beginning of the book. This is also the year he began his longest sustained endeavor, the garden diary that he stopped working on two decades later, six months before his death. At age sixty-three, William was still curious about nature in all of its parts, still working, apparently as hard as ever before, perhaps now in greater solitude, with the dog and the crow long since gone.[29]

What we see in all these writings from William's garden years are insights into the temper of a life led outside the bustle of politics and trade, somewhere between the urban and wilderness settings that served as stages for the great men of his time. By this point in his life, I could call him an eighteenth-century Thoreau who had found his Walden Pond on the banks of the Schuylkill. However, it makes more sense to see Thoreau as a nineteenth-century heir to William Bartram's naturalistic legacy.

The parallels between the lives of our first two great natural historians are instructive. Neither was a scientist. Both were Romantics. Each considered himself a failure in the eyes of the world. They both experienced a prolonged adolescence plagued by identity struggles; neither ever did secure a living, settle into a career, or marry. Each had just one, unconsummated romance. Both kept journals and revised their lives through their writings. Popular appreciation of their work came after death. Although there may be some coincidence in the parallels—both their fathers were named John—the leisured isolation that is the core of their artful engagement with nature was a product of rejection, flight, and a prolonged return to the environs of their youths. Neither could make it in the urban world of commerce or, for that matter, in the wilderness open to men of enterprise in each of their times. Bartram and Thoreau fled to rural settings from which they celebrated the wilds and denounced the civilized life.[30]

The meaning of William's life was in the days, as was true for Thoreau's sojourn at Walden, and not in accomplishments and events. As William himself said, in a passage of his commonplace book immediately following the account of his nap, with words that sound Thoreauvian to those who haven't heard Bartram before,

> The works of a person that builds begin immediately to decay; while those of him who plants begin directly to improve. In this planting promises a more lasting pleasure than building.

There would be no peripatetic construction for William, no quest to define himself by building a mansion on a hill, like Jefferson, or on a cliff, like Washington, with a superintending view that asserts human dominance over nature. William was no nation builder, either, as were the delegates to the Constitutional Convention and officials of the new federal government that they created, those who toured the garden and sought his advice about making plants grow. He would not try to capture nature's elements with a kite or in a bottle, like John's good friend Benjamin Franklin, who offered to make William a printer half a century before. He did not share the ambitions of Charles Willson Peale to confine nature in a cabinet, of Alexander Wilson to capture an entire species in a book, of Benjamin Rush to alter nature's biological course, of Benjamin Smith Barton to achieve fame through his writings about nature, or of Charles Brockden Brown to plumb the darker side of human nature in various settings.

William knew all these men, who, with the exception of Franklin, visited him in his retirement. The garden became an intellectual salon in which he was sought out by the great men of politics, science, and literature. William, in his role as a local wise man, was even the subject of Federalist satire, as the philosopher of the Schuylkill in Benjamin Silliman's Shahcoolen letters, where he is portrayed as a Republican anarchist who advocated return to a state of nature. Whether there was, in fact, a partisan slant to William's associations seems more a product of shared temperaments than of politics in the more literal sense, although he did attend at least one Republican political meeting late in his life, long after the Federalists and the federal government had left Philadelphia for good.[31]

In any event, although William shared his knowledge and wisdom with Republicans and Federalists alike, he wasn't one of them. His ambitions were more personal, his battles more inner-directed, his tasks more sensual—a plant nurtured, a bird observed, a hole dug, another nap taken on the lawn, honey collected, a pear picked and eaten on the spot, a tree admired for its beauty, with no thought to its utility, a day savored for its serenity—and performed at a more leisurely pace than was the norm in the bustling world of the great public men of his day. His satisfactions were becoming simpler, more spiritual, more natural he would say, but whether his days were less fruitful, his life less meaningful, his thoughts any less wise than those of his peers is a judgment that each of us must make for her- or himself.

One difference, to be sure, between William and the great men who sought him out in the garden was his largely successful quest to subdue ambition. While Franklin claims, unconvincingly, in his *Autobiography* to have vanquished his appetites, William's later writings suggest that the struggle was real, the setbacks significant, but the conquest of personal ambition is one in which he rightly took pride. "Ambition," he cautioned himself in his commonplace book, "eager in the pursuit of riches and power what oceans of blood hast it not shed." "Envy and avarice, the grand enemies to human happiness. . . . Let us . . . discountenance superfluities, avarice, ambition and inordinate gratifications," he pleaded in a passage that he excised from the *Travels*, perhaps because it seemed too preachy even for him.[32]

According to William, the closer we are to nature, the closer we come to achieving our best selves. Avarice, book learning, and cities begin his alphabet of vices, and ambition stands at the head of his list of cardinal sins. "O may those unviolated retreats ever remain in their present state of youthful innocence," he wrote of Florida's pine forests,

> unpolluted by the violent hand of invidious industry, avarice, and ambition, false politeness, and cruel civilization, which refines and sublimates humanity quite away leaving in its place a subtle, restless firey spirit, a malicious powerful principle, continually watching to enslave mankind and destroy the happiness of a future state.[33]

It was failure that quenched William's appetites in a way that success never satiated his father or even Franklin. Living, as William did, one step ahead and two steps behind his contemporaries made for an uncomfortable fit in the public world of the Founding Fathers. Failure as a merchant and planter led to flight, exploration, and ultimately withdrawal, which, in turn, contributed to a self-discovery that he otherwise would never have enjoyed and the articulation of his unique vision of the natural world, which he would never have written and we would have missed.

Intimately related to William's battle against ambition were his efforts to shed the personal possessions by which people generally define who we are. The great men of his day, including his father, were accumulators on a grand scale—of books, correspondence, and an incalculable array of other objects. William was notable for his disposal of things, giving away books, drawings, knowledge, essays, and good advice. When he died, William owned his clothing, which fit in two chests, the feather bed and bolster on which he slept, two glasses and a tray, a tin letter box, some books, and a purse with some cash.[34]

His destination had long been clear to William. He knew the pit-
falls; he knew the right paths. The journey was a long, difficult one, but
he was making progress.

> Be sure your bosom be serene;
> Devoid of hate devoid of strife
> Devoid of all that poisons life
> And much it 'vails you in their place
> To graft the love of human race.

This crude poem was one of the first things he ever wrote in his commonplace book, when he was young. Serenity continued to be the goal
in his mid-forties and long after that, the measure of accomplishment
and shortfall that he could feel inside. Self-knowledge is an essential
step, since the journey to serenity begins and ends inside our hearts.
"To know ourselves is to know what sort of creatures we are, what is
our duty and business and what we shall be," William wrote, drawing
upon both classical Roman wisdom and the Bible to sustain, to deepen
his own insights. We are composed of three parts, as William understood himself and the rest of us,

> the body, which is the earthly or mortal part of him; the soul which
> is the animal or sensitive part; and the spirit or mind which is the
> rational and immortal part. . . . A man acts becoming himself,
> when he keeps these three separate parts employ[ed] in their
> proper functions and preserves their natural harmony.

What he gained from such self-exploration was a knowledge of his
weaknesses, which he'd discovered in his plantation swamp and in the
other failures of his adult life. "He that take[s] up a burden that is too
heavy for him," William learned painfully, "is in a fair way to break his
back." "In every business consider first what it is you are about," he
advised himself, "and then your own abilities, whether they are sufficient to carry you through it." That's the inspiration for William's
refusal during his last forty-seven years to venture very far from the
garden, to take on burdens that he thought too great, to plunge out of
his depth. He had declined to lecture on botany, perhaps because he
was shy, to travel great distances into the wilderness, believing himself

physically and perhaps emotionally too frail. He had wanted to write his one book, draw, and share with others what he knew about nature; continue to till, think, and observe; and focus his internal resources on the important task of improving himself.

William also remained willing, indeed eager by all accounts, to help others find their bliss, too. In his mid-sixties, William took on a protégé, the Scottish poet, schoolteacher, and now neighbor Alexander Wilson, who wanted to learn how to draw birds. Wilson had no training in art or in nature. "If from the rough draughts here given you can discover what birds they are," Wilson wrote his teacher about one of the many sketches he sent for criticism, "please to give me their names. Any advice for their amendment from you will be truly welcome." Wilson was nothing if he wasn't diligent and sincere. He struggled to capture a rose bush with his pen, but "I have murdered your roses," he wrote in despair. He drew them over and over again.[35]

Wilson found himself transformed in the garden, under the tutelage of the gardener whose company he now kept. "I confess," he wrote to William on a day when they were apart,

> that I was always an enthusiast in my admiration of the rural scenery of Nature; but, since your example and encouragement have set me to attempt to imitate her productions, I see new beauties in every bird, plant, or flower, I contemplate; and find my ideas of the incomprehensible First Cause still more exalted, the more minutely I examine His work.
>
> I sometimes smile to think that while others are immersed in deep schemes of speculation and aggrandizement—in building towns and purchasing plantations, I am entranced in contemplation over the plumage of a lark, or gazing like a despairing lover, on the lineaments of an owl.

Wilson worked with a master, who instructed him in the ways of nature, of seeing nature, of valuing the truly valuable in the world. "While others are hoarding up their bags of money," the acolyte continued, showing that he had learned his lessons well, "without the power of enjoying it, I am collecting, without injuring my conscience, or wounding my peace of mind, those beautiful specimens of Nature's works that are forever pleasing."[36]

There was also a romance blossoming in the garden, between Wilson and Nancy—which is what the family called William's niece Ann. Notes from Wilson to William were ostensibly about pictures, but were also occasions to share his admiration for Nancy, whom he transformed into "Anna" for his poetic tributes.

> O dear to my heart in this deep shaded Bower
>> this snug little seat and this smooth Beechen Tree
> These old hoary Cliffs through the bushes that tower
>> And bend o'er the pool their resemblance to see
> The fountains the Grotto the Laurels sweet blossom
>> The streamlet that warbles to soothing and free
> Green solitude! dear to the Maid of my bosom
>> And so for her sake ever charming to me.
>
> Here seated with Anna what bliss so transporting
>> I wish every moment an age were to be
> Her taste so exalted—her humour so sporting
>> Her heart full of tenderness virtue and glee
> Each evening sweet Bow'r round thy cliffs will I hover
>> In hopes her fair form thro' the foliage to see
> Heav'n only can witness how dearly I love her
>> How sweet Beachen Bower thy shades are to me.[37]

The role of William in this aborted romance is implied rather than asserted in the surviving correspondence, but since family tradition recalls that it was Ann's father who dismissed the poet as a poor match, there is good reason to suspect that Uncle William was the young lovers' principal ally. As "Anna's" father watched the young schoolmaster with few prospects come under William's sway, he may have feared a future resembling his brother's past. Like his father and namesake, John Jr. wouldn't want such a life for his child, for any child, whom he dearly loved.

When he wrote his poem "A Rural Walk," in 1804, Wilson still dreamed that he could capture nature with his pen and Ann with his heart. The poem is again set in the garden and gives the reader a tour that links nature, romance, and God in ways visibly influenced by William's view of the world.

> The summer sun was riding high,
> The woods in deepest verdure drest,
> From care and clouds of dust to fly,
> Across yon bubbling brook I past.

The sounds, sights, and smells greet the traveler along his path with sublime scenes and a tortoise "in yellow coat of mail encas'd," as he reaches the chosen spot. There, he finds "the genius of this charming scene," tending nature's plot.

> To science, peace, and virtue dear,
> And dear to all their noble friends,
> Tho' hid in low retirement here,
> His generous heart for all expands.

This man who knows every flower's name, who risked his life to bring them to this charming setting, now nurtures everyone.

> And here their blooming tribes he tends,
> And tho' revolving winters reign,
> Still spring returns him back his friends,
> His shades and blossom'd bowers
> again.

It is not only William whom the poet celebrates, for there's "one flower, one sweet and faithful flower, worth all the blossom'd wilds can give." The woman who graces this scene so dear to Wilson's heart, which longs to call "that lovely plant his own," was not, he soon knew, to be his.[38] William and Ann would continue to help Wilson with his projects, an encyclopedia revision and his monumental *American Ornithology*, for which Ann hand-colored prints and her uncle advised. By 1813, the project was complete, the last volume in press, and the poet was dead. "Anna" had married the printer Robert Carr, a

man with prospects, who pursued a career that William might have
had for himself. Just as William's late father predicted, though, the
trade wouldn't bring prosperity to Carr's family.

William endured, outliving not only Wilson, but his brother John,
his friend Barton, and his nephew James. He was still, in the second
decade of the nineteenth century, "much laughed at in Georgia,"
among other places, for his alligators and "dubious" plants. With no
living specimens from his travels in the garden, he couldn't prove what
he had seen. He had outlived the seeds that he had collected; the
bushes and flowers were no longer his. The *Travels* was hard to come
by, so it seemed that William had outlived even his book.[39]

However, he lived on long enough that others began to retrace
his steps, locating rare plants that only he had seen. Curious men
who traveled through the swamps and savannas recognized that the
Travels could be used as a guide. "I have found his *Lantana Camara,
Crinum,* and a few others," William Baldwin reported, "not since
noticed by any botanist." "Could I only see a huge 'magnanimous'
rattlesnake," Baldwin wrote later, "it would help out my story very
much. During 5 years that I have been in this southern country, I
have seen but one living rattlesnake! But, had not Bartram been here
before me, I would astonish you with my account of the Alligators."
Vindication came slowly, glacially it must have seemed, but it was
coming at last.[40]

The Indians were now, in 1817, "far from numerous" and "no object
of dread," as they had been in William's day. In some quarters, sympathy for the Indians grew from mounting disgust for the way they had
been treated by "savage" whites. Baldwin found William's "authority"
good, contrary to the general suspicion for over a quarter century, and
couldn't wait to visit him upon his return.

> Though far advanced in the vale of years, I found him in the pos-
> session of good health; and all the faculties of his mind were as
> brilliant as in the morning of life. So pleased was he with the little
> details I gave him of East Florida, and so interested was I in the
> information which he was capable of affording me, that we parted
> with great reluctance, and mutual wishes for a further and more
> intimate acquaintance. Such, he informed me, was his partiality

for that delightful country, that he often fancied himself transported thither in his dreams by night. My being able to confirm several of his doubtful plants, was extremely gratifying to him; and he wished most anxiously that I would return and find others of them, before he descended to the grave. Aware of the suspicions which some entertain of his veracity, it was truly a feast to me to observe how his time-worn countenance brightened up at the vindication of his character, which I informed him I was prepared to offer. By this visit I am prepared to make his *Lantana Camara* a new species, without hesitation.[41]

One of William's most beautiful finds was now named after him, prospered in the garden, and graced the frontispiece of a botanical book that acknowledged his contributions to science. The plate was drawn by his dear niece and student, who was now an accomplished artist herself. Baldwin says that William "brightened"; I suspect that he glowed upon hearing the younger botanist's confirmation of his discoveries. He needed, somewhat desperately, for others to be rediscovered, too, which is why he begged Baldwin to go back again. "Mr. Bartram's still living," another botanist reported in 1818.

He resides at Kingsess gardens, where he hallows by his venerable appearance, and graces by his instructive converse and simple manners, the seat founded and supported by his family. He is one of the most unambitious lovers of nature I have ever seen.

How those words must have warmed William in the cold days ahead, when he read them or Nancy read them aloud in the copy of a book that the author sent him. An "unambitious lover of nature" is, after all, what he wanted to be, what others valued now in the man whom he was.[42]

William was still working in his seventy-eighth year, as a newspaper advertisement placed by Ann's husband proclaimed: "Fresh American Seeds, FOR SALE, at Bartram's Botanic Garden." Thus the ad beckoned prospective buyers to visit the house that John had built. One of the attractions was the venerable presence that customers would find there, whose role in their purchases enhanced the value, at least in the seller's eyes.

The Seeds have been carefully collected, and put up, under the immediate inspection of Mr. WILLIAM BARTRAM, and are warranted fresh and genuine. Each box contains four hundred species, with the generic and specific names affixed, and directions for their culture.[43]

This, too, was a vindication of sorts. Who would have thought, at least earlier in his life, that William's supervision would have counted for much? Certainly not the laborer whom he supervised by napping under a tree or his father, who saved him from snakes, creditors, himself, and from the swamp. Now, his knowledge and care were what distinguished the garden's produce. By living his way, the only way that he could, he had changed how people thought about him. He was a scientist and gardener of renown, revered for his demeanor and spirituality as much as he was for what he knew and the plants that he had found. Soon, but not soon enough to make a difference to him, William will also be discovered by Coleridge, Wordsworth, Emerson, and Thoreau; he'll become a literary figure, whose emotions in nature reveal to others great Truths.

Conclusion

THERE'S A PORTRAIT OF WILLIAM, but just one, and it's undoubtedly him. In his mid-sixties, the sage of the Schuylkill sat for Charles Willson Peale, who captured his subject's nature well. Gray, thinning hair, eyes averted modestly, his father's aquiline nose, ruddy-faced from time spent out of doors, a benign figure, kindly—one who's lived and has two decades to go. The only controversy about this portrait is the flower in William's lapel. Botanists have struggled over its name, unsure that it even exists. Perhaps the artist cunningly gave us two of nature's unique creations, William and a fictitious blossom, neither of which can be replaced. The portrait now hangs in Independence National Park, near the Liberty Bell and Independence Hall, two doors South of the building where the Free Quakers met, and across from the American Philosophical Society—of which William was a member, but whose meetings he never left his garden to attend.[1]

There's a body in the garden somewhere, even if William is not buried there. As a newspaper obituary reported in October 1820, when William still had a few years to live,

> DIED, on the morning of the 6th inst. in Bartram's woods, Kingsessing township, five miles from Philadelphia, JACK SNAKE, an Indian chief, one of the nine Cherokees travelling from Philadelphia to their nation. He is said to have been a warrior under Gen. Jackson, and fought at the celebrated battle of Horse Shoe. A coffin was procured and he was decently buried by the

Charles Willson Peale, William Bartram
(Independence National Historical Park Collection)

neighbors; at the request of his companions, his bow, arrows, &c. were buried with him, according to the custom of the nation.[2]

We can only wonder what brought Jack Snake to the banks of the Schuylkill to die. Perhaps he'd met William some time in the past, maybe during Puc-Puggy's travels, heard that the garden was a good place to camp, that a man lived there who would treat him well, who had written admiringly of his people a long time ago. Whether or not it's ironic, it's certainly poetically just that Snake died on a farm

259

purchased with money inherited from a man his ancestors had killed. After all the dangers faced by the Bartrams in the wilderness that was once this Indian's home, he was buried in a garden within sight of the house that John built.

The exact location of Snake's grave is unknown. He's believed, though, to rest beneath an apartment complex called Bartrams Gardens, which is anything but a garden or representative of what the Bartrams once were. The low, red-brick buildings are on the other side of the railroad tracks from John's house, tracks that run less than one hundred yards from where the Bartram family lived. The apartments are part of the human/industrial ghetto that surrounds what's left of the gardens, which are accessible to those who seek the solitude of an urban park down its paved paths. What visitors leave behind is about what you would expect, the detritus of a culture that doesn't always value the trees or ourselves. Snake is buried in a place as "unnatural" as humans can devise and more dangerous to living creatures than the wilderness ever was.

At least one person who lived at the time was profoundly moved by Snake's demise. An anonymous poet saw the tragedy of a whole people buried in his earthen tomb. "The present condition of the Aborigines of this country is specially fitted to awaken the sympathy of every feeling heart," the poet said. As we know, this was untrue two decades earlier and was wishful thinking at the time Jack Snake died. "The Cherokee's Grave" testifies to the sadness that William, too, could have felt.

> Calm by thy slumbers thou heart broken stranger,
> And downy the hillock which pillows thy head,
> The grave is a refuge from sorrow and danger,
> Where wrong and oppression pursue not the dead:
> Though far from thy cabin, thy kindred, and nation.
> Unwept and unhonour'd thy relics repose,
> Ere sleep with her poppies shall steal o'er creation.[3]

The world was moving, changing as William stood still. Even as it was becoming less recognizable to him, his values and feelings were drifting closer to the mainstream.

A bookmark preserved in one of William's personal copies of the

Travels addresses some of the same themes—life, death, violence, injustice, nature, and man. Torn from a newspaper, it's a poem that reflects sublimely on pain. "La Morgue" depicts the bloodiness of the revolution in France.

> In the great and noisy city,
>   By the waters of the Seine,
> Where across her hundred bridges
>   Paris pours a living train;
> Far beneath the gloomy shadow
>   Of high arches overhead,
> Humid, dark, repulsive, sombre,
>   Stands the mansion of the dead.

The poet uses contrasting natures in an urban setting to evoke the true terror that mankind has wrought. He or she explores the inner reaches of anguish and the outward displays of horror, which are the consequence of mankind's violent ways.

> Onward rolls the sparkling water,
>   Gaily as if Father Time
> Ne'er had seen it red with slaughter,
>   In the Carnival of crime.—
> Onward by a stately palace,
>   And by gardens fair and green,
> Where, of old, the jewelled chalice
>   Met the kisses of a Queen.

We cannot know whether William tore this column from the page, who inserted it in his book, or when. The language, the mood, the imagery of the poet are so consonant with the author's voice in the *Travels,* though, that they belong together, are together still, perhaps for all time.

> When the bright tho' transient moments,
>   bubbles bursting as they rise,—
> Still went by a magic circle
>   Of recurring fantasies:

> And o'er all there sat in splendor
> She whose beauty from afar
> Flashed above the faint horizon,
> Like the joyous morning star!

Perhaps William identified, in a moment of emotional hubris, with Marie Antoinette or with Jack Snake; perhaps he, too, saw hope on the horizon only to have his throat slashed by critics, by strangers, by people whom he didn't know and who clearly didn't understand him. Such a wild leap of fantasy may lack a firm foundation in reality, but has an emotional veracity of the kind that William, as author and artist, often tried to evoke.

> But there is a massive prison
> Built upon the river side,
> From whose vaults have vainly risen
> Lamentations to the tide:
> And within its dusky portals,
> Passed this yet heroic Queen,
> To trace her footsteps never
> Till she seeks the guillotine![4]

The Seine is both a conduit of hope and a vessel of despair, a wonder of nature and a witness to unnatural acts. If the poem spoke to William, it was both the shared sense of nature and its melancholic nature that struck him.

In some of the books that William owned, there are leaves between pages, scraps of cloth and paper, petals, and blossoms as well. When he wanted to mark a page, he reached for what he had and didn't waste much. If he was on the lawn, a leaf came to hand; in the library, a corner of one of his father's old letters or of one of his own drafts would do just as well. Books were also a place to press blossoms and preserve leaves that he wanted to draw or later try to identify. Deeply immersed in the words, with the book carefully closed, perhaps with one of John's fossils placed gently on top to add weight, a flower could be reduced in dimension much as an artist flattens nature with his pen on a blank page.

William's story about an orphaned bear preserves the petals

between its pages, moistens them with a reader's tears, and adds emotional depth to a nature thus saved.

> Finding ourselves near enough, the hunter fired, and laid the target dead on the spot where she stood; when presently the other, not seeming the least moved at the report of our piece, approached the dead body, smelled, and pawed it, and appearing in agony, fell to weeping and looking upwards, then towards us, and cried out like a child. Whilst our boat approached very near, the hunter was loading his rifle in order to shoot the survivor, which was a young cub, and the slain supposed to be the dam. The continual cries of this afflicted child, bereft of its parent, affected me very sensibly; I was moved with compassion, and charging myself as if accessary to what now appeared to be a cruel murder, endeavoured to prevail on the hunter to save its life, but to no effect! for by habit he had become insensible to compassion towards the brute creation: being now within a few yards of the harmless devoted victim, he fired, and laid it dead upon the body of the dam.[5]

The image of an orphaned child resonates with John's loss as much as the bear's. Entreaties for mercy fall on a culture's deaf ears. Heartfelt pleas are answered by another cruel act. The hunter doesn't see, hear, or feel what's right before him. Habit has deadened his soul.

William sees himself as complicit in the double murder. He travels with the hunter, after all, and consumes what the hunter kills. Is his guilt any less, he asks, for not having squeezed the trigger himself? Could he have prevented the carnage—used different words, physically restrained the murderer, or perhaps shot his own weapon into the air to scare the mother and child away?

"Charging myself as if accessary," William writes. We are accessories, too. The questions come from his century as much as they do from ours, from our experience as much as from his, from our shared guilt. "Habit" is still the explanation; "others" remain the excuse. Have we heard William any more clearly than the hunter did? Can we see better, feel more?

I finished writing this book in a Nova Scotia village that didn't exist when William wrote the bear story. Bears were here then. There was a pine forest; now a small lawn and large meadow define the landscape. Raspberries, blueberries, chamomile, buttercups, wild roses, and Queen Anne's lace abound. Snakes slink through the garden and lawn; bees buzz in the field. We plant a red pine each year, perhaps encouraging a cycle that will make the meadow more what it once was than what it is now. My son's earth-moving toys uproot elders and buttercups and disturb ants, slugs, and worms. They also loosen the soil, making it more receptive to the seeds that his dump truck moves with its loads of soil and rocks. We trample the weeds with our steps, occasionally roust a pheasant from her nest, remove the refuse of the lobsterman's trade that previous owners left. We had a new well dug, sucking moisture from the earth for our "needs." In window boxes we plant geraniums that attract hummingbirds. We drive our car hundreds of air-polluting miles to see them each summer. We have a birdhouse in which swallows nest, wash and dry our clothes with machines, write on a computer rather than with a pencil or pen, create sewage, fill bags with other people's trash that washes up on the beach.

Is the place better or worse for human presence? Is it less beautiful than it was before people, before Euro-Americans, settled here? Not simple questions to answer for the Bartrams or me. They admired similar landscapes in their time, could have happily imagined my home in its setting as well. They would have appreciated this kind of development as part of a cycle, not "improvement" or "destruction" in a single, irreversible direction. Humans intruding as we do are not simply outsiders; we are natural, too.

The lobstering and fishing are in decline and humans are to blame. There are fewer boats polluting Port Maitland's small harbor each year. The fishermen's shanties are deteriorating—a "ghost town" to local children; a beauteous decay evocative of other civilizations, other pasts, to a local artist. Soon the shanties will be gone; the boathouses will wash into the sea; the artist's paintings alone will preserve the memories of beauty-in-death that she and William saw. Like the remains of Spanish forts, abandoned plantations, and Indian graves that John and William found, our civilization is being reclaimed by nature in this once wild, still beautiful place.

Two hundred years ago, there was no way—save by clambering down and up its steep banks—to cross the tidal creek that flows past our house on its way to the upstream forest or the Bay of Fundy below. A wood-and-iron bridge now saves our feet from getting muddy, our legs wet. It keeps us from encountering the eels, snakes, and other life that only intrepid exploring children now find. The bridge gives us access to the port, produce, and culture of a town, a world, larger than ours.

The road that crosses the bridge is paved, at least for another mile or so; then earth, rain, hooves, feet, and wheels create a bumpier landscape, where people have helped beavers build a dam and lodge that shelter the animals without flooding our path. Across a field, down a cliff, on the rocky beach, the carcass of a whale rotted last year; are we to blame? People scavenged the mammal's teeth and bones as souvenirs—of what?—of nature, death, our connection to something larger than ourselves? Another mile past the beavers and the beach where the whale came to rest, a tranquil lake laps the road's edge; swimmers pluck leeches from their legs, a blue heron fishes, a pair of loons float between dives. Around the bend is a farm where horse-drawn rakes turn grass to hay, where organic fertilizers grow the largest, most succulent rhubarb around.

Is my story John's, William's? Are their stories mine? It's not just the cyclical elements of our tales that coincide. The rural development in mine is on a scale that rests compatibly with their assumptions about what human presence means. The environmental threats to the complacent assumptions of their stories lie beneath the surface of mine—in the sea, and elsewhere, more visibly in the environs of my New Jersey home than in the Nova Scotia village where I spend summer months.

The Bartrams never anticipated development on the scale that transformed the Philadelphia skyline visible from their house, polluted the Schuylkill that flows past their dock, ran railroad tracks through their garden, and built an apartment complex in the fields that they tilled. Neither imagined we could ever kill all the snakes, rid the forests of bears—or of trees, for that matter; that we could ever catch and eat all the fish in the sea. John wouldn't be surprised, though, that we are learning to conserve better, waste less, than we once did. He trusted our ingenuity, our ability to husband more wisely, to reckon the true costs of environmental profligacy and the better uses to which nature can be put. He would be hopeful, indeed confident, that efforts to save the river will succeed, pleased that weeds and trees are taking over the abandoned rail bed.

William knew that our problems are more those of the heart than of the head. He feared the hunter's desire to shoot the bear although he isn't hungry, to stomp the snake that poses no threat. He warned us, just as he warned himself, that unbridled ambition and violence for violence' sake are the ways of civilization, but not of the earth. He would be more pessimistic about our future, less sanguine about our past, than his father. He would retire to the Nova Scotia village, abandoning the postindustrial urban world.

Both John and William would marvel, though, at the tomato plant that sprouted through a crack in the concrete driveway of my Trenton home. They would find it remarkable, as I do, that the untended plant bore fruit during a terrible drought. They would be curious, as I am, about the sumac tree that grows through a wall adjacent to track five at the Trenton train station on the New York–Philadelphia line. Ten feet up from the ties, a dozen or more down from the street above, it's a testament to nature's persistence, to the indomitable spirit that the Bartrams saw in all of us—animals and plants alike.

As I write these words, my son plays in the next room. Dinosaurs, Tigger, and Mickey Mouse attack his toy trains, leaving carnage that an ambulance, firefighters, and tow trucks will clean up. No weapons in our house, but the death tolls are catastrophic nonetheless. This time, Tigger kills tyrannosaurus; Mickey is done in by a diesel engine, against which Tigger achieves revenge. I express some dismay when Moses strides into my den to report the latest body count. "It's only pretend, Papa," he assures me. "The dinosaurs are not extinct," he adds to cheer me. "Well, they are alive in your imagination," I offer supportively. "No, their bones are here," he retorts confidently.

My hopes and fears for him share much with John's for his sons. I want to protect Moses from the snakes of our world, to teach him a reverence for all living things, no less than for himself. I, too, care about my son's character and want him someday to make his own way in the world. But since the rattlers are gone and we need no longer ford flooded streams on horseback, since my son is African-American and we live in a city, my fears are also different from John's. My fathering differs from John's, too, which is no criticism of him. Just as our worlds are different, so are we and our sons. Although I wish that Tigger, Mickey, and Tyranna weren't battling anyone, I must admit some pride that they triumphed over the trains, at least this once in my son's fantasy.

Afterword

When, at various times over the past six years, people have asked what I was working on and I responded that it was a book about John and William Bartram, some have then enquired whether I was writing a biography. For a variety of reasons, some that I comprehend perfectly well and others of which I am only vaguely aware or totally ignorant, I was always more comfortable describing this book as a story than as a biography. This discomfort never represented a reluctance to associate with the genre, for I'm an avid reader of biographies, which entranced me as a child and young adult and undoubtedly played a significant role in my choice of careers. Indeed, I find such recent biographies as Nicholas Boyle's *Goethe*, Michael Holroyd's *Bernard Shaw*, and David Levering Lewis's *W.E.B. Du Bois* transcendent successes as history and literature.[1]

Edmund Morgan's biography of Ezra Stiles also belongs in this list, and is my favorite among my favorite early American historian's books. Morgan once told me that it's his favorite, too. No one tells stories about the past better than Morgan and no one captures the humanity of historical figures better than he. The biography of Stiles is a model of its kind, and innovative in a number of ways that I don't think readers have recognized. Experiments with voices; a fluid movement from the author's to the subject's perspective and then back again; the use of italics, quotation marks, and block quotes in close proximity to isolate, integrate, and blend voices break ground most recently tilled by John Demos, Richard Price, and Simon Schama.[2]

Demos's *Unredeemed Captive*, Price's *Alabi's World*, and Schama's *Dead Certainties, Unwarranted Speculations* bring us to the frontiers of the narrative arts. Demos experiments with historical storytelling and the relationship between an author's and a historical subject's voice, provocatively blurring identities in ways that address the largely unexplored psychological and emotional dimensions of narrativity. In Price's case, the perennial battle among anthropologists about the boundaries of perspective and the place of analysis is given new life as the voices of various actors, as well as the historian, are boldly differentiated in contrasting typefaces. Schama explores contested terrain, too, between history and fiction, what we can know and what it makes sense to make up. All three authors tell stories in challenging ways designed to urge thoughtful readers and writers to imagine ourselves into the minds of others and to admit without apology or embarrassment when that's what we are about.

In other ways, Laurel Thatcher Ulrich's *A Midwife's Tale* is closer to what I'm after—the interior lives of people who are less visible in the historical record than the great men of their day, but nonetheless significant in ours for what their experiences reveal about the past and the present. Several recent biographies have also contributed to my growing comfort in associating this project with the genre. I read these books very late in my consideration of the Bartrams, after I had written over half the manuscript and had a clear sense of the structure of the whole, so their influence is more one of identifying kindred spirits. Julia Blackburn's *Daisy Bates in the Desert* entwines the lives of author and subject together more explicitly than I do; Richard Holmes's *Dr. Johnson and Mr. Savage* is more focused in time and theme than my book; and Benedetta Craveri's *Madame du Deffand and Her World* is even more of an interior study than mine, but all are histories of emotion and intellect as much as they are recountings of lives. In that sense the books by Blackburn, Craveri, Holmes, and Ulrich are models of what I have in mind.[3]

My enduring attraction to "story" as a description of this book is also one of association as well as my independent sense of what I'm up to. As a graduate student fifteen years ago, I was greatly influenced by what Lawrence Stone had to say about narrative, by the other storytelling historians whose work he introduced us to in his seminar, and by his own storytelling talents honed on *The Family, Sex, and Marriage* and more recently in his three books on marriage and divorce. LeRoy Ladurie was a frequent visitor to Princeton during my four years there,

Carlo Ginsburg a palpable presence in the books that I read, and Natalie Davis and Clifford Geertz were visible fixtures on the local landscape. All were telling stories in those days. John Murrin, my principal graduate school advisor, is widely and rightly reputed to be the nation's leading teller of tales based on his unsurpassed knowledge of early American history. These scholars have by example influenced greatly the three books that I have written since leaving graduate school, and Murrin directly inspired my first book with his observation that the world was probably ready for a retelling of the story of the Whiskey Rebellion.[4]

Voices from outside the academy have had an equally profound influence on the course of my work and the shape of this book. The novels of Cormac McCarthy, N. Scott Momaday, and Wallace Stegner have contributed much to my sense of nature and landscape as central to all stories and to my desire to tell stories well. And the late Norman Maclean has led me to reconsider the relationship between storytelling and history, both by his monumental talents as a storyteller and by a distinction he makes between storytellers and historians. "If a story-teller thinks enough of storytelling to regard it as a calling," he writes in *Young Men and Fire,*

> unlike a historian he cannot turn from the sufferings of his charac-
> ters. A storyteller, unlike a historian, must follow compassion
> wherever it leads him. He must be able to accompany his charac-
> ters, even into smoke and fire, and bear witness to what they
> thought and felt even when they themselves no longer knew.[5]

If Maclean is right, and in a descriptive sense he certainly does capture the rules and limits of historical vision, then I'm a storyteller and this book is a story.

As we embark, with Maclean, on expeditions into nature's emo-tional unknown, the Bartrams become polestars of eighteenth-century culture. No less than scientists, historians have feared emotions, both our own and those of our subjects, defining them as beyond our pro-fessional terrain. The landscape is changing, though, as ethologists and ethnologists chart new directions for the rest of us.[6] Charles Darwin, after all, tried to set us on the right track with *The Expression of the Emotions in Man and Animals* (1872), but "science" has had little room for such "unreliable" endeavors since the Enlightenment. Conrad Lorenz, Jane Goodall, and others less known to the rest of us have stood outside the professional fear of anthropomorphizing and have jousted with the lingering influence of Descartes.

Recognizing the emotional linkage of other animals to us should lead to a greater appreciation of the science practiced by the Bartrams, each in his own way. John's legacy is surely a clear-sighted sense of connections that link species together, while William's is a deep appreciation of our shared feelings across the entire emotional spectrum. As scientists and historians rediscover the lost wisdom of "anecdotal" evidence, the "truth" and "fact" reported by individual observers of emotionality's nature should be valued more highly.

A science that dismisses evidence such as that of animal emotions as "mere" anecdote fails to learn much that nature teaches us. A self-interested denial of animal feelings plays a significant role in such blindness, because the moral of such stories as William's about the orphan bear advocate for our time an ethical opposition to caging and experimenting on our fellow creatures. A culture unmoved by such disregard of life and ecological systems that support it, which "others" animals in such violent ways, reaps the fruit of its own violence. Violent habits beget violence, othering creates others whom we value less. When we "other" on the basis of species, race, gender, or class, we create caste systems that protect us from and desensitize us to the suffering that we foment and tolerate, isolating us from the natural community of which we are a part.

That's what the Bartrams have left us, a recognition of connections across all life, which includes, but isn't confined to, the emotions that animals share. Our world is perhaps better prepared to consider their philosophy and observational insights than it ever has been since William died. Environmentalists, literary critics, and cultural historians may be open to extending backward in time their location of origins for modern earth-centered thought. Although knowledge of the Bartrams' existence has never been lost, there remains in the literature an overwhelming sense that American environmental history *really* begins with Thoreau and urban-industrial growth. Nods toward an eighteenth- and seventeenth-century past do not adequately integrate those experiences historically. Surely, a more complex history, which doesn't look like a straight line—either ascending or descending—

would represent gains more than compensating for sacrifices in simplicity. The modernization trajectory, a view of history as either strictly improvement or loss, which we find so emotionally attractive in stories about us isn't true. A historiography that splits optimists from pessimists, patriots from critics, will not serve us well in the times ahead. Environmentalists, at least, are showing signs of entertaining such changes in habits of thought.[7]

The story of the Bartrams as father and son also speaks to our world across time. So little has been written about eighteenth-century fatherhood, with the works by Greven, Demos, and Rotundo standing almost alone, that biography cannot help but add something to our knowledge, even if just one exceptional case. John and William's relationship means more than that, though, transcending the eccentricities of personality that they represent. Ultimately, there are similarities between their experiences and ours, which show that continuities are sometimes more meaningful than change. Historiographies thrive on "revolutions" and are prone to discount evidence of incremental change and continuities as less interesting, less revealing, and exceptional in a dismissible way. Nonetheless, the Bartrams' relationship illustrates both similarities and differences over time, the unique and the commonplace, and our need to know more about the emotional lives of people, in this case men, before any of us can say with assurance where they and we fit.

Bibliographic Note

For simplicity's sake, I have listed in the Notes the publishers only of books that exist in multiple editions, such as Bartram's *Travels*, Crèvecoeur's *Letters*, and Kalm's *Travels*. Also, I have not listed the location of John Bartram's correspondence, because it is available in three places. Unless otherwise noted, John's letters are in the Bartram Papers at the Historical Society of Pennsylvania and in Edmund Berkeley and Dorothy Smith Berkeley, eds., *The Correspondence of John Bartram, 1734–1777* (Gainesville, 1992). The Berkeley edition is almost comprehensive, but is unreliable in a number of ways that I discuss in my review of the volume in the *William and Mary Quarterly* 3d ser., 50 (1993):440–443. Darlington's *Memorials* also contains the bulk of the correspondence but in a form that edits out the less attractive side of John's nature, making it the least useful of the three sources. There are a few letters now lost, however, for which Darlington is the only source.

There are two recent editions of William Bartram's writings. *William Bartram on the Southeastern Indians*, edited by Gregory A. Waskelov and Kathryn E. Holland Braund (Lincoln, Nebraska, 1995), focuses on his writings about Indians. The annotations are extensive and constitute a major contribution of the volume. *William Bartram: Travels and Other Writings*, edited by Thomas P. Slaughter (New York: Library of America, 1996), is a comprehensive edition of his published writings and a selection of his more remarkable drawings. Since the Library of America and Penguin Books editions of the *Travels* are both in print, William's book is more widely available now than at any time since he wrote it. The largest published collection of his art is in Joseph Ewan, ed., *William Bartram: Botanical and Zoological Drawings, 1756–1788* (Philadelphia, 1968). William's correspondence, commonplace books, garden diaries, and the vast majority of his drawings have never been published.

Abbreviations Used in the Notes

AHR   *American Historical Review*

APS   American Philosophical Society

BP   Bartram Papers, Historical Society of Pennsylvania

cpb   William Bartram, commonplace book, privately owned

EAL   *Early American Literature*

gb   William Bartram, garden book, Academy of Natural Sciences

HSP   Historical Society of Pennsylvania

LC   Library Company of Philadelphia

JB   John Bartram

JHI   *Journal of the History of Ideas*

NEQ   *New England Quarterly*

NYHS   New-York Historical Society

PC   Peter Collinson

WB   William Bartram

WMQ   *William and Mary Quarterly*

Notes

INTRODUCTION

1   Raymond Williams, *Keywords: A Vocabulary of Culture and Society* (New York, 1976), 184, 186.

CHAPTER ONE: ENDS

1   Copy of birth entry, Darby Monthly Meeting, Academy of Natural Sciences, MSS/Archives, Coll. 15.

2   This method of dating was according to the "old-style" calendar in use until 1752, when the British Empire adopted the dating methods that we use today.

3   JB to WB, July 15, 1772.

4   WB, cpb.

5   Ibid.

6   Cormac McCarthy, *The Crossing* (New York, 1994), 129.

7   WB, cpb.

8   Donald Hall, *Life Work* (Boston, 1993); WB, cpb.

9   Ibid.

10   Alexander Wilson to WB, March 31, 1804, Clark Hunter, ed., *The Life and Letters of Alexander Wilson* (Philadelphia, 1983), 209–210.

11   WB, gb.

12   WB, "Some account of the late Mr. John Bartram, of Pennsylvania," *Philadelphia Medical and Physical Journal*, 1, 2d ed. (1804): 121–122.

13   On William's death, see [Robert Carr] to Mr. [John Doughty] or Mr. Stavely, Printer, [1833], University of Pennsylvania, Van Pelt Library, Miscellaneous Manuscripts; R[obert] Carr, Kingsessing, to Major James N. Barker, June 27, 1833, University of Pennsylvania, Van Pelt Library, Miscellaneous Manuscripts; Robert Carr to Dr. Wm. Darlington, Aug. 29, 1850, NYHS, Darlington Papers, APS microfilm, 607; Thomas Meehan, *The American Handbook of*

Ornamental Trees (Philadelphia, 1853); [John Doughty] "Biographical Sketch of William Bartram," *Cabinet of Natural History and Rural Sports*, 2 (1832): i–vii.

14 WB, gb.

15 *Poulson's American Daily Advertiser*, July 23, 1823.

16 Report of lunar eclipse, *Poulson's American Daily Advertiser*, July 26, 1823, 3; quotations from reviews of WB's *Travels*, *The Monthly Review*, 10 (1793): 13–22, 130–138; *Massachusetts Magazine, or, Monthly Museum*, 4 (November 1792): 686–687; *The Universal Asylum and Columbian Magazine*, 5 (1792): 195–197, 255–267.

17 Bartram Reunion address by Caroline Bartram Kelley, June 8, 1893, HSP, Bartram Papers, Misc. MSS; Meehan, *American Handbook*, 123.

18 "John Bartram, (Botanist), and Descendants of his son John," Francis D. West Collection of Material on John Bartram, APS, B: B28.w1, box 1.

19 JB to PC, April 27, 1755.

20 *Bulletin of Friends' Historical Association*, 17 (1928): 16–22; 24 (1935): 56.

21 BS Barton to WB, November 30, 1805, APS, Barton Papers, B:B284.d.

22 *The Morals of Confucius* (London, 2d ed., 1724); "Life & character of the Chinese Philosopher Confucius In the hand Writing of John Bartram the Elder the American Botanist and Philosopher," Pierpont Morgan Library, Autograph MSS.

23 JB to his children, [1758], HSP, BP.

24 J. Hector St. John de Crèvecoeur, *Letters from an American Farmer* (1782; New York: Penguin Classics, 1986), 189.

25 E. Anthony Rotundo, *American Manhood: Transformations in Masculinity from the Revolution to the Modern Era* (New York, 1993), 3; John Demos, "The Changing Faces of Fatherhood: A New Exploration in Family History," in Stanley Cath, Alan Gurwitt, and John M. Ross, eds., *Father and Child: Developmental and Clinical Perspectives* (Boston, 1982), 425–445.

26 "The Last Written instructions of John Bartram to his Children in order to incourage them to the practice of piety & Virtue, 1777," HSP, Society Collection.

27 JB to [?], untitled draft of letter from JB to one of his children, HSP, Society Collection.

28 "Will of John Bartram," [1772], (copy) APS, Francis D. West Collection, box 1.

29 WB, "Some Account," 124.

CHAPTER TWO: FOUNDATIONS

1 Last Will and Testament of William Bartram, Will Book C, Chester County, Pennsylvania, 335; JB to Archibald Bartram, 1761.

2 Hugh T. Lefler and William S. Powell, *Colonial North Carolina: A History* (New York, 1973), 65–79.

3 JB to PC, December 10, 1745; February 21, 1756; August 8, 1763.

4 JB to PC, February 21, 1756.

5   JB to PC, February 21, 1756; October 23, 1763; November 11, 1763; August 8, 1763.

6   On intercultural "othering," see Edward Said, *Culture and Imperialism* (New York, 1993) and *Orientalism* (New York, 1978); Mary Louise Pratt, "Scratches on the Face of the Country: or, What Mr. Barrow Saw in the Land of the Bushmen," *Critical Inquiry*, 12 (1985): 119–143; Eve Kornfeld, "Encountering 'the Other': American Intellectuals and Indians in the 1790s," *WMQ*, 3d ser., 52 (1995): 287–314.

7   JB to PC, September 30, 1763.

8   JB to John Fothergill, November 26, 1769; JB to [?], untitled draft of letter to one of his children.

9   Philip Greven, *The Protestant Temperament: Patterns of Child-Rearing, Religious Experience, and the Self in Early America* (New York, 1977); Barry Levy, *Quakers and the American Family: British Settlement in the Delaware Valley* (New York, 1988).

10   JB to PC, December 15, 1757.

11   Londa Schiebinger, "Why Mammals Are Called Mammals: Gender Politics in Eighteenth-Century Natural History," *AHR*, 98 (1993): 409.

12   Londa Schiebinger, "The Private Life of Plants: Sexual Politics in Carl Linnaeus and Erasmus Darwin," in Marina Benjamin, ed., *Science and Sensibility: Gender and Scientific Enquiry, 1780–1945* (Oxford, 1991), 125.

13   PC to JB, December 14, 1737.

14   E. Charles Nelson, *Aphrodite's Mousetrap: A Biography of Venus's Flytrap* (Aberstwyth, 1990), 5.

15   Daniel L. McKinley, "'Wagish Plant as Wagishly Described': John Bartram's Tipitiwitchet: A Flytrap, Some Clams and Venus Obscured," in Nelson, *Aphrodite's Mousetrap*, 125–126, 131, 137–138.

16   McKinley, "Wagish Plant," 131; JB to PC, [August 29, 1762].

17   The stepmother's half share was undoubtedly the consequence of her losing the North Carolina property and possessions. William's intentions apparently were that his two older sons by his first marriage would share his Pennsylvania wealth and his new family would share the North Carolina estate.

18   Account of William Smith, executor of the testament of William Bartram, Orphans' Court of Chester County, Pa., Chester County Historical Society; Francis D. West Manuscripts, APS; Tax Assessment Records, Chester County Historical Society; Deed Book H2, Philadelphia County Records, 252. The information on Kingsessing Township's 1769 tax assessment is taken from Joel T. Fry, "The 'Barn' at Bartram's Garden, An Historic Structures Report," July 1992, charts between pages 20 and 21. For additional details about John Bartram's life, see Edmund Berkeley and Dorothy Smith Berkeley, *The Life and Travels of John Bartram* (Tallahassee, 1982); Emily Read Cheston, *John Bartram, 1699–1777: His Garden and His House* (Philadelphia, 1953).

19   Jeff L. Kenyon, Stan M. Hunter, and Helen Schenk, "Basic Historic Research and Archaeological Feasibility Study of Bartram Park," Museum Historic Research Center, University of Pennsylvania, 1975.

20   JB to PC, [July 8, 1753].

21   John St. Clair to JB, November 4, 1761; Thomas Bond to JB, February 20, 1739; PC to JB, January 26, 1739; JB to PC, [summer 1738?]; JB to PC, July 29, 1757.

22   JB to Ann Bartram, September 4, 1765.

23   JB to PC, May 10, 1762; PC to JB, June 1, 1764.

24   PC to JB, April 6, 1759.

25   JB to Jared Eliot, January 24, 1757.

26   JB to PC, May 30, 1763. Although the letter is from 1763, the reference is to the previous year.

27   JB to Benjamin Franklin, April 29, 1771.

28   Joel T. Fry, "Room Function in the Bartram House with Special Attention to the Location of John Bartram's Library," (May 30, 1991), Bartram's Garden; list of specimens written on back of letter, John Bush to JB, June 8, 1764, HSP, BP, box 3, file 52.

29   Crèvecoeur, *Letters*, 188; "Historic Structures Report"; conversation with Joel T. Fry.

30   Crèvecoeur, *Letters*, 188.

31   Ibid., 188–189.

32   WB, "Some Account of the late Mr. John Bartram," 122.

33   Crèvecoeur, *Letters*, 196.

34   JB to PC, July 22, 1741.

35   WB, "Some Account," 122.

36   JB to PC, July 22, 1741; JB to WB, April 5, 1766; April 9, 1766.

37   JB, Journal of a trip to Maryland and Virginia, [fall 1738?]; JB, "Diary," 29, 30, 36.

38   Crèvecoeur, *Letters*, 188–194.

39   JB to Jared Eliot, February 4, 1752.

40   Crèvecoeur, *Letters*, 194.

41   JB to Alexander Catcott, May 26, 1742; JB to PC, May 1, 1764; Thomas Woody, *Early Quaker Education in Pennsylvania* (New York, 1920; 1969), 190–203; Berkeley and Berkeley, *Life and Travels of John Bartram*, 4–5.

42   Crèvecoeur, *Letters*, 194.

43   JB to PC, May 1, 1764; JB to Alexander Catcott, May 26, 1742.

44   Crèvecoeur, *Letters*, 194–195.

45   JB to PC, December 6, 1739; JB to PC, July 6, 1742; JB to PC, May 27, 1743.

46   PC to JB, May 20, 1737, August 28, 1736, May 20, 1737, January 20, 1737/8, December 14, 1737.

47   William T. Stearn, "Linnaean Classification, Nomenclature, and Method," in Wilfred Blunt, *The Compleat Naturalist: A Life of Linnaeus* (New York, 1971), 242–249; Wolf Lepenies, "Linnaeus's *Nemesis divina* and the Concept of Divine Retaliation," *Isis*, 73 (1982): 11–27.

48   JB to PC, May [?], 1738; JB to PC, July 6, 1742.

49   JB to PC, April 27, 1755.

50   Joseph Kastner, *A Species of Eternity* (New York, 1977), 49.

51   JB to PC, April 27, 1755.

CHAPTER THREE: VISIONS

1　John Berger, *Ways of Seeing* (New York, 1973, 1977), 9; Marjorie Hope Nicolson, *Mountain Gloom and Mountain Glory: The Development of the Aesthetics of the Infinite* (New York, 1959), 1; D. W. Meinig, "The Beholding Eye: Ten Versions of the Same Scene," in Meinig, ed., *The Interpretation of Ordinary Landscapes: Geographical Essays* (New York, 1979), 33; John L. Allen, "Lands of Myth, Waters of Wonder: The Place of the Imagination in the History of Geographical Exploration," in David Lowenthal and Martyn J. Bowden, eds., *Geographies of the Mind: Essays in Historical Geosophy* (New York, 1976), 58; Clarence J. Glacken, *Traces on the Rhodian Shore: Nature and Culture in Western Thought from Ancient Times to the End of the Eighteenth Century* (Berkeley, 1967), 3.

2　PC to Cadwallader Colden, March 7, 1742, NYHS; Francis Harper, ed., JB, "Diary of a Journey Through the Carolinas, Georgia, and Florida," *Transactions* of the American Philosophical Society, new series, 33 (Philadelphia, 1942), Introduction, 2.

3　JB to PC, May 10, 1762.

4　On this last point, see James P. Ronda, "Dreams and Discoveries: Exploring the American West, 1760–1815," *WMQ*, 3d ser., 46 (1989): 147.

5　JB to PC, [November 14, 1751]; reprinted, with date, in the *Gentleman's Magazine*, 26 (1756): 474–475.

6　JB to Dr. John Fothergill, August 12, 1769.

7　JB to PC, July 22, 1741.

8　William C. Braithwaite, *The Beginnings of Quakerism to 1660* (1912; Cambridge, 1955); Braithwaite, *The Second Period of Quakerism* (1955; York, 1979); Jack D. Marietta, *The Reformation of American Quakerism, 1748–1783* (Philadelphia, 1984); H. Larry Ingle, *First Among Friends: George Fox and the Creation of Quakerism* (New York, 1994).

9　Abraham Rees, *The Cyclopedia, or, Universal Dictionary of Arts, Sciences, and Literature*, 41 vols. (Philadelphia, 1806–1822), IV, entry for Bartram, John.

10　JB to PC, June 16, 1758.

11　Thomas Burnet, *The Sacred Theory of the Earth: Containing an Account of the Original of the Earth, And of all the General Changes which it hath already undergone, or is to undergo, till the Consummation of all Things*, 2 vols., 6th ed. (London, 1726), I, xviii, xx, 6, 8, 9, 11, and passim.

12　John Ray, *The Wisdom of God Manifested in the Works of the Creation* (1691; 9th ed., 1727), 30, 54, 136, 161–165, 215.

13　JB to Benjamin Rush, December 5, 1767; JB to PC, April 26, 1737; JB to PC, October 23, 1763.

14　JB to PC, January 1738[?].

15　François Delaporte, *Nature's Second Kingdom: Explorations of Vegetality in the Eighteenth Century*, trans. by Arthur Goldhammer (Paris, 1979; Cambridge, MA, 1982).

16　JB to Benjamin Rush, December 5, 1767.

17　JB to Alexander Garden, March 25, 1762.

18　Ibid.

19 JB to PC, May 10, 1762.
20 JB to Alexander Catcott, May 26, 1742.
21 JB to Cadwallader Colden, April 7, 1745.
22 PC to John Custis, December 24, 1737, American Antiquarian Society.
23 Levy, *Quakers and the American Family.*
24 Barbara Maria Stafford, *Voyage into Substance: Art, Science, Nature, and the Illustrated Travel Account, 1760–1840* (Cambridge, MA, 1984).
25 Robert Boyle, *General Heads for the Natural History of a Country, Great or Small; Drawn out for the Use of Travellers and Navigators* (London, 1692), 3–10.
26 Richard Holmes, *Dr. Johnson and Mr. Savage* (New York, 1993), 85.
27 Patricia McClintock Medeiros, "The Literature of Travel of Eighteenth-Century America," Ph.D. diss., University of Massachusetts, 1971, 192.
28 John Bartram, *Observations* (London, 1751; Ann Arbor, 1966), 9–10.
29 Allen G. Debus, *Man and Nature in the Renaissance* (New York, 1978).
30 JB, "Diary," 15.
31 Nicolson, *Mountain Gloom and Mountain Glory,* vii, 3, and passim.
32 Harper, ed., "Diary," 4–5.

CHAPTER FOUR: BUSINESS

1 On eighteenth-century ways of seeing, see Michel Foucault, *The Birth of the Clinic: An Archaeology of Medical Perception* (New York, 1973). For a dissent from Foucault's understanding of the eighteenth-century gardener's gaze, see Stafford, *Voyage into Substance,* 320.
2 [Samuel Hartlib,] *Samuel Hartlib His Legacy of Husbandry* (London, 1655), 223.
3 Thomas Barnes, *A New Method of Propagating Fruit-Trees, and flowering Shrubs: Whereby The common Kinds may be raised more expeditiously,* 2d ed. (London, 1759), 10; James Justice, *The Scots Gardiners Director, containing Instructions to those Gardiners, who make a Kitchen Garden, and the Culture of Flowers, their Business,* 2d ed. (1754; Edinburgh, 1759), v, 1.
4 JB, untitled essay on reforestation published as Preface to Benjamin Franklin, *Poor Richard Improved . . . 1749* (Philadelphia, 1748).
5 Alexander Garden to Cadwallader Colden, November 4, 1754.
6 PC to JB, January 1736; February 12, 1736; December 14, 1737; April 12, 1739.
7 PC to JB, January 24, 1735; March 1, 1735; February 3, 1736.
8 PC to JB, April 21, 1736.
9 PC to JB, December 20, 1737; JB to PC, May 1738.
10 PC to JB, September 8, 1737; PC to JB, February 17, 1738.
11 JB to PC, [1738?].
12 PC to JB, [1739?].
13 JB to PC, July 18, [1739].

14 PC to John Blackburne, October 20, 1742, Oxford University; PC to John Custis, December 24, 1737, American Antiquarian Society.

15 Berkeley and Berkeley, *The Life and Travels of John Bartram,* 9; Crève-coeur, *Letters,* 188.

16 WB, "Some Account of the Late Mr. John Bartram," 122.

17 Robert G. Stewart, "A Portrait of John Bartram Identified," *The Garden Journal,* 17 (1967): 11–14; Ralph S. Palmer, "The Spurious Portraits of John Bartram," *Bartram Broadside* (Fall 1993): 3–5; Robert Carr to William Darlington, August 20, 1856, NYHS, Darlington Letters. The formal portrait is in the National Portrait Gallery, Smithsonian Institution, Washington, DC. The "Peale" portrait of the wigless man is in the library of the Pennsylvania Horticultural Society, Philadelphia. Apparently Charles Coleman Sellers, a biographer of Peale, believed the wigless portrait was not painted by Charles Willson or any of his artist offspring.

18 Stewart, "A Portrait of John Bartram Identified," 13; JB to PC, October 23, 1763.

19 WB, "Some Account of the Late Mr. John Bartram," 122; JB to his children [1758]; Rees, *Cyclopedia,* IV, entry for John Bartram.

20 Rees, *Cyclopedia,* IV.

21 Garden to John Ellis, November 19, 1764, *Correspondence of Linnaeus,* I, 522.

22 Custis to PC, [August 12?] 1739, in E.G. Swem, "Brothers of the Spade: Correspondence of Peter Collinson, of London, and of John Custis, of Williamsburg, Virginia, 1734–1746," *Proceedings of the American Antiquarian Society,* 58 (1948): 77; Alexander Garden to John Ellis, March 15, 1755, in Smith, *Correspondence of Linnaeus,* I, 286; Peter Kalm, *Travels in North America* (Stockholm, 1753; London, 1770; 1937; Mineola, NY: Dover Publications, 1987), 63.

23 PC to JB, January 24, 1735; August 12, 1737.

24 JB to James Logan, August 19, 1737; JB to Cadwallader Colden, October 4, 1745; JB to PC, November 3, 1754.

25 Garden to Ellis, July 15, 1765, in Smith, *Correspondence of Linnaeus,* I, 537; PC to Colden, March 5, 1741; Colden to Gronovius, May 30, 1746; Colden to PC, June 1744.

26 Garden to Ellis, March 25, 1755, in Smith, *Correspondence of Linnaeus,* I, 344–345; BF to JB, July 9, 1769, ms. list in Department of Special Collections, Stanford University Libraries; Kastner, *A Species of Eternity,* 54.

27 PC to JB, December 10, 1737; Colden to JB [October 24, 1744]; BF to JB, January 9, 1769; BF to JB, July 9, 1769.

28 PC to JB [February 3, 1767?].

29 JB to PC, May 27, 1743. The cup is now in the collections of the University of Pennsylvania, Van Pelt Library.

30 JB to Sir Hans Sloane, November 16, 1743.

31 John Hope to BF, January 23, 1772; BF to JB, February 10, 1773; Garden to John Ellis, in Smith, *Correspondence of Linnaeus,* I, 531–532; PC to JB, February 3, 1767[?].

32   JB to Peter Bayard, [June 1741?]; JB to Gronovius, December 6, 1745.

33   JB to PC, October 15, 1764; JB to PC, December 5, 1766.

34   JB to PC, [December 1739?]; JB to Dillenius, December 5, 1739; JB to Colden, November 10, 1744; Peter Kalm to JB, August 6, 1749.

CHAPTER FIVE: BEGINNINGS

1   Alexander Garden to John Ellis, July 15, 1765, in Smith, *Correspondence of Linnaeus,* I, 538.

2   JB to PC, June 24, 1760; JB's Bible, LCP. This is one of several Bartram family Bibles that survive. Printed perpendicular to the inscription in the margin, "JOHN:BARTRAM." On rear flyleaf, apparently in her hand, the signature of "Mary Bartram" and "John Bartram his Book 1761." The Bible is a 1613 London edition.

3   JB to WB [brother], December 27, 1761; JB to PC [fall 1753?].

4   JB to PC, [1745?]; August 14, 1761.

5   JB to PC, May 22, 1761.

6   JB to PC, August 14, 1761; [1735 or early 1736]; JB to John Clayton, September 1, 1744; JB to PC, November 1739; JB to Cadwallader Colden, September 25, 1742.

7   JB to PC, December 18, 1742; JB to Cadwallader Colden, January 16, 1743; JB, "Diary," 29, 33, 34.

8   Kalm, *Travels,* 61.

9   Crèvecoeur, *Letters,* XI, 191.

10   JB to Gronovius, December 6, 1745; JB to PC, [June 10, 1755]; JB to Philip Miller, February 18, 1759.

11   JB to Mark Catesby, [March 1741?].

12   JB to PC, May 30, 1763; May 10, 1762.

13   PC to CC, March 7, 1742; the "figur" is in HSP, BP, box 1, 1–16.

14   S. Peter Dance, *The Art of Natural History: Animal Illustrators and Their Work* (Woodstock, New York, 1978), 52.

15   PC to JB, August 10, 1753; JB to PC, August 20, 1753.

16   JB to PC, [fall 1753?].

17   Kalm, *Travels,* 36.

18   PC to CC, October 5, 1757.

19   JB to PC, November 3, 1754.

20   JB to PC, [fall 1753?].

21   JB to Gronovius, December 16, 1754; JB to PC, March 6, 1755; April 27, 1755.

22   *Pennsylvania Gazette,* August 12, 1756; Saul Sack, *History of Higher Education in Pennsylvania,* 2 vols. (Harrisburg, 1963), I, chapter 14.

23   JB to PC, April 27, 1755.

24   JB to PC, September 28, 1755; PC to JB, [January 20, 1756?].

25   PC to JB, February 1756; JB to PC, May 30, 1756.

26   JB to Garden, March 14, 1756.

27 Shirley Streshinsky, *Audubon: Life and Art in the American Wilderness* (New York, 1993).
28 George Edwards, *Gleanings of Natural History*, 6 (London, 1760), 172–173, 190–192.
29 Receipt, HSP, general collections.
30 [Anonymous,] *A New Introduction to Trade and Business; Very Useful for Young Gentlemen and Young Ladies* (London, 1758), LCP.
31 JB to PC, November 7, 1756; PC to JB, July 20, 1756, February 10, 1757.
32 PC to JB, March 18, 1757; JB to PC, September 25, 1757; PC to JB, March 10, 1759.
33 JB to William Bartram [brother], December 27, 1761.
34 JB to PC, May 22, 1761; WB to JB, May 6, 1761.
35 WB to JB, May 20, 1761.
36 JB to WB, [June? 1761].
37 JB to WB, September 1, 1761.
38 JB to WB, October 5, 1761; George Edwards to WB, Jr. [sic], November 15, 1761; William Darlington, ed., *Memorials of John Bartram and Humphry Marshall* (Philadelphia, 1849), 419–420; Samuel Eldridg to WB, 1761, HSP, BP, box 3, 104.
39 JB to WB [brother], December 27, 1761; JB to WB, December 27, 1761.
40 Berkeley and Berkeley, *Life and Travels*, 193, 202.
41 JB to PC, November 8, 1761; William Bartram [brother] to JB, June 11, 1762.
42 Receipt signed by WB, HSP, Etting Collection.
43 JB to Moses and WB, November 9, 1762; JB to PC, May 30, 1763.
44 JB to PC, March 4, 1764; PC to JB, March 7, 1764.
45 JB to PC, September 23, 1764.
46 JB to WB, June 7, 1765; Isaac Bartram to JB, August 15, 1765.

CHAPTER SIX: SNAKES

1 Alexander Hamilton, *Itinerarium* (St. Louis, 1907), 94; Albert Matthews, "Rattlesnake Colonel," *NEQ*, 10 (1937): 341–345.
2 JB, *Observations on the Inhabitants, Climate, Soil, Rivers, Productions, Animals, and other matters worthy of Notice Made By Mr. John Bartram, In his Travels from Pensilvania to Onondago, Oswego and the Lake Ontario, In Canada* (London, 1751; Ann Arbor, 1966), 11–12, 26, 65, 68; JB, *Diary of a Journey Through the Carolinas, Georgia, and Florida: From July 1, 1765, to April 10, 1766*, edited by Francis Harper, *Transactions of the American Philosophical Society* (Philadelphia, 1942), 18, 26, 35; JB to PC, July 17, 1734.
3 JB, draft letter, on back of letter, Lionel Chalmers, Charleston, to John Bartram, April 1, 1773, HSP, BP, box 1, 102.
4 JB to PC, February 27, 1737.
5 JB, part of draft letter, on back of letter, Lionel Chalmers to JB, April 1, 1773, HSP, BP, box 1, 102.

6   Ibid.; JB to PC, April 27, 1755.
7   JB to PC, June 11, 1743.
8   JB to PC, February 27, 1737.
9   JB to PC, June 13, 1737.
10   JB to PC, [fall 1753?].
11   PC to JB, October 5, 1762; JB to PC, August 8, 1763; JB to PC, May 1, 1764.
12   WB, *Travels Through North and South Carolina, Georgia, East and West Florida, The Cherokee Country, the Extensive Territories of the Muscogulges, or Creek Confederacy, and the Country of the Chactaws* (Philadelphia, 1791; London, 1792; New York: Penguin Books, 1981), 224.
13   Ibid., 224–225.
14   Ibid., 222.
15   JB to PC, February 27, 1737.
16   WB, *Travels*, 222.
17   Ibid., 218–220.
18   WB, Report, 144.
19   WB, *Travels*, 188, 221.
20   Ibid., 223.
21   Benjamin Smith Barton, *A Memoir Concerning the Fascinating Faculty which has been Ascribed to the Rattle-Snake, and other American Serpents* (Philadelphia, 1796), 33–34.
22   Ibid., 26.
23   WB, *Travels*, 222.
24   Ibid., 221.
25   Barton, *Memoir*, 9, 12.

CHAPTER SEVEN: JOURNEYS

1   JB to PC, June [30?], 1766.
2   JB to WB, April 5, 1766.
3   Ibid.
4   Ibid.
5   JB to WB, April 9, 1766.
6   JB to WB, July 3, 1766.
7   Henry Laurens to JB, August 9, 1766.
8   William Styron, *Darkness Visible: A Memoir of Madness* (New York, 1990), 16–17.
9   Ibid., 17–18.
10   JB to PC, August 26, 1766.
11   WB, cpb.
12   Ibid.
13   Ibid.
14   PC to JB, May 28, 1766.
15   PC to JB, April 10, 1767; PC to JB [February 3, 1767?].

16 WB, cpb.
17 HSP, Bartram Papers, box 1, folder 41.
18 Thomas Lamboll to WB, April 28, 1767, HSP, BP, box 4, file 66.
19 PC to JB, April 10, 1767, July 28, 1767, December 1767.
20 PC to WB, February 16, 1768, HSP, BP, box 3, file 73.
21 PC to JB, February 17, 1768, February 29, 1768, May 17, 1768, July 6, 1768.
22 Fothergill to JB, October 29, 1768, May 1, 1769, November 26, 1769, January 13, 1770.
23 JB to Fothergill, September 30, 1770.
24 JB to WB, April 25, 1771, July 21, 1771.
25 Ibid.; JB to Charles M. Wrangel, July 6, 1771.
26 JB to WB, July 15, 1772.
27 Fothergill to JB, [?] 1772.
28 Fothergill to WB, October 22, 1772, HSP, BP, Box 4, 23; Fothergill to Dr. Chalmers, October 23, 1772, HSP, BP, box 4, 26; Fothergill to WB, September 4, 1773, HSP, BP, box 4, 27; Fothergill to JB, July 8, 1774.
29 Lionel Chalmers to JB, April 7, 1773.
30 Chalmers to WB, May 17, 1774, Darlington, *Memorials,* 464–465; Chalmers to JB, July 12, 1774; Thomas Lamboll to WB, November 9, 1773, HSP, BP, box 4, 68.
31 WB to JB, March 27, 1775.
32 WB to Lachlan McIntosh, July 15, 1775 [*sic*], HSP, Dreer Autograph Collection; WB, Report, 188.

CHAPTER EIGHT: PERSPECTIVES

1 On influences, for the debate over William's poetic versus scientific visions, and for characterization of his authorial identity within the context of existing genres, see Larry R. Clarke, "The Quaker Background of William Bartram's View of Nature," *JHI,* 46 (1985): 435–448; Bruce Silver, "Clarke on the Quaker Background of William Bartram's Approach to Nature," *JHI,* 47 (1986): 507–510; Thomas Vance Barnett, "William Bartram and the Age of Sensibility," Ph.D. diss., Georgia State University, 1982; Samuel Robert Aiken, "The New-Found-Land Perceived: An Exploration of Environmental Attitudes in Colonial British America," Ph.D. diss., The Pennsylvania State University, 1971; Charlotte Porter, "Bartram's Travels and American Literature, or Why Did He Wait so Long to Publish?," The Bartram Trail Conference and Symposium, *Proceedings of the Symposium* (1991): 59–64; L. Hugh Moore, "The Aesthetic Theory of William Bartram," *Essays in Arts and Sciences,* 12 (1983): 17–35; Pamela Regis, *Describing Early America: Bartram, Jefferson, Crèvecoeur, and the Rhetoric of Natural History* (DeKalb, 1992); Robert McCracken Peck, "William Bartram and His Travels and Books from the Bartram Library," in Society for the Bibliography of Natural History, *Contributions to the History of North American Natural History* (London, 1983), 35–50; James Rosen, "William Bartram's Sketches: The Field

and the Image," Bartram Trail Conference, *Proceedings of the Symposium* (1991): 41–54; William L. Hedges, "Toward a National Literature," in Emory Elliott, ed., *Columbia Literary History of the United States* (New York, 1988), 190–191; John Seelye, "Beauty Bare: William Bartram and His Triangulated Wilderness," *Prospects*, 6 (1981): 37–54; William Gummere, "William Bartram, A Classical Scientist," *Classical Journal*, 50 (1955): 167–170; Bruce Silver, "William Bartram's and Other Eighteenth-Century Accounts of Nature," *JHI*, 39 (1978): 597–614; N. Bryllion Fagin, *William Bartram: Interpreter of the American Landscape* (Baltimore, 1933); Charlotte M. Porter, "The Drawings of William Bartram (1739–1823), American Naturalist," *Archives of Natural History*, 16 (1989): 289–303; Mary S. Mattfield, "Journey to the Wilderness: Two Travelers in Florida, 1696–1774," *Florida Historical Quarterly*, 45 (1967): 327–351; Clive Bush, *The Dream of Reason: American Consciousness and Cultural Achievement from Independence to the Civil War* (London, 1977); Myra Jehlen, *American Incarnation: The Individual, the Nation, and the Continent* (Cambridge, MA, 1986); Christopher Looby, "The Constitution of Nature: Taxonomy and Politics in Jefferson, Peale, and Bartram," *EAL*, 22 (1987): 252–273; Berta Grattan Lee, "William Bartram: Naturalist or 'Poet'?" *EAL*, 7 (1972): 124–129; Edward Nygren, "From View to Vision," in Nygren, ed., *Views and Visions: American Landscape before 1830* (Washington, D.C., 1986), 3–81; Catherine L. Albanese, *Nature Religion in America: From the Algonkian Indians to the New Age* (Chicago, 1990); William Martin Smallwood, *Natural History and the American Mind* (New York, 1941); Glacken, *Traces on the Rhodian Shore;* Roxanne M. Gentilcore, "The Classical Tradition and American Attitudes Towards Nature in the Seventeenth and Eighteenth Centuries," Ph.D. diss., Boston University, 1992; Kastner, *Species of Eternity;* Richard Slotkin, *Regeneration Through Violence: The Mythology of the American Frontier, 1600–1860* (Middletown, CT, 1973); Larzer Ziff, *Writing in the New Nation: Prose, Print, and Politics in the Early United States* (New Haven, 1991); Patricia McClintock Medeiros, "The Literature of Travel of Eighteenth-Century America," Ph.D. diss., University of Massachusetts, 1971; Amy R. Weinstein Meyers, "Sketches from the Wilderness: Changing Conceptions of Nature in American Natural History Illustration: 1680–1880," Ph.D. diss., Yale University, 1985.

2 WB, *Travels*, 64–65.

3 Amy R. W. Meyers, "Imposing Order on the Wilderness: Natural History Illustration and Landscape Portrayal," in Edward J. Nygren and Bruce Robertson, eds., *Views and Visions: American Landscapes before 1830* (Washington, D.C., 1986), 105–131. I owe my initial insight into William's drawings of the Alachua Savanna to Meyers, who sees his linkage of animals and plants "through reflections of form" (121).

4 WB to Lachlan McIntosh, July 15, 1775 [*sic*, 1774], HSP, Dreer Autograph Collection. The corrected dating was made by Francis Harper, ed., WB, "Travels in Georgia and Florida, 1773–74: A Report to Dr. John Fothergill," *Transactions* of the American Philosophical Society, new series, 33 (Philadelphia, 1943), 188.

5 WB, Report, 140.

6 Francis Harper to Charles F. Jenkins, June 25, 1939; March 31, April 19, May 18, 1940; February 12, 1941, Academy of Natural Sciences, MSS/Archives, Coll. 15.

7 WB, Report, 123.

8 Ibid., 134.

9 Ibid., 136, 138.

10 Ibid., 160, 164.

11 Outline, BP, box 4, 24, identified in finding aid: "seems to be Wm. Bartram's notes re book on travels (1772)." It is unclear how the document was dated 1772, but it was certainly written before 1777.

12 James Dickey, Introduction, WB, *Travels*, viii–ix.

13 Francis Harper, "Proposals for Publishing Bartram's *Travels*," *The American Philosophical Society Library Bulletin* (1945): 34.

14 Moore, "Aesthetic Theory of William Bartram," 27–28; WB, Report; Francis Harper, ed., *The Travels of William Bartram: Naturalist's Edition* (New Haven, 1958).

15 Jay Fliegelman, *Declaring Independence: Jefferson, Natural Language, and the Culture of Performance* (Stanford, 1994), 60, 76, and passim.

16 Immanuel Kant, *Observations on the Feeling of the Beautiful and Sublime*, John T. Goldthwait, trans. (1764, 1799; Berkeley, 1960); Archibald Alison, *Essays on the Nature and Principles of Taste* (Edinburgh, 1790); William Smellie, *The Philosophy of Natural History* (Edinburgh, 1790; Philadelphia, 1791); Gilbert White, *The Natural History and Antiquities of Selborne, in the County of Southampton* (London, 1789).

17 Virgil, *The Eclogues*, trans. by Guy Lee (New York, 1984); Virgil, *The Georgics*, trans. by L. P. Wilkinson (New York, 1982); Gentilcore, "The Classical Tradition"; Tuveson, "Space, Deity, and the Natural Sublime."

18 Tuveson, *Imagination as a Means of Grace*, 1, 6, 26.

19 Mark Akenside, *The Pleasures of Imagination. A Poem in Three Books* (London, 1763), v, vi, 15, 16.

20 Edmund Burke, *A Philosophical Enquiry into the Origin of Our Ideas of the Sublime and Beautiful* (London, 1767), 7–8.

21 Ibid., 58.

22 WB, Report, 164.

23 Ibid., 95 and passim.

24 Tuveson, *Imagination as a Means of Grace*, 26.

25 WB, MS journal, "A Journey from Spaldings lower Trading House to Cuscowilla & the Great Alachua Savanna," HSP, BP, small Bartram volumes.

26 *Cabinet of Natural History and American Rural Sports*, 2 (1832), iii; Francis Harper, "William Bartram and the American Revolution," *Proceedings* of the American Philosophical Society, 97 (1953): 571–577.

CHAPTER NINE: TRAVELS

1 WB, *Travels*, 141, 24–25.

2 Ibid., 47–48, 107, 143, 150.

3 Ibid., 151.
4 Ibid., 119.
5 Ibid., 115–116.
6 WB, Report, 151–152, 154.
7 Joseph Conrad, *Heart of Darkness* (1902; New York, 1983), 40, 41.
8 Bill of sale for Negro woman, Jenny, APS, B:C692.1.
9 WB, *Travels*, 80, 84, 133, 164, 256, 268, 329.
10 Ibid., 277, 350, 351.
11 WB, essay, written on the back of printed "Catalogue of American Trees, Shrubs and Herbacious Plants, most of which are now growing, and produce ripe Seed in John Bartram's Garden, near Philadelphia," [1783], HSP, Broadsides, Abnd-251.
12 Jean R. Soderlund, *Quakers and Slavery: A Divided Spirit* (Princeton, 1985); Jack D. Marietta, *The Reformation of American Quakerism, 1748–1783* (Philadelphia, 1984).
13 WB, Report, 155.
14 WB, *Travels*, 44–45.
15 WB, cpb.
16 WB, "Observations," 18–19. On the eighteenth-century rhetorical revolution that favored "natural" communication, see Fliegelman, *Declaring Independence*.
17 WB, "Observations," 20.
18 Ibid., 21.
19 Ibid., 39; Crèvecoeur, *Letters*, XII, 200–227.
20 WB, *Travels*, 58–59.
21 Ibid., 113, 164. For other examples of "skulking" or violent Indians in William's writings, see WB, Report, 137, 143, 157.
22 WB, *Travels*, 183–184.
23 Ibid., 182.
24 Ibid., 199; WB, Report, 157.
25 WB, "Observations," 18.
26 WB, *Travels*, 88.
27 Ibid., 288–290.
28 Ibid., 290.
29 Ibid., 214.
30 Ibid., 215.
31 Ibid., 110–111.
32 Ibid., 111.

CHAPTER TEN: GARDENS

1 Johann David Schoepf, *Travels in the Confederation*, Alfred J. Morrison, trans. and ed. (Philadelphia, 1911), 92.
2 *Pennsylvania Packet and Daily Advertiser*, April 22, 1785.
3 William Shakespeare, *Twelfth Night*, act 5, scene 1.

4 [Johann Georg von] Zimmermann, *Solitude Considered with Respect to Its Influence upon the Mind and the Heart* (London, 1791), i, 1–2, 6, 57, 58, 59; WB to Moses Bartram, n.d. [1791 or 1792], HSP, BP, box 1, 80; WB to James Howell Bartram, September 23, 1804, copy in recipient's hand, Bartram's Garden, Philadelphia. The notes on Zimmermann are in "William Bartram's Commonplace Book, 1797–1802," HSP, Bartram Papers, small Bartram volumes.

5 WB, "Anecdotes of an American Crow," *Philadelphia Medical and Physical Journal,* 1 (1804), 90.

6 What I know about the problems of publishing in the 1780s is based entirely on information generously shared by James Green.

7 B. S. Barton to WB, August 26, 1787, HSP, BP, box 1, 1–3.

8 Thomas Say to WB, December 15, 1786, HSP, Gratz Collection, case 8, box 17; Barton to WB, December 30, 1787, HSP, BP, box 1, 8; Barton to WB, February 19, 1788, HSP, BP, box 1, 1; WB to Barton, March 3, 1793, APS, Barton Papers, B:B284.d. William describes his injury briefly in a letter to Lachlan McIntosh, May 31, 1796, NYHS, BP.

9 WB to Mrs. Mary Bartram Robeson, September 7, 1788, HSP, Gratz Collection.

10 F. Parke to WB, November 15, 1788, HSP, BP, box 4, file 94; WB to Robert Barclay, November 1788, British Museum (Natural History), Book E, in Joseph Ewan, ed., *William Bartram: Botanical and Zoological Drawings, 1756–1788* (Philadelphia, 1968), 164.

11 WB to Benjamin Smith Barton, December 15, 1789, in E. G. Squier, ed., WB, "Observations on the Creek and Cherokee Indians," *Transactions of the American Ethnological Society,* 3 (1853): 9.

12 WB, "Anecdotes of an American Crow," 89–95.

13 Philip Greven, *Spare the Child: The Religious Roots of Punishment and the Psychological Impact of Physical Abuse* (New York, 1991); Alice Miller, *For Your Own Good: Hidden Cruelty in Child-Rearing and the Roots of Violence* (New York, 1984).

14 WB to A. Laribore, 1795, HSP, Gratz Collection.

15 Gilbert White, *The Natural History and Antiquities of Selborne, in the County of Southampton* (London, 1789).

16 WB, draft letter on back of B.S. Barton to WB, September [?], 1795, HSP, BP, box 1, 1–9.

17 This copy of the *Travels* is in the collections of the Morton Arboretum, Lisle, Illinois.

18 Copy in Library Company of Philadelphia, inscribed "W. Hamiltons Book given to him by the author June 9th 1799"; Fagin, "Bartram's Travels," 289.

19 Peter Eisenstadt, "The Weather and Weather Forecasting in Colonial America," Ph.D. diss., New York University, May 1990.

20 The second personal copy of the *Travels* is in the collections of the Library Company of Philadelphia.

21 Anonymous review, *The Universal Asylum and Columbian Magazine,* 5 (1792): 255–267, with excerpts, 8, 22, 89–97, 195–197.

22 *The Monthly Review,* 10 (1793): 13–22, 130–138. See also *Massachusetts Magazine, or, Monthly Museum,* 4 (1792): 686–687.

23 John Pearson, Richard Willing, Hugh Lloyd, to WB, March 14, 1793, HSP, BP, box 1, 84.

24 William Dunlap, *A History of the American Theatre* (New York, 1832), diary entry for May 9, 1797, 170–171.

25 David John Jeremy, ed., *Henry Wansey and His American Journal, 1794* (1796; 1798; Philadelphia, 1970), diary entry for June 9, 1794, 112.

26 WB to·Lachlan McIntosh, May 31, 1796, NYHS, BP; Elaine Forman Crane, ed., *The Diary of Elizabeth Drinker*, 3 vols. (Boston, 1991), II, 900, entry for March 23, 1797.

27 WB, cpb, 1797–1802, HSP, BP, small Bartram volumes.

28 WB to Barton, April 3, July 11, 1800; July 13, August [?], August 23, September 27, October 25, 1801, APS, Barton Papers, B:B284.d; Barton to WB, Saturday, 24 [? apparently 1801, but finding aid says 1804], August 8, 1801, HSP, BP, box 1, 1–13.

29 WB, "Account of the Species, Hybrids, and Other Varieties of the Vine of North-America," *The Medical Repository*, 2d ser., 1 (1804): 19–24; WB to Barton, [?], 1802, May 25, 1802, APS, Barton Papers, B:B284.d; WB, Manuscript copy of "Entomology from Gmelin's [?] last addition [*sic*] of the celebrated Systema Naturae by Sir Charles Linne, and Translated by William Turton, M.D. London, printed 1802," University of Pennsylvania, Van Pelt Library, Special Collections, B595.7 L647.

30 Walter Harding, *The Days of Henry Thoreau* (New York, 1970; 1982); Richard Lebeaux, *Young Man Thoreau* (Amherst, 1977); Lebeaux, *Thoreau's Seasons* (Amherst, 1984); Robert D. Richardson, Jr., *Henry Thoreau: A Life of the Mind* (Berkeley, 1986).

31 Benjamin Silliman, *Letters of Shahcoolen, a Hindu Philosopher, Residing in Philadelphia; to His Friend El Hassan, an Inhabitant of Delhi*, introduction by Ben Harris McClary (1801; 1802; Gainesville, 1962), viii–ix, 138–152; Donald Jackson and Dorothy Twohig, eds., *The Diaries of George Washington*, vol. 5 (Charlottesville, 1979), entries for June 10, 1787, and September 2, 1787, 166–167, 183; *Aurora and General Advertiser*, September 29, 1812. I thank Joel Fry for generously calling the newspaper article to my attention.

32 WB, "A Journey from Spaldings lower Trading House."

33 Ibid.

34 City of Philadelphia, Register of Wills, file no. 174, administration book M, 404; McKinley, "The End of William Bartram," 6–7.

35 Wilson to WB, March 4, [1803], [1803], October 30, 1803, November 10, 1803, November 17, 1803, November 20, 1803, December 19, 1803, March 29, 1804, May [1 or 21], 1804, May 22, 1804, June 15, 1804, June 16, 1804.

36 Wilson to WB, March 31, 1804.

37 Wilson, "The Beechen Bower," June 18, 1804.

38 Wilson, "A Rural Walk," *The Literary Magazine, and American Register*, 2 (August 1804): 377–379.

39 Manuscript memorandum of B. S. Barton, October 4, 1811, in Harper, ed., Introduction, "Report," 127; Henry Muhlenberg to William Baldwin, November 4, 1811, April 20, 1813; Baldwin to Muhlenberg, March 20, 1813, in

William Darlington, ed., *Reliquiae Baldwinianae: Selections from the Correspondence of the Late William Baldwin, M.D.* (1843; New York, 1969), 52, 72, 79–80.

40 Baldwin to Darlington, January 15, 1817, March 30, 1817; Baldwin to A. B. Lambert, February 7, 1817, in Darlington, ed., *Reliquiae Baldwinianae*, 195, 197, 212, 186.

41 Baldwin to Darlington, April 19, 1817, May 27, 1817, July 3, 1817, August 20, 1817, November 10, 1817, in Darlington, ed., *Reliquiae Baldwinianae*, 215, 230, 234–235, 238, 247.

42 Baldwin to Darlington, August 14, 1818, ibid., 277; William P. C. Barton, *Vegetable Materia Medica of the United States; or Medical Botany* (Philadelphia, 1818), II, 107–108.

43 *Poulson's American Daily Advertiser*, December 2, 1817. I thank Joel Fry for generously calling this ad to my attention.

CONCLUSION

1 Rubens Peale, memorandum [1856], APS, Peale Papers.

2 *Poulson's American Daily Advertiser*, October 11, 1820.

3 *The Rural Magazine, and Literary Evening Fire-Side*, 1 (1820), 478.

4 Reprinted from the *Southern Literary Messenger*, Library Company of Philadelphia.

5 WB, *Travels*, 22.

AFTERWORD

1 Nicholas Boyle, *Goethe: The Poet and the Age*, vol. 1 (New York, 1991); Michael Holroyd, *Bernard Shaw*, 3 vols. (New York, 1988–1991); David Levering Lewis, *W.E.B. Du Bois*, vol. 1 (New York, 1993).

2 Edmund S. Morgan, *The Gentle Puritan: A Life of Ezra Stiles, 1727–1795* (Chapel Hill, 1962); John Demos, *The Unredeemed Captive: A Family Story from Early America* (New York, 1994); Simon Schama, *Dead Certainties, Unwarranted Speculations* (New York, 1991); Richard Price, *Alabi's World* (Baltimore, 1990).

3 Laurel Thatcher Ulrich, *A Midwife's Tale: The Life of Martha Ballard, Based on Her Diary, 1785–1812* (New York, 1990); Julia Blackburn, *Daisy Bates in the Desert: A Woman's Life Among the Aborigines* (New York, 1994); Richard Holmes, *Dr. Johnson and Mr. Savage* (New York, 1993); Benedetta Craveri, *Madame du Deffand and Her World* (Milan, 1982; Boston, 1994).

4 Lawrence Stone, *The Family, Sex, and Marriage: In England, 1500–1800* (New York, 1977); Stone, *Road to Divorce: England 1530–1987* (New York, 1990); Stone, *Uncertain Unions and Broken Lives* (New York, 1992); Natalie Davis, *The Return of Martin Guerre* (Cambridge, MA, 1983); Clifford Geertz, *The Interpretation of Cultures* (New York, 1973); Carlo Ginsburg, *The Night Battles: Witchcraft and Agrarian Cults in the Sixteenth and Seventeenth Centuries* (Baltimore, 1983); LeRoy Ladurie, *Montaillou: The Promised Land of Error* (New York, 1978); Ladurie, *Carnival in Romans* (New York, 1979).

5   N. Scott Momaday, *The Ancient Child* (New York, 1989); Wallace Stegner, *Angle of Repose* (1971); Cormac McCarthy, *All the Pretty Horses* (New York, 1993); McCarthy, *The Crossing* (New York, 1994); Norman Maclean, *Young Men and Fire* (Chicago, 1990), 102.

6   Jeffrey Moussaieff Masson and Susan McCarthy, *When Elephants Weep: The Emotional Lives of Animals* (New York, 1995); Donald Griffin, *The Question of Animal Awareness: Evolutionary Continuity of Mental Experience* (New York, 1976); Paola Cavalieri and Peter Singer, eds., *The Great Ape Project: Equality Beyond Humanity* (London, 1993); Peter N. Stearns, *Jealousy: The Evolution of an Emotion in American History* (New York, 1989); Stearns and Carol Z. Stearns, *Anger: The Struggle for Emotional Control in America's History* (Chicago, 1986); Stearns and Stearns, eds., *Emotion and Social Change: Toward a New Psychohistory* (New York, 1988).

7   Gregg Easterbrook, *A Moment on the Earth: The Coming Age of Environmental Optimism* (New York, 1995).

Index

Italicized page numbers indicate illustrations.